Dedication

For the Palestinian Resistance which preserves
the honour of the nation.

For Abd al-Moneim Riyad, Chief of Staff of the
Egyptian Armed Forces, who died on the battlefield defending Ismailiyyah on 9 March 1969.

For the workers of Abu Zaabal, our comrades,
massacred at work on 12 February 1970 for
expressing the national will of Egypt.

Contemporary Arab Political Thought

Anouar Abdel-Malek (editor)

Other Books by Anouar Abdel-Malek

In Arabic

Madkhal ila'l Falsafah, Cairo, Al-Dar al-Misriyyah lil-Kutub, 1959.

Maktabat al-Afkar, Cairo, Al-Dar al-Misriyyah, li'l Kutub, 1959.

Dirasat fil-Thaqafah al-Wataniyyah, Beirut, Dar al-Taliah, 1967.

Al-Gaysh wal-Harakah al-Wataniyyah, Beirut, Dar Ibn Khaldun, 1974.

Al-Mugtama al-Misri wal-Gaysh, Beirut, Dar al-Taliah, 1974.

Al-Fikr al-Arabi fi Marakat al-Nahdah, Beirut, Dar al-Adab, 1974.

Rih al-Sharq, Dar al-Mustaqbal al-Arabi, Cairo, 1983.

Nahdat Misr, Al-Hayah al-Misriyyah al-Amah lil-Kitab, Cairo, 1983.

In Other Languages

Peuples d'Afrique, Monte-Carlo, Éditions du Cap, 1961.

Égypte, société militaire, Paris, Le Seuil, 1962.

Anthologie de la littérature arabe contemporaine - vol II: *Les Essais*, Paris, Le Seuil, 1965; 2nd edition, 1970.

Kultûr Emperyalismi (with G. and A. Dino, P.N. Boratav), Istanbul, Kitabevi, 1967.

Idéologie et renaissance nationale: l'Égypte moderne, Paris, Anthropos, 1969; 2nd edition, 1975.

Sociologie de l'Impérialisme, Paris, Anthropos, 1971.

Renaissance du Monde Arabe (ed. with A.-A. Belal and H. Hanafi), Algiers, Duculot, Gembloux, 1972.

La Dialectique sociale, Paris, Le Seuil, 1972.

L'Armée dans la nation, Algiers, Duculot, Gembloux-S.N.E.D., 1975.

Spécificité et théorie sociale, Paris, Anthropos, 1977.

Intellectual Creativity in Endogenous Culture, edited by Anouar Abdel-Malek; co-edited by Amar Nath Pandeya, The United Nations University, Tokyo, Japan; 1978.

Science and Technology in the Transformation of the World, edited by Anouar Abdel-Malek, Gregory Blue, Miroslav Pecujlic, The United Nations University, Tokyo, Japan; 1979.

Contemporary Arab Political Thought

Anouar Abdel-Malek (editor)

Translated by Michael Pallis

Zed Books Ltd., 57 Caledonian Road, London N1 9BU

B+W 10.75 Oct.84

Contemporary Arab Political Thought was originally
published in French by Editions du Seuil, 27 Rue Jacob,
75261, Paris in 1970 (revised and expanded edition 1980);
first published in English in an updated edition by Zed
Books Ltd., 57 Caledonian Road, London N1 9BU in 1983.

Cover design by Lee Robinson
Typeset by Forest Photosetting
Printed by The Pitman Press, Bath

British Library Cataloguing in Publication Data

Abdel-Malek, Anouar
Contemporary Arab political thought
1. Arab countries—Politics and government—1945–
I. Title   II. La pensée politique arabe
contemporaine. *English*
320.917'4927   JQ1850.A3

ISBN 0-86232-077-1
ISBN 0-86232-074-7 Pbk

US Distributor
Biblio Distribution Center, 81 Adams Drive, Totowa,
New Jersey 07512

Contents

Glossary

Caliph:	Lieutenant ("successor") to the Prophet Muhammad; in principle, leader of the Islamic community (umma).
Fatwa:	judicial or religious verdict delivered by a mufti, on consultation.
Figh:	Islamic canon law.
Hadith:	Tradition, a body of accounts telling of the sayings and actions of the Prophet, and having a normative value.
Iltizam:	Responsibility for the collection of taxes.
Imam:	Religious leader.
Jahiliyyah:	Pre-Islamic period.
Kharijites:	Secessionists who broke away from the Islamic community in 657: a minority Islamic sect, most widespread in certain areas of North and East Africa.
Mahjar:	Emigration, especially from Syria and Lebanon, to the United States.
Mutazilites:	8th and 9th Century rationalist school of theology, repressed and decimated by Caliph Al-Mutawakkil.
Mutakallimoun (from kalam):	Muslim theologians.
Nahda:	Renaissance, term used to designate the cultural revival of the Arab countries, beginning in the early 19th Century.
Umdeh:	Village mayor.
Quraish:	The tribe of the Prophet Muhammad.
Shariah:	Islamic religious law.
Sheikh al-balad:	Mayor or administrator of a small town.

Shia (Shi'ites):	Politico-religious Islamic tendency, dominant notably in Iran; followers of Ali, the Prophet's son-in-law and cousin.
Souq:	Market, fair.
Sunnah (Sunni):	The majority tendency within Islam; Sunni Islam claims to be the only orthodoxy.
Umma:	The Islamic community.
Waqf:	*mainmorte* assets held by religious foundations.
Watan:	Motherland.
Zakat:	Tithe.

Introduction

The texts presented here have been chosen as a way of answering one main question: what is the content of contemporary Arab thought?[1]

There is no longer any doubt that such thought exists. Ever since 1945, and particularly since 1952, the Western social sciences — invariably rooted in the Eurocentrism which issued from the Renaissance and the Enlightenment — have begun to seek ways of understanding the ideas, the mentalities, the way of thinking, the motivations, and sometimes the theories and visions of the new social forces and political movements operating within a colonial world struggling for its liberation and national rebirth. Within the three 'forgotten continents' themselves, the drive to reconquer an identity has forced the autochthonous intelligentsia to look at themselves, to conduct an increasingly objective and rigorous analysis of their own national society and thought.

The present work seeks to contribute to this task: to shed some light on the contemporary Arab world.

The texts selected and presented here constitute the main elements of this book, as the title indicates. It did, however, seem appropriate to introduce the collection as a whole, in order to draw out the main lines of contemporary Arab thought and to explain why and how the selection was made. Such an introduction cannot, of course, amount to a comprehensive survey: it simply aims to light up the edifice, from the inside, once it has been situated historically.

An introduction of this kind inevitably requires of the reader some familiarity with the texts in question, as will be evident from the final section: they are, after all, the real object of the endeavour. No synthesis of a whole domain of contemporary civilization, however precise and penetrating, can lay claim to be scientific if it does not presuppose a critical study of the sources and the patient collection of data. And in the field we are concerned with here, the necessary work has only just begun.

On the Cultural and National Unity of the Arab World

Two fundamental factors orient the entire course of contemporary Egyptian

1

and Arab thought. Both have deep historical roots, but their character is nonetheless very different. Philology teaches us that Arabic, along with Greek and Chinese, is one of the few languages which has maintained its fundamental structures from the tribal era right up to the 20th Century, whatever the regional or national cultures it was used to express. What is in question is the content of the culture so expressed; that culture has often been denigrated as lacking in originality, value and depth. The rebirth of historical studies in Egypt, the Arab world and the West has, however, gradually demonstrated that in practice, this millenarian language has been a means of unifying the cultures of the peoples and nations which were swept up by Islam and the Islamic empire, ever since the first conquests. Egypt is a case in point: once the country had been converted to Islam and had adopted the Arabic language, Egyptian culture continued to carry within it the cultural legacy of historic Egypt, now enriched by new formulations and contributions. Communality of language has created a communality of culture and a very strong awareness of that communality amongst all the peoples of the various Arab countries. The interactions between specifically Arab and Islamic cultural inputs on the one hand, and the autochthonous national cultures of the Arab empire on the other, form a whole field of study in themselves. These interactions are usually particularly pronounced, as elements within the more widely shared Arab culture, in those cases where the peoples whose identity and thought they express have long lived an autonomous national existence endowed with its own specificity, and have managed to maintain their continuity as a distinct entity throughout history. The most obvious example is Egypt, but in many ways, the same applies to Morocco and Yemen.

Indeed, the cultural disarray of certain Arab intellectual elites which have been deeply penetrated by the West — notably in the Maghreb — bears witness to the objective and subjective existence of this stable cultural base. Their disarray is a reaction to a powerful new influence which has created a dichotomy in sensibility and attitude. It is their underlying sense of belonging which is in turmoil.

The second factor dominating contemporary Arab thought is historical and political. Nobody nowadays would contest the importance of an Arab national movement which embodies both a national liberation struggle and the accompanying striving towards that national renaissance, which constitutes the long term objective of reconquered independence.

The National Movement: The Two Stages

This Arab national movement falls into two main stages: the 1939-45 war, epitomizing the general crisis of a worldwide imperialist system, serves as a dividing line.

During the first stage, stretching from the early 20th Century to the Second World War, the main problem was to promote the emergence of the autochthonous social classes and groups, which were evolving, each in their own very different ways, from oriental feudalism into a backward, predominantly agrarian, form of colonial capitalism, and to ensure access to political and economic power for these groups. The central struggle was the one against the imperialist occupying force, and the principal demands centred on the restoration of a formal sovereignty, on which basis the power of a national state enjoying real decision-making authority over significant domains could gradually be built up. This debate, which often turned into a more or less sustained struggle against the occupying power, was generally led by the autochthonous bourgeoisie of the various Arab countries. During this period the *Wafd*, the *Kutlah*, the *Istiqlal* and the *Destour*, amongst others, began to assume a national role.

Meanwhile, the ground was shifting fast. The struggle waged by the autochthonous bourgeoisie at an official level relied heavily on the action of the popular masses. The latter — the *fellahin*, workers, artisans, shopkeepers and the influential intelligentsia of town and countryside — were progressing gradually, slowly gaining access to a more modern lifestyle. The promised land could be glimpsed in the distance and it was no longer seen as exclusively within the gift of the occupier. But the poor soon came to perceive the new autochthonous authorities as primarily concerned with maintaining their own power and privilege. The ordinary people of town and countryside, who had always been ready and willing to devote themselves to the cause, to risk their lives even, slowly began to organize themselves. Trade unions and popular national political parties started to emerge, especially after the wave of revolts and revolutions which followed the 1914-18 war.

Amongst the autochthonous ruling elites the desire to preserve and extend their own privileges, rather than to improve the conditions of others, gradually led various influential groups to form alliances with the occupying power, or even to become its instruments.

The factors influencing this overall social polarization were by no means confined to a national framework. The 1917 socialist revolution in Russia, the activity of the Comintern, and then, after 1945, the emergence of several socialist states in Europe, followed by the victory of the popular revolution in China and the creation of new socialist states in Asia — in short the advance of the world socialist revolution under the banner of Marxism and the leadership of Communist and Workers' Parties, along with the constitution of a bloc of socialist states — could not but have dramatic repercussions on an Arab world which was itself in the midst of a profound transformation.

A second stage began, and this time the issues were authentic independence, the creation of independent national states, and, within those states the possibility of securing access to all the material and cultural resources of the nation, perhaps even to state power, for the various popular social classes and categories. Socialism had gained a place on the agenda: but in what terms?

Socialism has a quite different meaning for the people of Europe and North America: their very existence as a nation is not at stake. In the Arab countries, on the other hand, an accelerating economic, social, political and economic renaissance, as well as the advance of socialism throughout the world, have polarized matters and placed socialism right at the heart of the *nationalitarian* processes — as we shall see later. Socialism thus has a very specific character in the Arab countries. The cultural and the political are intertwined and interact at many levels.

In the Arab world, Marxism, along with the other political tendencies, has striven to revive national culture and autochthonous civilization by subjecting them to an historical and comparative critique, in the effort to animate a national rennaissance rooted in the popular classes. The nation had only just been repossessed by its people, was not yet fully itself and was already undergoing profound changes: it was in this context that the Marxism of the Arab countries took on a national role and approach. Arab Marxists understood that only by being fully itself, rather than a mere imitator of others, can a nation become a full member of the international community. Given this prerequisite, socialist action and thought could orient and enrich the general course of a popular national renaissance, which needed such a contribution if it was not to fall back into the new blind alley of nationalism.

Contemporary Arab thought has its own content, its own themes. The effort made by various groups to provide a theoretical account of the society's evolution, and to influence that evolution in accordance with the interests and aspirations of different classes and social categories, naturally led to considerable diversification. Yet two main tendencies can be distinguished.

Islamic Fundamentalism

The first of these tendencies drew its inspiration from Islam. There has been much talk of an Islamic 'revival', Islamic 'traditionalism' and 'nationalism'. It would be more accurate to define this new development, launched by Jamal al-Din al-Afghani and Muhammad Abduh, as an *Islamic fundamentalism*. In essence, it consists of a return to the wellsprings of the faith, purified of all the deformations and dead weight which, according to the advocates of this tendency, have accumulated as a result of centuries of decadence.[2] Supposedly, the original truths, once they have been rediscovered, will clear the way for a dialogue with the new era premised on careful but constant application of common sense. As the reader will realize, what we are describing is a form of pragmatism, not a rationalism as it has so often over-hastily been called. It is a pragmatism firmly rooted in the framework of orthodoxy, of the faith, the only ideology recognized as appropriate for the *Umma* as a whole. Implicit or explicit debate is permitted, but it must never degenerate into a dialectical struggle which could lead to disunity.

Such is the common basis of this major current, from which neither right nor left variants have substantially departed, at least until very recently. The common cultural heritage, especially its religious component, remains fundamental. The goal is a restoration of past glory, by means of a reworking of the historical legacy in terms of the most urgent and inevitable requirements of modern times, rather than by progressive transformation of present realities.

Yet it is worth noting that it was the great confrontation with modern ideas — the impact and contribution of Europe — which provoked this critical reassertion of identity. As its epigones see it, Islamic fundamentalism permits the integration of these new and efficacious ideas without being swamped by them: in the event, they opted for a conservative interpretation which effectively cut the growing fruit off from the roots it needed, namely a renovated Islam.

Liberal Modernism

The second main tendency of contemporary Arab thought, *liberal modernism*,[3] was quite different. It took as its starting point the rebirth of Eastern civilization, analysis of which was supposed to lead to great changes in every aspect of life in the Arab world. The stress was on the scientific approach, philosophical rationalism and political liberalism. The aim was to create a modern society, similar to those of Europe and North America, resolutely forward looking and open to progress, yet preserving those aspects of past traditions and customs which would not hamper the envisaged advance. The spectrum encompassed everything from the conservative liberalism of the land-owning bourgeoisie to Marxism, which steadily gained in influence amongst the intelligentsia, the working class and even, albeit to a lesser extent, in the countryside.

One should remember that this differentiation goes back to the last third of the 19th Century, to the phase in which contemporary Arab thought first emerged. The principal divergence in turn determined several further differences: in style, attitude and frame of reference; in the nature and type of problems considered; in what was deemed worthy of investigation; and in the possibility of the ideas in question changing and evolving into a real alternative. Each of these two great currents fitted into a specific sociological context, a set of aspirations and a vision of the world which it expressed and only occasionally transcended.

Naturally enough the archaic, traditional and less dynamic sectors of 20th Century Arab society recognized themselves in the activist groups adhering to Islamic fundamentalism in its various forms.

Artisans, shopkeepers, religious figures and their clientele, small landowners, even aristocratic landlords and religious leaders, were all receptive to this first great current, epitomized by *Al-Urwah al-Wuthga*, by the Muslim Brotherhood, by *Al-Manar*, by Middle Eastern and North African Islamic nationalism and even, especially at first, by the 'Free Officers'. But Islamic fundamentalism also attracted more dynamic elements: the officer corps, certain sections of the working class, nationalist intellectuals raging against imperialism, even a few captains of industry — the most notable example being Muhammad Talat Harb, founder of the Misr Group — who were searching for some autochthonous ideological base.

The second tendency was more common in those sectors most directly affected by changes in the economy and by commercial competition and trade with the outside world: urban intellectuals, factory workers, government employees, professionals, entrepreneurs, the industrial and financial bourgeoisie and sections of the state bureaucracy.

But it should not be assumed that any simple one-to-one correspondence or uniformity exists from which one can extrapolate. The countries which embarked upon the nationalitarian phase in the middle of the 20th Century were marked, even more than the established nations, by that often underestimated phenomenon, the autonomous development of ideologies, each with its own dialectic. This process unfolded in different ways in each Arab country: according to the evolution of economic structures, the nature of the political regime, the depth of colonial penetration, the degree of genuine independence, the quality of national culture and the role of the popular classes, amongst other factors. The reader will understand that an introduction such as this can only try to establish a few general criteria, in terms of economic and social infrastructure and in terms of cultural development; the study of specific cases calls for specialized investigation of each particular area.

A Socio-Ideological Domain in the Protracted Change

The numerous, apparent contradictions which will emerge should thus disturb only those who hold to a unilinear methodology —be it vulgar economism or one of the ethnic typologies so decisively discredited both by the resurgence of the three continents which, until recently, had been grossly overlooked, and by the new challenges they posed to the hypotheses, postulates and paradigms of the humanities and social sciences.

Our research will tend to concentrate on how each of these two great currents have changed, and on the ways in which, to some extent, they have converged. The starting point was the crisis of a formal independence — notably in Egypt and Iraq after 1919 — which did nothing to resolve the fundamental problems of social development on any level. A return to the wellsprings of faith may seem out of touch with the new realities of our century, but mere imitation of a culturally and historically alien modernity also proved incapable of meeting the needs of the Arab world, and especially the needs perceived by the people of that world. Consequently, in the early 1930s, certain eminent representatives of the liberal-modernist current turned back to Islam and provided a conveniently rationalist interpretation. Others, especially from the younger generation, saw Marxism as the natural extension of this liberal current which had never been taken to its logical conclusion by its older epigones. Conversely, young radicals steeped in Islam began to investigate the requirements of the historical development process, albeit in terms which had little to do with the models put forward by European social science. Their efforts were well received by the mass of ordinary people, who had become deeply politicized and receptive to the key ideas of socialism. The majority of this Islamic current's thinkers, however, continued to fight for orthodoxy and against any evolving conceptualization.

Each of these currents can be further divided into two sub-groups. Islamic fundamentalism split, on the one hand, into the orthodox, the *salafiyyah*, who harked back to the past and were resolutely opposed to any 'intrusion'; and on the other hand, those groups whose sincere faith was inseparable from an equally sincere desire to promote a national renaissance in contemporary terms. It is in the latter group that Abduh's influence was most marked, reaching its apex where the two great currents crossed — in the political thought and work of Gamal Abdel Nasser.

For its part, the liberal-modernist wing brought together forces attracted by the efficiency of Eurocentrism, especially in its more left-wing formulations. They naturally hoped for similar results and effects at home. But the tendency also attracted other forces which had been developing rapidly since 1945-52: those who conceived of the march towards modernity and socialism in terms of a nationalist renaissance to which they sought to give a rationalist and democratic character. These forces gradually abandoned an imitation of Europe, however socialist, and became more firmly wedded to that evolving sense of national history which the multiple and contradictory influences of the West had stimulated.

Once again, we see how the two great currents overlap. In many ways this is the most striking aspect of the present phase; the essential nature of the renaissance of the entire Arab world depends on the success of this fusion between these radical and convergent wings of the two great tendencies of contemporary Arab thought.

As the national movement gained in momentum from 1919 onwards, but especially after the great turning point of the Second World War, a new balance of forces was established and again new forces emerged. Naturally, many of the elements of differentiation outlined above remained relevant; indeed they were brought to their paroxysm by the requirements of the industrial age. Yet within each of these facets one can observe a process of change which accords with an evolution towards national liberation and renaissance, a process rooted in the increasingly sociological polarization of the Arab peoples.

In fact one could argue that this differentiation between tendencies, at least in the terms we have described, no longer constitutes the fundamental contradiction within the Arab thought of the present period, even if it continues to be one of its fundamental aspects. Perhaps it should now be replaced by an analysis of the shared ground and the changes currently in process, including the emergence of a new kind of fundamental contradiction.

For instance, the more recent Arab thought — say from 1939 to 1970 — could be said to fall into two new major tendencies, each of which is becoming more and more firmly established. These are, firstly, that body of thought which works to promote a renaissance of a 'civil society' attuned to the 20th Century; and, secondly, all those currents which situate themselves outside the framework of the independent national state, and outside the present great debate between the autocratic and democratic proponents of this national state, a debate which was given such impetus by the Egyptian revolution of 1952, the Algerian war of liberation (1954-62) and the Palestinian resurgence in the era of superpower confrontation. The theoretical problems posed by this evolution certainly warrant further investigation.

What is the Nationalitarian Phase?

To begin with, we need to elucidate the concepts by which we can characterize the historical stage the Arab world has been passing through during the 20th Century.

The term currently used to designate both its content and its various manifestations is 'nationalism'. In the traditional terminology of European political history, the concept suggests both a negative and a positive element: on the one hand a rejection of the outside world, a withdrawal into oneself, a negation of universalism; and on the other, the active frontier quarrels and expansionist aims which have been the root cause of European wars for four centuries. Enlightened opinion in the West now condemns both phenomena: nationalism is outdated, interpenetration, interdependence, the broader community have come into their own; or at least that is what people say, even though the national question and the national aspect of problems have recently been increasingly and strikingly prominent throughout the world, notably in Western Europe itself. But does the term 'nationalism' really describe the process which is unfolding before our eyes in the Arab world?

Let us take a closer look. In practice, the activist manifestations of European nationalism were most characteristic of nations which had long been self-assured, sovereign and independent national states in their struggles for control over the sources of wealth in Europe and throughout the world. It was not to establish their autonomous national existence that the European powers fought the great wars of 1914-18 and 1939-45; it was in order to attain hegemony over the other European powers and the peripheral continents. Hence the present denigration of nationalism and nationalisms, those synonyms of aggression, chauvinism, inhumanity and anti-universalism.

In the Arab world, on the contrary, the aim of the struggle waged against the imperialist occupying powers — apart from the reconquest of national sovereignty and the eradication of the ex-occupier's power base — was to win the right to decide upon every aspect of national life, as a prelude to recovering that identity which lies at the heart of the desired renaissance and which has been constantly assailed by every means and on every terrain.

Obviously the two processes have points in common, notably certain negative features. In order to free oneself from the alien oppressor's penetration, it is vital to distance oneself, to refuse all amalgamation, to define oneself as an authentic *other* on the basis of one's own history and autonomous aims. But in doing so, one must stress the fact that it is natural for peoples engaged in struggle to seek support from many sources: from non-colonial states as well as from international organizations, parties, institutions and schools of thought which transcend frontiers. The break, the rejection of the oppressor's influence, is not necessarily a withdrawal into oneself. On the contrary, it should be a quest for those others with whom one can develop a relationship which in no way restricts one's desire to be genuinely oneself.

So even in this 'negative' sense, in which one might expect certain similarities to emerge, there is an important difference between the Arab and European forms of nationalism. In the 'positive', radical sense, there is even less in common between what happened in Europe and what is happening in the Arab world: there are no expansionist aims, no generalized wars in the Arab world. True, there are plenty of conflicts, but at present the central axis remains the struggle against the foreign occupier or invader. The struggle is fundamentally a national liberation struggle, the instrument of that reconquest of identity which is so central to everything in this domain. It thus seems worth marking this conceptual difference by defining what is happening in the Arab world — and in Asia, Africa and Latin America — as a 'nationalitarian' process rather than a nationalist one.[4]

Of course, this distinction does not mean that the newly independent countries have a completely different attitude towards other nations than have those countries where the national problem has long ceased to be so pressing. Another way of putting it would be that the nationalism of the period of national construction — the 'nationalitarian' period — is positively oriented and creates progressive values and institutions, while the nationalism of the colonialist powers is a form of political aggression geared to ethnic and racial domination.

In other words, there is no essential difference between the two, simply a difference in the effects produced as a result of an historical time-lag. The nationalitarian phase in Europe was marked by the struggle of European peoples to assert their own national existence against the constraining influence of the European great powers; this movement went hand in hand with the great bourgeois and democratic revolutions against feudalism which swept Europe from the 16th to the 19th Century. The process at present underway in the Arab countries and in the nations of the three 'forgotten continents' is far more radical: the struggle against European imperialism hardened the respective national movements, and the independent national states which eventually emerged were strongly oriented towards political radicalism, which in the present historical phase means socialism.

Modernism and Modernity

The interaction between the renaissance of the Arab world and the contemporaneous environment poses a second set of problems. How can the new beginning be launched? How can one act to remain oneself in a world dominated by the 'other'?

Certain Arab thinkers — in fact one whole section of the liberal-modernist current — originally opted for imitation of the West. It has to be remembered that at the time, wars and generalized crises had not yet tarnished the achievement of the age of revolutions and the Enlightenment. Western influences, pressures and solicitations constantly promoted the process, providing the historical framework of 'modernism' throughout the first half of this century. Imitation of the West was seen as desirable in every domain, from clothing to philosophy, from the alphabet to political institutions, from sexual mores to the economy. Supposedly, only a decisive break with the Arab past, a total negation of decadence, could halt catastrophic decline. Then, once the decadent national 'selfhood' had been completely eradicated, it would be possible to transplant the West into the Arab world and thereby ensure a renaissance.

It was not long, however, before those who supported this view ran into deep-seated resistance. Naturally, certain structures emerged —indeed they are still emerging — which were, at first sight, favourable to the process of Europeanization. But the heart of the matter lay elsewhere. Through political struggle and contact with new ideas, the mass of the people themselves, and the intellectual groups living in close contact with them, were becoming aware of their society's decline and relative backwardness. But these forces' attachment to their own essential and historical being, to their own humanity and to their own form of humanism — that national consciousness which is also the class consciousness of the popular masses — led them to reject the godown economy, cultural plagiarism, unquestioning acceptance of foreign infiltration and denial of their true self — in other words they rejected the servility which invariably marks 'compradors', wherever they may be.

Yet the century and its events itself were manifestly unavoidable. Criticism had to be brought to bear both on oneself and on the others, on the historical selfhood in crisis and on the seminal but enslaving foreign contribution. It gradually emerged that the task at hand was neither a simple extension of historical selfhood nor the imitation of the constraining 'other': rather, what was called for was to study and understand the reconquered national territory, both historically and sociologically, to expose its specificity and enrich it with those aspects of Western industrial civilization likely to promote progress and development, thereby accentuating a specificity which could evolve without being deformed, forced or alienated. To do all this it was essential that genuine independence should follow on from formal independence, through the construction of an independent national state primarily committed to this extensive reconquest of decision-making power at every level relevant to the life of the nation.

This process is precisely what we mean when we talk of *modernity*. The relevant reference points are, of course, different from those in Europe or America, since they are determined by national forces in terms of their own specific objectives. In this sense it is clear that those foreign observers who seek to judge 'others' entirely in the light of their own privileged history have understood very little. The quest for novelty and ingenuity is relevant only in a particular context, and even then not just for its own sake.

To talk of 'acculturation' is to imply that the only task facing the peoples of the Arab World is to carry out some benign graft on to their own cultural corpus. This one-sided view, so typical of Eurocentrism, ignores the fact that the renaissance of the three forgotten continents, Africa, Asia and Latin America, is not simply a political operation. What in fact is at stake is the entire content of our contemporary civilization. If this renaissance can genuinely be accomplished, present and future Western generations will cease to be so self-centred and will be enriched by having relearnt how to welcome and appreciate the contributions of the denigrated and marginalized world of the periphery. Mutual enrichment and interaction between different cultures, even if they are at different stages in their historical evolution, cannot be reduced to ensuring that peoples with their own distinct and specific history gain access to the culture and industrial civilization of Europe and North America.

This should not, of course, be taken to mean that Europe and North America do not partake of this modernity. That would be an absurd over-extension of the distinction we are trying to make. In particular, it would be to forget that modern science and technology have elicited modes of social organization and thought in Europe and North America which pertain more to a certain kind of civilization — industrial society — than to some Western specificity.

It is all too easy for uncritical observers, both at home and abroad, to take this fact simply as a cause for contentment or alarm. The reality is that the convergence of the way material life is organized throughout the world is strongly tempered by the influence of the respective cultural backgrounds, in other words by specific national cultures. To the extent that the ex-colonies have genuinely reconquered their identity and decision-making power, they can move forward, keeping in step with the times without having to exchange their colonial status for a faceless cosmopolitanism. The path to a true world civilization will have to encompass all the various avenues that the different nations have explored throughout their history.

In any case, which Europe are we talking about? Until the First World War the question hardly arose, outside Communist circles at least. But after the great crisis of 1929-32, and then under the influence of the Popular Front in France, Marxism began to make headway in several Arab countries. The war, Bandoeng and Suez, the conflict in Palestine, all fuelled the left's meteoric rise. And it was not long before socialist republics were actively collaborating with the Arab states within the framework of Afro-Asian international bodies.

There are thus two Europes, the old imperialist one and the socialist one. Since we live in the era of the cold war, we have to choose between the two. Naturally, no institutionalized choice is possible for a national state in the Arab world which is truly working to promote the future of its national culture and civilization. Sympathy and alliances with friendly powers cannot preclude state realism, renegotiation of old forms of trade, the creation of a new international context more in keeping with the aspirations of the new states; such is, after all, the essential content of that political neutralism which, in its various interpretations, is well suited to the demands of the nationalitarian phase.

Arab Unity: The Two-Tier Nation

A third group of theoretical notions bears upon the problems of the Arab peoples' *common* existence. In this context, any honest appraisal reveals both efforts and failures, each of which has been a pretext for fierce polemics. The peoples of the Arab world have been united by a common or interconnected history since the 8th Century, and share a common language and for the most part profess a single religion, namely Islam. They are the inheritors of a long tradition of struggle against foreign invasion dating back to the Crusades, a tradition which has, for a century, taken the form of a direct struggle imbued with a revolutionary content. Europe has never been willing to accept the fact that this history, and the multiple affinities it gives rise to, demand that the Arab peoples seek out ways and means to realize their unity, perhaps even on the state level. North America on the other hand, saw this aspiration as a useful means of blocking the advance of communism. Yet Europe itself is searching for its own unity: the multiplicity of languages, the centuries of war, the territorial grievances, the religious conflicts and the racist venom do not deter an enlightened public. On what basis, then, can Europe condemn the process of Arab unity?

The usual argument is based on the diversity of the historical national formations, and it is indeed true that the desire for unity does not stem from precisely the same motivations in each and every case. In the territories of Greater Syria, which were carved up following the 1919-21 treaties, the aim is to recover a cohesion which, within the present artificially imposed frontiers, is precluded by regionalism, parochial quarrels and the instabililty of state power. From the Egyptian point of view, this same unity is seen as the only means whereby to create an Arab regional entity endowed with the raw material resources indispensable to the development of the Arab territories; the objective is a level of economic complementarity which will enable the Arabs to approach the era of the cold war and super-power rivalry on a firm footing. In North Africa, where the notion is not so central, the purpose is to secure immediate and fraternal support, to draw on new forces following the great haemorrhage.

The left-wing of the Arab national movement takes a more militant view of the matter. Here the accent is not only on the unity of culture, but also on the struggle against imperialism. The envisaged unity is more flexible: a federation or confederation which would respect the national particularities and the achievements of each people within the Arab world.

The concept of a two-tier nation is relevant here. Nothing can stop Egypt being itself, the first nation in history to have achieved a centralized state which endures to this day. But nor can anything detract from the fact that, since AD 640, Egypt has been an Arab country, indeed, the Arab world's main national state formation, the centre of modern Arab culture and of Islam. All the peoples of the Arab world, and especially those endowed with a national tradition predating the Arab conquest, recognize themselves simultaneously as Arabs and as Egyptians, Moroccans, Iraqis, Syrians and so on.

There is thus no need to renounce one's lineage in order to rejoin one's distant brothers. A dialectic has been established between the two poles, following the hard lessons of the failure of the first, insufficiently mature, attempts at unity. But the process is now irreversibly underway, as is borne out by the constant polemic, the attempts at theoreticization and the growing power of the movement towards a universally cherished unity.

The analysis of these various dimensions of the nationalitarian phase naturally also proceeded in stages. At first, we find vast syntheses, constructed before the work of analysis and preliminary investigation had been adequately carried out.

At best, these serve as an overall introduction, where intuition and sensitivity shore up an architecture severely deficient in information; at worst, we find works inspired purely by the requirements of political activism — lacking in objectivity, over-hasty and frequently specious. The most that can be expected from this early stage then, is impressionist syntheses, usually based on extrapolation and typology. More often the writings are propagandist tracts serving the cause of one or other of the ideologies warring within and against the Arab world at the time.

More recently, specialized works — theses, handbooks, essays on the culture, the literature and the thought of a given country, era, school, discipline or author — have been published. What is striking here is that the initiative came from those concerned themselves, that is from the universities of the various Arab countries and from the Arab League's Institute of Advanced Arab Studies; also, naturally enough, there has been a plethora of individual efforts, both in the Arab world and abroad.

It is this second type of writing that we have concentrated on in this volume, drawing on works published in Cairo from 1952 to 1959, and in Paris from 1960 onwards.

Philosophers and Combatants

As is to be expected, this infrastructure of contemporary Arab thought we have been describing has evolved a specific style of its own.

Few, if any of our authors, pursue the merely gratuitous. Practically every one of them is engaged, each in his or her own way, in the quest for the new renaissance. Of course, in the last two generations, and especially in the last few years, efforts have been made to break this tradition of commitment, by rallying certain marginal intellectuals, strangers to their own country, who are eagerly attentive to all the blandishments from across the sea. We have thus witnessed occasional bursts of aestheticism, the most recent being the work of Arab appendages of a Western international institution dedicated to a crusade against socialism. But for once, all the various Arab tendencies, schools of thought and rival political groups were unanimous in their condemnation of this orchestrated 'decommitment', which in any case evoked practically no response in the Arab world, despite all the efforts of its backers.

The interpenetration of the Arab political and intellectual elites remains a notable feature of all the Arab countries. The vast majority of creative intellectuals, al-*muthaqqifoun*, indeed of all intellectuals in the broad sense of those who work by the brain, al-*muthaqqifoun*, have always been and still are deeply involved in the national movement. Gramsci's theses on intellectuals have perhaps never received more resounding confirmation than in the Arab world. Inevitably, one consequence has been a limitation of the scope of the Arab contribution to the work of theoretical elaboration on the more general level. But in compensation, political and social thought has been fecundated by the contributions of philosophers and specialists in the various natural and human sciences, who, in other times, would have concentrated exclusively on their own professional tasks. In the Arab world today, the philosopher is king, an oft-crucified king who neither governs nor sits in judgement.

Before one condemns this commitment for the limitations it imposes, one must appreciate what it has meant for those who have accepted it, and understand what it has done for the evolution of the countries concerned, on every level. The historic achievement of the Arab intellectuals of this century will have been to re-evaluate history and historical destiny, rather than simply to become better specialists. This imbrication of theoretical thought in practical action, in the life and tumult of the city, the towns and the countryside could not but enhance a normative aspect. The problem of the nature and hierarchy of values constantly recurs in all the texts presented here, as in so many others. One might even say that 'pure' formal research is still unknown in contemporary Arab thought.

The Socio-Cultural Ethos

What then are these values?

When thought, all thought, aims to fecundate the substrata from which it arises, ideological differences and the struggle between the various tendencies and intellectual movements will inevitably bear precisely on the social value of a given intellectual endeavour. When national renaissance is so central, inevitably it also becomes the criterion of all thought. And this is what happens in the Arab world: accusations and anathemas are invariably promulgated in the name of the good of the nation as a whole, envisaged in different ways.

A closer examination reveals a second form of communality integral to this normative aspect. In order to achieve the goals of the nationalitarian stage, work and struggle — joint effort in other words — are indispensable. Meditation and contemplation alone cannot break the alienation of the colonial era. There is in effect an objective convergence between the scale of values relevant to the ex-colonial world as a whole, including the Arab world, and the one adopted by socialist movements. The fact that great stress is usually put on most immediate tactical and political aspect should not obscure the roots of a *rapprochement* which has so deeply marked the reorganization of international relations during our generation. An ethic based on profit, or even on hedonism, simply cannot be reconciled with the demands of national renaissance. What we are touching upon here concerns the philosophical foundations of the great struggles of our time — struggles which in the Arab world, as in all the ex-colonial countries, are framed in terms of principle.

One consequence of all this has been the polemical, ardent and combative tone characteristic of men and women wrestling with foreign influence and with themselves and their own national identity, in an era dominated by the general crisis of the imperialist system, the emergence of socialism and the struggle between the two great power blocs, as well as by constant technical upheaval and fundamental new discoveries and questions.

15

It is no easy matter to steer a course from the Middle Ages to the nuclear era, from feudalism to socialism, from servitude to renaissance; this is especially the case when one is under constant fire from the masters of yesterday, who still hold the main sources of wealth, influence and power in the world, and who do everything to sidetrack the best intentions and to break the will of those who oppose them. Let the terrain to be reconquered be poor in resources, hard to cultivate —as is the case in most Arab countries — and it is only to be expected that the voice of analysis should often rise to a raucous tirade.

Towards the Reconquest of Identity

The immediate European response has been to characterize the Arab of today as archetypally resentful. One aspect of Arab human experience is isolated, magnified and treated as a permanent typological essence: appearance substituted for content, historical or sociological analysis going completely by the board. Even the fact that resentment was a notable feature of Western post-nationalism — once the old Empires had collapsed — has been blithely overlooked.

The reality is that the distinctive feature of the Arab today is the drive to reconquer an identity, the identity of that national community within which he can develop his own subjectivity; first, he has to partake individually of a common humiliation. The starting point, as we have already pointed out, is negation of the 'other'; resentment, rejection and anger are simply some modalities amongst others of this first step.

But the essence lies elsewhere, in the irreversible and prodigiously complex process of nationalitarian construction. Once the disjunction has been made, a different, autonomous course will emerge: future encounters between cultures will be all the richer and more authentic when that happens.

Two Roads to Universality

All this shows the extent to which contemporary Arab thought is the thought of transition, both historically and formally. Should we then conclude that it has no other historical value than to witness and illustrate the era of the *Nahda*, and thereby to extend the impetus of that era into the future? The question raises the problem of the universal value of ideas. The historicist conception has deeply penetrated into every domain of critical reflection since the last century, and decisively so since Hegel, Marx and Darwin. Our efforts here to illustrate the specific historical context of the body of thought we are presenting constitute just one example amongst many. Yet that does not release us from the obligation to seek the connection between the historicity and the universality of this thought, and indeed of all thought.

We can do this on two levels: firstly, in terms of the transformation of the terrain from which that thought arises. One has only to compare the Arab world's starting point, towards the mid-19th Century, with what has been achieved since then. By this means some idea can be grasped of the efficacity of this thought, its suitability for the human communities of the Arab world, the speed of the resultant action and the impetus it gave to Arab progress.

It could be argued that all in all, this contribution was merely regional. But that would be to refuse to understand that the very fact of dragging an entire cultural world out of its stagnation and restoring it to the life of our epoch in all its complexity, in itself constitutes a form of universalization, an integration with the wider body of the world, an enrichment of contemporary civilization and an extension of the great movements of fraternity which are the key to mankind's future. Secondly, contemporary Arab thought has made a considerable contribution to an innovatory form of synthesis: between the contemporary and the ancestral, between the systems and ideologies of industrial society, be they capitalist or socialist, and the context of a national terrain.

A second type of synthesis is embodied in the contribution of Islamic fundamentalism (from Muhammad Abduh to Alal al-Fasi), which has much to teach us and can usefully be compared with the *aggiornamento* currently underway in the Christian world. Given the profoundly different historical circumstances, Abduh's efforts nonetheless show him to have been a pioneer, and not simply in the Islamic context. Similarly, the eruption of historicity into religious and literary reflection based on the Koran, thanks to Taha Hussain, clearly marks the beginning of that convergence between the more advanced wings of the two main currents we spoke of earlier. Hussain qualifies as a precursor: his breakthrough has become the general rule.

Three other endeavours illustrate this second type of synthesis. To begin with, there are the socialist analyses conducted in the Arab world, notably in Egypt, Sudan, Algeria and Morocco. Generally speaking, the tendency has been to integrate Marxism into the national movement, to approach problems in terms of national experiences rather than through an automatic transposition of revolutionary schemes evolved elsewhere.

Next in line, chronologically speaking, we have the emergence of 'Nasserism' as the movement and political ideology of the independent autocratic national state in the 'Kemalist' tradition; the experience has had a lasting impact on several regions of the Arab world, Asia and Latin America. Finally, one notes the peasant socialism based on self-management put forward by the new Algeria, and the eruption of socialist ideologies and revolutionary action in Palestine from 1967 onwards.

A third type of synthesis is to be found in a range of autobiographies which together constitute a valuable body of critical reflection upon the process of social evolution as a whole; the effect is reminiscent of the Russian tradition. Also, at the very limits of the genre, at the confluence of history, philosophy and aesthetic reflection, we find a few exceptional works in which erudition, rigour and great literary skill combine to produce master-pieces such as Hussain Fawzi's recent *Sindbad Misri*.

We have described a few areas in which the historical value of contem-porary Arab thought attains to universality. It was not an easy transition: its effects are only now beginning to be felt in the metropoles which command the great cultural sectors of the West. The comparative study of other cul-tures, both in the three forgotten continents and in certain European coun-tries, will eventually enable us to approach the matter from an universalist perspective and to detect what is specific to the very problematic of Arab thought.

Within the Arab world itself, the critical study and historical appraisal of this thought are still at an early stage. For the moment we can provide only an inevitably incomplete first outline.

But there are other obstacles. Recent years have seen a harden-ing of the national movement, and, even more so, of the dangers which threaten it. The climate of political liberalism which once prevailed has not survived this crisis. The scope of debate has been narrowed down at the pre-cise moment when a fundamental requirement of the Arab world's renaissance is the restoration of a dialectic of ideas as an integral part of the social dialectic between the new national structures. In religious, philosophical, political and aesthetic matters, the range of permissible topics is steadily being reduced in the name of the defence and protection of independence.

1964, however, saw a political resurgence, notably in Egypt, Algeria and Yemen. Above all, the June 1967 war forced all the political forces and all the ideological tendencies to adopt a necessary critical rigour. The Palestinian resistance, the radicalization of the independent national states, the 1969 revolutions in Sudan and Libya, the implantation of socialism in southern and eastern Arabia — from Aden to Dhofar — were so many milestones along this Arab long march. From Suez to Palestine — from 1956 to 1967 — new structures were beginning to emerge.

From Liberation to Revolution

The Israeli aggression on the morning of 5 June 1967 — the third such act in 20 years — and the subsequent defeat of the Egyptian, Syrian and Jorda-nian armies, brutally disrupted all our euphoric calculations. The Arab world's political re-emergence was suddenly plunged into the most pro-found and dangerous crisis since the imperialist eruption a century before. Imperialism seemed committed more resolutely than ever to maintaining its advance post in the Middle East in order to control Arab oil and the southern marches of the Soviet bloc, and to obstruct the path of the Arab long march with iron and fire. It took three wars in 20 years for the broad masses of the Arab world to become aware of the Zionist state's true nature.

An empire was waiting to be carved out, from the Euphrates to the Nile, under the protection of hegemonic imperialism and with the almost unanimous open or tacit connivance of the West. But it could only come into being by uprooting and dispersing a nation, by condemning the Palestinian people to live out their lives in refugee camps. The terrible and implacable bloodletting finally destroyed all faith in outside help or intercession. The form of coexistence agreed upon at Yalta weighed down upon the Middle East and the Mediterranean like a pall of iron.

Everything accentuated a despair which the liberal West — relieved at last of its culpability and guilt towards the Jewish communities it had persecuted — seemed all too willing to treat with commiseration or sympathy. In the Arab world, but especially in the Middle East and above all in Egypt (still first in line in imperialism's sights, as in the days when Europe banded together to restrain Muhammad Ali) and amongst the Palestinian people, the temptation was very great. There was no shortage of well-placed individuals in the military and political leadership, notably in Cairo, who saw the defeat as an ideal opportunity to bring down the head of state, decry an unsuccessful alliance and, in exchange for a liberation of Sinai, offer to return to the American fold; this in the context of that US-led joint Middle East defence policy which the entire national movement — from Iran to the Sudan — had so resoundingly rejected after the Second World War.

Everything indicated despair. And then, from the heart of the night, there came a gleam of hope. The people of the tents, the anonymous men and women, children and old people of Palestine embarked upon the only valid course open to a nation stripped of its homeland and faced with that ethnic, cultural and political racism which lies at the core of all imperialism. The people of Palestine endowed themselves with resistance organizations charged with the co-ordination, definition and pursuit of a campaign of armed national liberation.

The long period of formal independence had been characterized by the strategy of reformist, often parliamentary, national fronts, which sat back and watched while imperialism implanted a racist fortress of militaristic aggression in the heart of the Arab Middle East, wiped out the Palestinian homeland and brought the second phase of the Egyptian renaissance to a sudden halt. History now unambiguously indicated the course to be taken in future: the armed national liberation struggle had come into its own. Given the realities of peaceful coexistence and the geopolitical equilibrium throughout the region and the world, that struggle would have to be a war of attrition, a broad, long-term action by the Arab popular masses and all the states most directly involved. The historical merit of the Palestinian resistance, led by Al-Fatah (founded by Yasser Arafat on 1 January 1964), is to have objectively shown the national movements of the Arab world that the time had come to replace the armoury of criticism with the criticism of arms. Of course this thesis had long been current amongst the more radical elements of the national movement, inspired as they were by revolutionary socialism. But now the call to arms was no longer the watchword of any one faction, party or class; it had emerged as the only possible course if the nation as a whole was to survive. The battle of Karameh (21 March 1968) marked the end of a process by which defeats and reversals engendered a demoralization that the enemy had hoped would be irreversible.

As we have pointed out, the imperialist offensive was poised to strike at Egypt's heart. To this day, Israeli atomic weaponry has no other function. The endogenous problems, however, were quite another matter. It was crucial, and it still is, to ensure that the popular masses would genuinely control the national revolution, in other words, the state. Until June 1967, the latter, rotted by the growth of the state capitalist class under the military regime, seemed unlikely to evolve. The bloodbath shook the entire edifice. The Cairo trials exposed the corruption, the ineptitude, the treason of the leaders of the political and military apparatus. The occupation of the national territory east of the Suez Canal, which was itself paralyzed, opened up a chasm between the army and the people. The watchwords of popular armed struggle and prolonged war gradually won almost unanimous support throughout the country, notably during the huge demonstrations mounted by the workers and students in February, and then in November 1968 — demonstrations reminiscent of Spring 1946 and the 'National Workers' and Students' Committee'.

Was the army left out of this upheaval? The officer corps, taken in hand by a tough uncompromising General with a reputation for great courage, Abd al-Muneim Riyad, was forced to remake itself in the image of its chief-of-staff. It soon became obvious that the so-called political option no longer found an echo within the military apparatus, which was now wholly committed to the course of armed struggle and prolonged war, in keeping with the aspirations of the people. When Riyad died in the line of duty on 9 March 1969, his funeral marked the coming together of all the forces of the Egyptian nation: the popular masses side by side with the now rehabilitated officers, the fellahin alongside the workers, intellectuals and officials of the towns; the citizen-soldiers were once again the focus of the people's affection and expectations. Unity was being reforged, and not just at the affective level. From now on that unity was based on the watchwords so strikingly put forward by five million demonstrators during the 11 hour demonstration in Cairo on Monday 10 March 1969: armed struggle against the invader, a war of attrition against imperialism, no compromise. National unity meant an end to any possibility of disengagement. An era had come to an end, another had begun. But at what cost?

Freedom as an Historical Necessity: the Primacy of the Political

Armed action, the starting point of the renewal in question, cannot be reduced to gratuitous violence. Rather it was the logical culmination of a rigorous scientific analysis of the entire process of national renaissance, including its disruption. The thought which stemmed from this analysis found expression in political documents — manifestos, articles, reports — as well as in literature proper, notably in poetry. Works in preparation will no doubt eventually provide an account of the endogenous reasons for the disjunction and an outline of the mental framework within which it took place. The theses presented here date back to 1964; they have undergone their baptism of fire. More recent works will elaborate upon the new elements brought into play and further the contradictory task of analysis.

The axis of that analysis has now shifted dramatically. The other — imperialism — is no longer set up as the sole or even the main problem. Determinant factors endogenous to socially and historically specific contemporary Arab societies are now the main focus for analysis. True, even before 1967, both levels were considered, especially by Arab Marxists, ever-attentive to issues of class struggle. But the primacy of the united national front against imperialism meant that endogenous criticism had to be relegated to the background — or at least that was the prevailing sentiment at the time. The June 1967 war broke that reticence completely. Since then, the Arab masses and the Arab intelligentsia have critically scrutinized the structure of national life in its entirety, from the economic to the ideological, and not excluding the apparatus of state, the centrepiece of any society, whatever cabinet may be in power. That scrutiny was like a blade turned in the wound, and orientated the Arab people towards a revolution lying beyond the national liberation which would have to be won through political armed struggle.

The problem was to discover the causes of a defeat which threatened our national existence itself. Until recently, two answers had been put forward. The apparatus, as well as some modernist intellectuals, had argued that the Arab world was on its knees because it had failed to raise itself to a Western level of technology: this position implied that only an industrial, technical and scientific revolution could remodel the public mind and endow the national states and movements with the necessary cadres and impetus. But in practice, this was no answer at all: if technology took precedence over the political, how was one to account for Vietnam, that 'backward' country where the greatest military power of all time was floundering? At best, such an answer permitted one to put the problem more clearly: given the importance of technology, the question became how to carry out the revolution in a technologically and economically backward country.

How else but by attacking the very root of the political problem, the nature of state power? The facts show that backward colonial-type capitalist regimes, as well as those set up by the new militarily dominated state capitalist class, have proved incapable of achieving the goals of the nationalitarian phase, to say nothing of the required social revolution. The reasons are various, but they all point to one essential factor, namely that all these regimes have kept the popular masses at a distance from the exercise of state power. Should the people — the armed people, under the leadership of the workers of town and countryside and the revolutionary intellectuals — assume responsibility for the whole social system, through the state, it would then be possible to pose the problems of liberation and revolution in a far more radical way, without having to go to great lengths in order to protect the interests of the wealthy classes who so often are quick to declare their conversion to 'socialism'. Such a departure would permit the development of a social philosophy, a non-productivist, authentically revolutionary and humanist ethic, and a general strategy adapted to the real needs of the people; in short, we would be in a position to make choices, both in domestic and foreign policy, which were really suited to the potential which is just waiting to be realized: the response to a course genuinely desired by the people themselves. We could then harness and mobilize the human energy of our countries, rely on our own strengths, take responsibility for our own actions. It goes without saying that none of this obviates the need to take the constraints of geography and geopolitics into account: Egypt is not Vietnam; the war has not spread to the interior, to blight the lives of the peoples of the Nile delta; classical military methods are therefore indicated by the situation itself.

The reorganization of the country's socio-political structure thus has as its first objective the consolidation of the domestic front. The debate is well underway. Already one can distinguish the basic premises of an historical choice of strategy; the Palestinian resistance and the radicalization of national unity in Egypt and throughout the Arab Middle East are necessary preconditions if the Zionist victory is to be eroded. The weapon of criticism thus provides an essential accompaniment to the critique by arms, even if only the latter is capable of breaking down present obstacles.

The most general problems can now be posed on the basis of a concrete reality rather than in terms of myths; they can be framed in terms of practical politics, rather than mere ideology. This applies equally to the central problem, the underlying nature of the state apparatus, which in practice determines the measures governments can implement. Arab unity is another problem which can now be treated more realistically. Since 1956, we have defended the idea of 'national specificity' as epitomized by Egypt and Morocco; this approach is now generally accepted, though it was long seen as the cranky notion of a small group of stubbornly 'provincial' thinkers. In the interim, of course, there was June 1967, the tragedy of defeat and the hard lesson inculcated by a Zionist apparatus determined to bring down Egypt in particular: nobody missed the point, least of all the Palestinians. The idea of a two-tier nation, as developed here, emerged as a means of harmonizing national specificities with membership of a broader historical and cultural whole, namely the Arab world in all its diversity, from the Maghreb and the Nile Valley to Greater Syria and the Arabian Peninsula. Paradoxically, the Zionist offensive reinforced solidarity and the drive for a common project of national renaissance from one end of the Arab world to the other, precisely by re-emphasizing the specific role and importance of national centres within the Arab world. The victorious national revolutions in Sudan and Libya amply confirm the point.

The Zionist operation, the most intense form of imperialism the Middle East has ever known, seeks above all to divide the Arab world, and in particular to isolate Egypt. For Egypt, with its millenarian culture, its resources, cadres and prestige, remains the only country capable of breaking out of the decadence the West seeks to impose on the Arab world. Arab intellectuals, and indeed the Arab people as a whole, are only too aware that Egypt must not be allowed to become the Bantustan of a new South Africa, thereby enabling the West to maintain its hold on the continent at both ends. The Arabs know they must do everything in their power to foil this masterplan which underlies all conceivable Israeli strategy. An isolated and weakened Egypt, a Middle East undermined by constant raids, such as those against Lebanon — aimed at proving that the Arabs' desire to live together peacefully, despite confessional differences is impossible — and the mobilization of world racism against a Palestinian resistance cut off even from its friends; these are surely effective steps towards dismantling the Arab tactical infrastructure from within. But the opportunity will not be available forever. The present worldwide geopolitical equilibrium, established at Yalta, represents the apogee of five centuries of modern history, marked by the great maritime explorations of the 15th Century, the rise of bourgeoisies, the development of philosophical rationalism, scientific methodology and materialism, the industrial revolution and the advent of socialism. New forces have now begun to restructure this equilibrium: China, the oil-rich states, those countries whose giant populations and territory earn them a place as middle ranking powers, the Arab national movement itself — all these now have to be taken into account. The Middle East — South West Asia — is central to this reorganization of world power relations. Renaissance and revolution in the East is gradually becoming the historical pivot of a new world order.

In the dark days following the summer of 1967, this was the background against which ideas were put forward in the Arab world. Everything converged, objectively and inexorably, to deepen a radicalization of political and ideological debate. This intense and rapid evolution, affecting tens of millions of young people, was particularly noticeable amongst those committed to the struggle, be it within the Palestinian resistance, the Arab armies (especially in Egypt) or the ranks of the intellectuals, then as always the most sensitive linkage between the state and the people, tradition and modernity, reflection and action.

Then came the October 1973 war. Military and political contingencies aside, it is undeniable that the action launched by Egypt and Syria, backed by the entire Arab world and supported by all the non-aligned countries, fundamentally altered the course of events. The October war did away with the 'logic of contempt' and replaced it with the honour of action, the courage of initiative, the national will, the primacy of the political. It broke the downward momentum, halted the slide into decadence and imposed a reappraisal of the problem in terms of concrete historical realities, thereby

23

dissipating the endless fascist insistence that the Arabs were marginal to what happened in the world. How else is one to explain the unprecedentedly warm welcome proferred by an almost unanimous UN General Assembly to the leader of the Palestinian resistance on 13 November 1974? The Arabs now have to meet the challenge, to live up to it in terms of their own civilization.

As in the days before 1967, it is now essential to make the transition from a state of siege to civil society, from martial law to political normality. There can be no truly efficacious national existence without a genuine social dialectic, a dialectic which unfortunately will have to develop in the context of imperialism and racism exacerbated by the energy crisis. This difficult equation dominates the Arab thought of our time. The course of our long march may be uncharted, but the essentials are clear: a struggle to displace the all too often conservative and privileged classes from the leadership of the national movement and to replace them with radical national forces drawn from the people themselves, from the great spiritual families which alone can create a true united national front dedicated to the project of national renaissance — a project which already has close associations with socialism. Without such progress, Arab thought and national existence cannot subsist. For those who are committed to the endeavour, it represents a vision of history which they themselves can shape — the wellspring, the dignity, the principle of their very being.

We have chosen 63 texts, representing 59 thinkers from the following Arab countries: Egypt, Lebanon, Syria, Libya, Palestine, Iraq, Sudan, Tunisia, Algeria, Morocco, Saudi Arabia, North and South Yemen. It is hoped that they will enable the reader to judge for himself the validity or otherwise of these introductory remarks.

Making the selection was no easy matter, given the flourishing of Arab culture during the period in question, notably the important role played by the press and journals. We have had to observe certain strict criteria so as to avoid purely arbitrary decisions. Naturally, our choice remains just one amongst many possible such selections.

Our first and most important criterion was to be representative in our choice. Although Islamic reformism has been the subject of countless writings, they are not all equally representative of its affective and ideological content. The same applies to Arab nationalitarianism, Marxism, liberal ideology and right-wing thought. In seeking to make choices which were representative we were led to the second criterion, namely, the social import of the works concerned. Forced to choose between several thinkers of the same tendency, all equally representative of a particular vision of the world, we have opted for those on whom recent or contemporary history has conferred the most influence in their respective domains.

The third criterion was originality of approach or style. This was assessed in terms of the frame of reference specific to the Arab world, although some of these Arab thinkers have also made a broader innovative contribution to contemporary thought as a whole.

The texts have been broken up into eight main sections, according to theme, as follows: (1) History and Present Times; (2) political Islam: Fundamentalism and Integrism; (3) the National Liberation Struggle; (4) the Reconquest of Identity; (5) the Problem of Power: the Popular Masses, the Intellectuals and the Army; (6) Arab Unity; (7) the Problematic of Socialism; and (8) War and Peace: the Project of Renaissance.

Within each section the texts have been arranged according to the publication date of the author's central works rather than by country or date of birth. Each section begins with a text by a great precursor. Amongst the names which heralded the contemporary cultural revival — Khaya al-Din, Faris al-Shidiaq, Butrus al-Bustani, Rifah Rafai al-Tahtawi — we chose the latter, who, from the humble Muslim *kuttab* of his native village, attained a rationalist vision, tinged with socialism, of the nation's future. As *Imam* of the first Egyptian mission to Europe, his intellectual progress took him through many unexpected stages, and his prolific writings are perhaps more varied and more useful than those of his peers, whom he represents in this work.

Notes and references have been kept to a minimum. Most of them serve to illustrate the relation of certain terms and proper names to Arab reality today. It did not seem useful to artificially burden the texts with biographical notes about every personality mentioned, especially the mediaeval ones. The introductory pieces should provide an adequate contextualization. Notes in the original text are fixed with an (A); our own references are simply numbered. In most cases, the only date provided is that of each author's birth. A glossary of the most commonly used Arab terms is included at the beginning of this introduction.

We have drawn up a select general bibliography, in three parts, as follows: (1) General works (in Arabic and European languages); (2) Periodicals (in Arabic); (3) Monographs (in Arabic and European languages).

The extremely rapid evolution of contemporary Arab culture since the time of the *Nahda* — as outlined in this introduction — inevitably also had an effect on the style, the conceptual vocabulary, the very rhythm of linguistic expression. The texts written during the first stage of the national movement, are notably different on all these levels from those written after the Second World War and later. It seemed useful to reproduce this variety of styles rather than to seek an artificial homogeneity. After all, we are studying the second half of 150 years during which the Arab world has passed from the Middle Ages into the atomic era. Hence our desire to respect historicity, even in matters of style; but we have also made sure that all the texts are intelligible to contemporary non-Arab readers.

This work was made possible by the interest expressed in it by the Centre National de Recherche Scientifique, and especially by its Commission on Sociology.

Readers who have found this work interesting may wish to consult the author's *Anthologie de la litterature arabe contemporaine, II, Les essais* (Le Seuil, 1970), which covers a much wider field than the specifically political.

Our special thanks to those friends and colleagues who have helped with this work in various ways, especially Abd al-Rahman Badawi, Mahmoud Amin al-Alem and Shafiq Mitri, in Cairo; Michel Chodkiewicz, Ahmad Bayoud Abdal-Ghani, Mmes Meuvret and Jacqueline Trabuc in Paris; Albert Hourani and J.D. Pearson in Oxford and London; Muhi al-din Azzouz and Salih al-Garmadi in Tunis; Yusif Asad Dagher, Tawfiq Touma and Mikhail Souaya in Beirut; Faisal al-Samer, Salah Khalis and Abd al-Wahab al-Bayati in Baghdad; Dr Ahmad Taleb Ibrahimi and Mustafa Lacheraf in Algiers; and all the editors and directors of Arab cultural magazines and journals who have helped throughout the preparation of this collection.

Our thanks also to Mireille Demaria and Claudine Paulignon who edited the texts for publication at Editions du Seuil.

Finally, our special thanks to our friends and comrades who are directly involved in political action, who helped us at every stage to a better understanding of the reality and thought which is our common concern.

Anouar Abdel-Malek
Paris, 1970 – Cairo, 1983

Notes

1. This volume takes up many of the themes outlined in the author's first doctoral thesis in sociology at the Sorbonne, 'Matériaux pour l'étude de la pernsée arabe contemporaine; l'Égypte', presented 29 April 1964. The core of the Introduction, many of the Egyptian texts and sections of the Bibliography are reproduced from the earlier work, along with many new texts by thinkers representing other Arab countries. The more recent period has, however, been the object of special attention in the present volume.
2. One recognizes here the resurgence of a theme which had already become manifest in Wahabite puritanism (18th-19th Centuries) and, even earlier, in the thought of Ibn Tamiyyah (?-1328).
3. 'Modernist', from 'modern', defined in its primary sense as 'a term used frequently ever since the 10th Century in philosophical or religious polemics, nearly always either pejoratively or with laudatory intent (openness and freedom of thought, knowledge of the most recent discoveries or formulations, absence of indolence and routine), A. Lalande, *Vocabulaire téchnique et critique de la philosophie*, 8th edition, (Paris, 1960), p.640.
4. We will therefore render the term 'qawmiyyah' as 'nationalitarian' or 'nationalitarianism'.

1. History and Present Times

RIFAH RAFAI AL-TAHTAWI
(1801-1873, Egypt)

For his day, the course of Rifah's life was quite extraordinary. He left his native village of Tahtah in 1817 for Cairo, where he studied at the University of Al-Azhar. From there, he went to Paris, as *Imam* of the first Egyptian mission to France sent by Muhammad Ali, in 1826. During his five years in Paris, Rifah worked furiously, striving to acquire as encyclopaedic a culture as possible; he was particularly influenced by the ideas of the 1789 Revolution and by Saint-Simon. He was present, a fascinated observer, during the 1830 Revolution.

When he returned to Egypt, he was appointed Director of the Royal School of Administration, as well as the School of History and Geography (1834), and the School of Languages (1835). In 1840 he became editor-in-chief of *Al-Waqai al-misriyyah* (The Official Gazette), and then, the following year, Director of the Department of Translations. Khedive Abbas I, as part of his efforts to dismantle the modernization undertaken by Muhammad Ali, transferred Rifah to the Sudan. Khedive Said appointed him *miralai* (Brigadier-General) and, in 1854, head of the Military Academy in the Citadel, which he turned into a full-scale university. Removed from public life a second time in 1861, when the Military Academy was dissolved, he was reappointed Director of the Department of Translations by Khedive Ismail in 1863, and remained there until his death.

His sizeable opus — 27 published original or translated works — and the many other works he encouraged, all aimed to integrate the cultural contribution of the age of revolutions in Europe with the renaissance of the Egyptian motherland. He saw that the Middle Ages were coming to a close, in Egypt as in the rest of the Arab world, and understood that a new era was beginning, the era of reconquered identity, the main goal of the nationalitarian phase. And he grasped that what was required was a critical approach both to the national heritage and to foreign contributions, so as to develop a radical way of thinking appropriate to the national framework.

Main works: **The Purification of Gold or the Abridged Overview of Paris** (*Takhlis al-ibriz ila talkhis Bariz*); **The Beauty of Grammar** (*Gamal al-agroumiyyah*); **The Faithful Messenger** (*Al-rassoul al-amin lil-banat wal-banin*); **The Egyptian Hearts' Road to the Joys of Contemporary Mores** (*Manaheg al-albab al-misriyyah fi mabaheg al-adab al-asriyyah*).

Complete works, edited by **Muhammad Amarah**, now being published in Beirut.

The latter work (1869), signalling the early impact of socialist thought on Egyptian and Arab writing, focuses primarily on three themes: the distinction between the political and the religious; labour as the source of all value; the equality of all citizens within the nation, irrespective of creed. The essential passages are reproduced below, in the archaic style of the period.

'Let the motherland be the site of our common happiness, which we shall build by freedom, thought and the factory.'[1]

In matters of religious law, the term *utility* should be interpreted as referring to all those forms of altruistic co-operation laid down by the *shariah*, such as loans, donations, the *sudaqah*,[2] the *wafq* and other similar institutions; it presupposes a familiarity and agreement with the way material life and time are organized. In practical domestic matters, a utility is whatever exists in a village, town or kingdom to promote the well-being of the inhabitants and the organization of their condition in such a way as to produce an effect which enriches the kingdom, serves the interests of the nation and benefits all the participants. It is thus a public affair.

Nowadays, this kind of utility is thought of as part of the political domain: the prescriptions of the *shariah* as followed within the kingdom, do not necessarily coincide with this political utility; one is therefore led to interpret the *shariah* so as to incorporate the utility in question.

The basis of utility as put forward by religious policy consists in the acquisition of money (but without transgressing the law), and its use for proper ends, as well as a commitment to remove everything detestable from the life of mankind — a striving to help and succour others as much as is humanly possible.

European administrations take utility to be the sum of all virtues. We have already seen that there are four sources of material well-being, namely: agriculture, industry, trade and stock-rearing. It is worth adding that where these sources exist within a kingdom, they will never run dry for as long as equity and justice prevail there. If, thanks to investment, savings and the accumulation of resources of all kinds, the people are able to satisfy their domestic needs, they will also be able to fulfil their duties towards the monarchy, recognizing that the latter owes it to itself to be rich and powerful, since it is responsible for their security and protection. Finally, they will be able to give freely in God's name, to help the needy

Thus, the domestic order and the political order are intertwined, the basis of both being economy and the rejection of excess, envy, avarice and waste.

The things of material life have two facets, one active, one passive. The first is labour, the second is agricultural land. The question then arises as to whether land is the source of all wealth and prosperity, while work is but a tool without value other than its application to agriculture; or whether work is the true source of wealth, happiness and profit. In short, whether work is the real basis for the religious community and the nation. In the latter case, happiness would stem from the fact that people draw away from the land what they need for profit and rest; the real merit would accrue to their labour, the merit of the land being only secondary and derivative.

Certainly most farmers would take the second view, arguing that the land becomes fertile only by dint of constant labour; let that labour cease and the land will lie fallow. It is work which gives value to all things which cannot exist without it. Even things which are not commonly bought and sold, such as air and water, gain in value by labour; to the extent that they are necessary to labour, they have the same value as labour itself . . . .

Work is thus the pivot of plenty. Through labour, man derives benefit from the spontaneous activity of the animals, to the greater benefit of his countrymen . . . . Through skilfully executed labour, human beings manage to exploit the movement of air and water, the hardness and softness of materials, the concentration of steam, everything which is endowed with force, all the secrets hidden in the particles of the universe. Experimentation, efficient industry, and the development of skill and knowledge, have given mankind access to the natural energies which God in his wisdom has spread throughout the universe.

Thanks to the existence of industry, which is the locus of labour, and land which is fertile or can be fertilized, man can profit from all these things.

All the virtues which the faithful must manifest towards their brothers in faith are also incumbent between those who share a motherland, in terms of their reciprocal rights and the patriotic fraternity which unites them. Those who share a motherland have a moral obligation to co-operate in order to improve the condition of their nation and to contribute to its greater glory, wealth and prosperity. This prosperity can stem only from the orderliness of social relations and the achievements realized in terms of public utilities. These benefits should be equally distributed between the members of the nation, so that all share in the advantages of pride in one's nation.

When injustice, cowardice, deception and contempt have disappeared, the virtues and their benefits will touch all men and happiness will prevail amongst them.

ABD AL-FATTAH SUBHI WAHIDA
(1912-1956, Egypt)

Holder of a doctorate in law from the University of Rome, Wahida's historical culture, his deep sense of identification with his native land and his solid training in economics, led him to elaborate the first major theoretical work on the general course of Egypt's progress. The book was greeted enthusiastically by the most prominent figures in Egyptian economics, notably Ismail Sidqi and Hafez Afifi, and in 1950 he was appointed Secretary General of the Egyptian Federation of Industries, where he represented the rising technocracy. He was assassinated by a subordinate in 1956.

Main works: **On the Principles of the Egyptian Question (***Fi usoul al-masalah al-misriyyah***).**

In the extract presented here, the author resumes his indictment of the predominance of the agrarian economy, the accompanying social structures and attitudes, and the repercussions for public life in Egypt, on the eve of the overthrow of the old regime. The text should help the reader to understand why the military regime found it easy to attract young technocrats yearning for a future characterized by industrialization and efficiency.

On the Eve of the Industrial Era[3]

A new Egyptian society is emerging. Its origins go back to the beginning of the 19th Century, and its basis can be traced to the weakening of the links between the Turkish Sultanate and Egypt, the dissolution of the Mameluke institutions and the growth of separatist tendencies, starting amongst the country's sheikhs, culminating in Muhammad Ali and achieving their goal at the end of the First World War. These factors converged towards the constitution of a new ruling dynasty and a form of local government serving national interests; eventually they provided the native sons of our country with the means to impose their supremacy over the other elements who had, till then, intermingled with them.

From its past, our society has inherited its Arab thought, its Islamic consciousness and its Mongol institutions, all of which became deeply corrupted under the domination of the Turkish state. It has also been exposed to the influence of the brilliant Western civilization which developed from the 15th to the 19th Centuries, precisely during the period of Turkish decline.

We are now confronted with rulers who assume the trappings of modernity but in reality constantly hark back to their Mongol origins, confusing power and tyranny, proceeding exactly as they choose and treating the people and the people's interests as instruments rather than as the *raison d'être* of a central authority. These rulers make almost no distinction between the general interest and their own personal interests, with the result that their administrations have become entirely based on favouritism, personal advancement and greed. Such systems allow no room for positive legislation; legal rights are extended or restricted according to the rulers' whims, without the slightest concern for correct procedure. The power of these rulers is recent, since none of those who exercise it, at any level of the hierarchy, have done so for more than a generation or two; at the same time such power is already out of date in terms of the institutions involved, given that the latter have remained unchanged and uninvestigated since the last century.

... We are now living that imitation of the West dreaded by Sheikh Muhammad Abduh, although not quite in the form he feared: it has not turned the new generation into the spokesmen of imperialism, but it has cost them an empty Western mould, a distortion which stems from their ignorance of the Eastern scientific heritage and their chaotic assimilation of Western science. Modern science has become a mirage to them, hazy and intangible. They do not study the works of the East, either ancient or modern, in any genuine way, nor do they absorb Western thought from its primary sources. Finally, they do not see the numerous sciences paraded in front of them as having any influence on everyday life. Hence their vacillation between, on the one hand, a negation of their own past and that of the previous generation, whom they hold responsible for present difficulties, and, on the other hand, a blind fanaticism which stems from inflamed emotion rather than from deep reflection, and thus amounts to little more than meaningless verbiage. Finally, there is that enthusiasm for the West which, in certain ex-pupils of foreign schools and institutions abroad, extends to a loss of national consciousness ....

This new generation diminishes itself by avoiding business and rushing into the public sector .... This flight is essentially due to the agrarian character of Egypt's economy, with everything that that involves in terms of the inertia of a society where exchange is limited, profits small and risks high. ... A further consequence is a greed for material possessions, leading certain members of the new generation into reprehensible practices. Corrupt officials, untrustworthy doctors, dishonest engineers are all too common .... This generation is in many ways the first which earns its living by industry and commerce alone and which meets the expenses of contemporary life without the benefit of a private fortune: it is thus inclined to increase its profits by any means available, with no regard for industrial and commercial traditions or for the norms of wise investment . . . .

This generation's awareness of the economic differences separating them from Westerners explains their coldness towards foreigners living in our midst, a coldness which is generally interpreted as hostility and which thus surprises those who contrast it with the generalization of Western life-styles in the country. The phenomenon is a complex one. Amongst its elements, one can number the minor satisfaction of the enfeebled who feel their strength returning, traces of old religious differences and the tension which inevitably arises between people who cross each other's path morning, noon and night without ever communicating. Above all, there is the imperious need felt by the younger generation to live in that semi-modern style which remains the privilege of the foreign residents. The coldness thus in no way contradicts a predisposition towards the West, in fact it is particularly pre-valent amongst those who have spent part of their life abroad and who thus find themselves open to accusations of having distanced themselves from the fundamentals of our oriental way of life.

. . . In conclusion, I believe the main root of our present situation is that loss of vigour, the staleness of the blood which afflicted every aspect of Egyptian life from the 15th to the 19th Centuries, shrinking our economic activity, reducing our social life to the sordid and leading our thought into *Azharist* dogmatism. We are talking of a society that has just emerged from extreme degradation and has begun to gain access to the most recent advances in human civilization, a society striving to accommodate itself to a new existence without drawing on any genuine traditions or foundations of its own. Consequently, it is a society which flounders between the debris of the past and the difficulties of the present, refuses to assess its specific conditions with the required objectivity, and fails to confront them with the determination they demand. The only way to remedy the situation is to purify, nourish and enrich the tired blood of the country, a task which requires a considerable effort from all the members of our society, since it bears on the activity of each and every one of us.

HUSSAIN FAWZI
(1900, Egypt)

After studying medicine in Cairo and Toulouse, Fawzi held the Chair of Oceanography at the Alexandria Faculty of Sciences, later becoming Dean of that faculty and Rector of the university. He was Under-Secretary of State at the Ministry of Culture and National Orientation (1957-59), where he launched many important projects, notably the second (cultural) programme of the Egyptian broadcasting service,

Al-Magallah **magazine, and projects for an Arab encyclopaedia and a general history of Egypt. He is now a member of the Egyptian Institute and cultural adviser to** *Al-Ahram*.

Historian, musicologist, traveller, Fawzi is also the author of a series of works in which he elaborates the problematic of East-West relations. His great interpretation of the history of the Egyptian personality, *Sindbad Misri* **(1961) is one of the masterpieces of contemporary Egyptian culture.**

Main works: **A Contemporary Sindbad (***Sindbad asri***); Sindbad goes West (***Sindbad ila l-gharb***); An Egyptian Sindbad (***Sindbad misri***).**

Continuity of the Egyptian Personality

All these monuments, the pyramids, the nilometer, the bas-reliefs, the churches, the mosques, the Mameluke sanctuaries, evoke the names of kings, caliphs and sultans, making us forget their true creators — the Egyptian people, whose presence one should feel in all these marvels, resolutely facing up to endless catastrophes and misery. We forget the Egyptian people because, unlike Ptolemy, Ramses and Al-Nasr Muhammad Ibn Qalaoun, they have no name. We forget them, even though they stand before us to this day, unchanged for a thousand, three thousand, six thousand years. The Egyptian *fellah* of today is just as he was thousands of years ago, not in his thought, his language, his faith or his dress — although it is generally thought that what he wears today is still the Greek Chlamys of Ptolemaic times — but in his relationship to the land, to irrigation and agriculture. He still goes to the fields and comes home to a primitive dwelling, takes a wife, has children who make up his labour force, sleeps alongside his children, his beasts and his chickens almost exactly as of old; the *sheikh al-balad* or the *umdeh* still loom large and powerful in his life. This continuity runs like a thread throughout Egyptian history; it is the continuity of life on the banks of the Nile. But there is also a more important continuity, the continuity of suffering at the hands of urban landowners, temple priests and the representatives of authority. The actors may change, the history of suffering does not.

A longstanding curse has weighed heavily upon the Egyptians, so often at odds with their Kurdish, Turkish, Circassian, Slavonic, Ferghanian and Maghrebian masters. The Turks spread confusion in the administration, followed by the Albanians and other heterogenous troops. The French — after their first aggression in the days of the Crusades, Amaury, Jean de Brienne and Louis IX — came back to Egypt three times, first under Bonaparte and then through the agency of Muhammad Ali's dynasty, when the Pasha, the family's founder, invited them to realize his selfish exploitative projects and to develop his various monopolies on agriculture, industry and even leisure. The third time, they brought the Zionist hoodlums with them.

But the most signal catastrophy to befall Egypt in the 19th Century was

that army of adventurers from East and West who came to Egypt with profit
as their only law. Such avidity soon turns into pillage when it is unleashed
upon simple honest folk. A gang of foreigners fell upon Egypt: traders,
industrialists, monopolists, usurers, thieves and pimps. Most started poor,
but eventually they became masters obeyed by all, thanks to the Pasha and
the Khedive, who craved an ostentatious veneer of civilization. Some of
these adventurers transformed themselves into intermediaries, then ministers; their arrogance culminated in heavy debts and the British occupation.
Then the adventurers became the agents of the occupier in the ministries
and the private sector . . . .[5]

The real miracle of this Egyptian people is thus not so much the civilization it has bequeathed to the world, but rather the fact that it has managed to
remain a living people, with a personality entirely its own, without ever
being swallowed up by the invaders and the exploiters. The Egyptians
remained at all times a people who planted, built and made things with their
own hands, a people who shaped a civilization,[6] whether they were
governed by a man who loved science and appreciated art or by a
debauched adventurer. They were a people who imposed civilization upon
their rulers.

How else is one to explain that throughout their history, they built *mas-
tabas*, pyramids and temples, monuments and mausoleums, churches and
monasteries, schools, mosques, palaces and sanctuaries, dug canals and
erected dams, linked the two seas, either through the Nile or, more directly,
between Al-Kulzum and Al-Ferma? Who was it who spun the *sharab*, the
debbeki and *tennissi* garb and the *qabbati*[7] cloth of Akhmim? Who
decorated the mosques and their pulpits, the churches and their altars? Who
painted the popular images on wood and placed them in the sarcophagi of
the Fayoum and Bahnasa? Who created the seminary at Heliopolis and the
school of Christian theology, the Didascald which resisted the paganism of
the School of Alexandria? Who founded the University of Al-Azhar? Was
it Pharaoh, the Fatimid chieftain, the Mameluke sultan, de Lesseps or some
other such personality whose name history has preserved along with the
memory of these great works of civilization? Or was it that unknown and
much slandered force whose name is the Egyptian people?

There can be no doubt that the unity of the Egyptian people is the oldest
and strongest unity ever achieved by any nation on earth. It has been
enriched by the silt of the Nile, invigorated by the brightness of the sun. The
civilized people, those who worked the land, have had to organize their lives
around the flood and fall of the Nile. Their calendar has been regulated by
the course of the seasons. They have had to unite to get the best out of the
Nile silt and the Egyptian sun, and in order to forestall the dangers of flooding, drought and the accompanying epidemics . . . .

Even if, as some historians claim, Egyptian civilization has had no direct
influence on the nations which have come into contact with it, it has certainly acted as a leaven in both the ancient and the modern world, by showing what man's physical, mental and social efforts can achieve. We are

talking of a civilization characterized by astonishing and admirable elements, given what we know of the human condition during the early days of this civilization. The Egyptians excelled in applied science, notably engineering and medicine; in the codification of traditions and laws; in governmental institutions, in irrigation, agriculture and stock-rearing; in domains such as architecture, construction, carving, sculpture, painting and the decorative arts, and last, but by no means least, in the spiritual adventure of man's quest for his creator, for his relationship with what lies beyond the universe, the natural world and this temporal life.

The detractors of our ancestors' civilization will point out the weaknesses of its spiritual and material activity: a certain sclerosis of individuality, an approach which remained unchanged over the 30 centuries for which this civilization endured, an inadequacy in those domains of pure reflection and intellectual adventure in which the Greek and Indian civilizations so distinguished themselves. The few changes that did occur only rarely went beyond the limits imposed by deep-seated beliefs and the original inventions of the people of the Old Kingdom.

Yet Egyptian art has survived 30 centuries, despite turmoil, revolution, the Hyksos[8] invasion, the Persian curse, the military might of the Macedonians and Romans. Is that not the real miracle in the history of all humanity's artistic endeavour?

Only the Egyptians' attachment to the traditions of their society and their government can explain this continuity, more, this regularly renewed openness and blossoming forth, not only during the Sait period under the 16th dynasty — reputed for its remarkable artistic achievements inspired by the works of the Old Kingdom — but throughout the centuries until the fall of the 30th dynasty, the last of the Egyptian dynasties. Their art could not have surivived for 3,000 years if the Egyptians had not always turned to their own past to imitate the accomplishments of their ancestors, whose works, especially those of the early dynasties, represented the summit of perfection. The real miracle is that the Egyptians should have so loved their past, remaining faithful to it until the very last.

MUSTAFA LACHERAF
(1917, Algeria)

After completing his classical and modern Arabic studies at Thaalibiyyah and the Sorbonne, Lacheraf was appointed to a *lycée*. As early as 1939 he organized the underground press of the Algerian People's Party, and in 1945 he reconstituted the Party's French federation. A leading member of the MTLD and then of the FLN, he was arrested with a group of the leaders of the Algerian revolution on board the plane taking them to Tunis. In 1962 he served as President of the Algerian

delegation to the Congress of Afro-Asian Writers in Cairo, and was appointed editor-in-chief of *Al-Moujahid*. After a spell as Algerian ambassador to Argentina, he became President Boumedienne's Counsellor for Cultural Affairs and dedicated himself to the study of Algerian culture.

In his stories and essays, he is clearly concerned to re-evaluate traditional themes in the light of modern historical criticism.

Main works: **Arab Heroism** (*Al-butoulah al-arabiyyah*); *Algerie, nation et societe*.

The Transformation of Arab Heroism[9]

What concerns us here is the new, difficult and tortuous road taken by heroism. Over and above the traditional values, new concepts were introduced, such as a spirit of sacrifice, a refusal to engage in reprehensible action and the duty to challenge such actions in others — both verbally and in practice, even if that meant exposing oneself to their hate and irrespective of their position of power. Loyalty, not simply in terms of keeping one's word but more importantly in matters of faith and belief — notably devotion to the bearer of the message, even after his death — became especially important. These notions barely existed in the pre-Islamic period, nor did the expressions which designate and describe the new man so expressively. Notable amongst the latter are 'direct action', 'fine patience', 'struggle in the name of Allah' and the 'sacrifice' of one's own life. Muslim heroism, be it that of the people or that of the elite, both in the rhythmic oral literature and in classical literature, is characterized by a particular concern for such values. Hardship, effort, tribulation, even sorrow and catastrophe, were closely associated with the new concepts.

I feel that the image of genuine traditional Arab heroism emerges clearly from such expressions . . . . . It is in this area that we can make the demarcation between the Western notion of heroism and our own.

Following the course of history, we discover other developments . . . which made heroism almost a matter of necessity, a collective rather than an individual quality. The reason was an endless series of major invasions, the huge, permanent and violent offensives launched against the Arab world by the Crusaders, the Mongols and the Tartars during three centuries. The heroism of Saladin, Al-Zaber Baybars and their companions was possible only because of the efforts of the nameless thousands who never failed to risk their lives and their possessions, animated by a sense of the immense peril threatening the very existence of the Muslim *Umma*. Such attitudes were completely new, even if they cannot really be called 'national' in the modern sense of the word: they represented an intense consciousness of the unity of Muhammad's *Umma* and of the magnificence of what he had bequeathed.

Today, we are witnessing a phenomenon which foreshadows a return to the desires which we first noted in the literature of the pre-Islamic period, even if these desires and physical needs have taken a new form. The grounds for pride are being buried in complacent evocation of them. One of the striking aspects of this phenomenon is that it is no longer restricted to the elite and their poets. It can now be found coming from the mouths of the people, or expressed in long screeds of popular writing, devoid of all measure and characterized by an imagination run wild, in which heroism is spoken of as something imbued with overwhelming appetite, bristling with desire. Such evocations are stamped with boundless futility; they prefer artifice to creation, mix reality and the ideal and make a mockery of order and historical accuracy.

The people live in the bosom of this experience of heroism as if by instinct, choosing as they see fit amongst eternal truths: the trunk without the branch or the branch without the trunk. They crave evocations of heroism to satisfy spiritual needs as pressing as thirst and hunger. By a strange coincidence, this phenomenon has manifested itself in the history of all peoples going through troubled times, and especially during periods devoid of any real heroism, after disastrous national defeats .... But it is particularly striking in Arab popular literature, with its ardent passions, overflowing imagination and long sagas full of heroes and men of action.

Foreign domination has surrounded each people with a wall, cutting them off from the other peoples. Yet powerful counter-currents surge forth from the heart of the Eastern and Muslim masses, wherever they may be, almost as if this were a necessary part of the thirst for a liberating heroism, operating on both the psychological and the political levels .... We have already noted that the Crusades and the Mongol and Tartar offensives transformed heroism by transferring it from the elite to the masses, changing an individualistic conception into a collective one and increasing its practical value by referring it back to the needs of a national, doctrinal or political entity, rather than to the quest for personal reputation and useless glory. Under the impact of the necessity imposed by changing circumstances and by the danger constantly hanging over the life of the Arab peoples, heroism became a commitment to constant struggle, a compulsion fired by the instinct of self-preservation. All this comes close to the sense and meaning of the word 'resistance'.

Notes

1. *Manaheg al-albad al-Misriyyah* .... (Cairo, 3rd ed., 1912), p.23-24.
2. Ritual aims.
3. Abd al Fattah Subhi Wahidah, *Fi Usoul* ...(Cairo, 1950), pp.209-224.
4. Hussein Fawzi, *Sindbad Misri* (Cairo, 1961), pp.139-41, 305-43.
5. The viceroy of Egypt nominated by the sultan bears the title 'Khedive'. The author is referring to the events which marked the reigns of Said, Ismail and Tawfiq, notably the chronic indebtedness which was eventually to serve as the

pretext, first for Franco-British financial control, and then for the British occupation. (1882).

6. In the sense of *homo faber*.

7. Types of cloth woven in the Delta during the Middle Ages.

8. Invaders of Egypt, from Asia, who dominated the country from 1730 to 1580 BC.

9. *Al-butoulah al-arabiyyah wa awamel nashatiba bayn al-waqai wal mithaliyyah* (Arab Heroism and the Factors of Its Birth, Between Reality and Idealization), *Al-Fikr*, Vol.V, No.4, 1960, pp.11-24.

2. Political Islam: Fundamentalism and Integrism

MUHAMMAD ABDUH
(1849-1905, Egypt)

After completing his studies at Al-Azhar, Abduh became the disciple and close companion of Jamal al-Din al-Afghani, and was eventually appointed to lecture at Dar al-Ulum. His reticent support for Arabi's 1882 revolution was enough to condemn him to exile after its defeat and the British occupation. He taught in Lebanon and then went to Paris, where he and Al-Afghani published *Al-Urwah al-Wuthqa* (1884) a journal which proved to be the crucible of Islamic national-itarianism.

On his return to Egypt, he took up various senior posts in the religious magistrature, and was finally appointed Mufti of Egypt in 1889. A distant supporter of the National Party, which enjoyed Cromer's backing, he dedicated himself to the task of elaborating the theoretical principles of Islamic fundamentalism and the spiritual renaissance of the Arab world: his ideal was a return to the wellsprings of the faith, combined with the application of common sense, which would enable Islam to adapt to the modern world. The theses he developed made him the true founding father of the Islamic revival, both in the Middle East and in the Maghrib.

Main works: **Treatise on Divine Unity**[1](*Rissalat al-tawhid*); **Islam and Christianity Face to Face with Science and Civilization** (*Al-Islam wal-nasraniyyah maa al-ilm wal-madaniyyah*); **Intepretations of the Noble Koran** (*Tusir al-Qur'an al-karim*); **Memoirs** (*Mudhakkirat*).

One particularly prophetic text sets out Abduh's programme of political action aimed to promote the renaissance of decadent Islamic society. It enables the reader to grasp the relationship between Islam and democracy during the period of national renaissance in its own context rather than in terms of extraneous situations which have resulted from different evolutions.

Only a Just Despot Will Ensure the Renaissance of the Orient[2]

The Orient needs a despot who would force those who criticize each other to recognize their mutual worth, parents to be charitable, neighbours to be fairminded, and people generally to adopt his view of their interests, be it by intimidation or by joyful consent; a despot who would never take any step without his primary consideration being the effect on the people he governs, so that any personal good fortune which befell him would be quite secondary, in that he would live more for them than for himself.

It would take only 15 years to bring the people to a point of no return — the time required for an infant to reach puberty and the age of reason, growing up under the protection of a benevolent godfather and becoming steadily stronger, until he could overcome any assailant. Fifteen years during which the powerful will be throttled for their own good and that of their descendants, and their souls will be purified by the most efficacious means available, by amputation and cauterization if need be. Fifteen years during which the spirit of the common folk will be elevated, their willpower reinforced, their aspirations strengthened by culture, their souls nurtured as if by a gardener training plants. Fifteen years during which an immense mass of people dedicated to reform will be mobilized, both those who have eagerly awaited it for years and the young who will have grown up expecting it, both those who have laboured intensely to bring it about and those who support it because they hope to benefit from its virtues.

When attitudes have evolved along the course set for them and people have reached the stage for which they have been prepared, when emotion has been tempered by judgement and the passions curbed, then men will be allowed to draw sustenance from as much freedom as the young can assimilate and their elders digest. To begin with, parish councils will be set up, to be followed a few years later by boards with wider powers: neither will be machines to be manipulated, rather they will serve as a focus for opinions and ideas. Eventually representative assemblies will be created. It may well be that no man will be able to follow the whole process from beginning to end. But the forerunners will pave the way for their successes; fifteen years are all that is required, a short period in which to educate a slave, let alone a nation.

Is the entire Orient unable to bring forth a single autocrat who would be just with his people and through whom justice would achieve more in fifteen years than reason alone has achieved in fifteen centuries?

ALI ABD AL-RAZEQ
(1888-1966, Egypt)

Brother to Mustafa Abd al-Razeq, the great Rector of Al-Azhar, he studied at first at Al-Azhar then at Oxford. In 1925 he published his book on the necessary historical separation between religion and political power. This was in response to his alarm at Ottoman and Hashemite attempts to bring Egypt under their hegemony, using the Caliphate as the pretext, following the Egyptian revolution of 1919. His work was condemned by Al-Azhar and his career seriously compromised as a result. He spent the rest of his life working at the Arabic Language Academy in Cairo.

Main works: **Islam and the Principles of Government (***Al-Islam wa usoul al-hukm***); Unanimity in Islamic Holy Law (***Al-ijma fil-shariah al-Islamiyyah***).**

The text below, inspired by Tahtawi, exemplifies the direct, incisive and powerful use of the fundamental tenets of Islam in the struggle against arbitrary power following the 1919-24 revolution. Yet it was precisely his application of the criteria of political sociology to the Caliphate which brought down such opprobrium upon the author. A generation later, Khaled Muhammad Khaled was to pursue a similar line of thought, this time influenced by socialist ideas.

The Caliphate as a Political Institution[3]

(1) We have not been able to establish with any certainty who forged the title '*Caliph* of God's Prophet' used by Abu Bakr; we only know that Abu Bakr accepted and adopted it.

(2) There can be no doubt that, as we have already explained, the Prophet was the leader of the Arabs and the keystone of their unity. Abu Bakr then set himself up as King of the Arabs — as the artisan of their unity, to use a modern political phrase — so one may indeed call him caliph of God's prophet, or even just caliph, given the meaning of the term in Arabic. It is in this sense that Abu Bakr was the caliph of God's Prophet; no other possible meaning of the term caliphate can be sustained.

(3) The term is imbued with prestige, strength and magnetism. It is thus not in the least surprising that Al-Siddiq[4] adopted it; after all, his aim was to bring a new state into being out of a raging tempest of sedition and contradictory ambitions. The people had only just emerged from the *Jahiliyyah* and were still marked by remnants of fanaticism and bedouin wildness. Furthermore it was not long since the people had given their complete allegiance to God's Prophet, offering to do his bidding in every way. His memory was still fresh in their minds. The title was thus likely to make it easier to control and direct them, and this may well have been the reason it came into being.

Some of these people believed that since Abu Bakr had assumed the caliphate of God's Prophet, he should be recognized as a caliph in the full sense of the word. Since Abu Bakr was Muhammad's caliph and Muhammad was God's caliph, they reasoned, it followed that Abu Bakr must be God's caliph as well. They would not have been wrong if the title of Muhammad's caliph assumed by Al-Siddiq had really meant what they took it to mean and what many people still think it means. But Abu Bakr rejected the notion and announced 'I am not God's caliph, only the caliph of God's Prophet'.

(4) The title nonetheless led a great many Arabs and Muslims to accept Abu Bakr's principate as sovereignty by divine right, just as they had done in the case of God's Prophet. His royal rank was thus heightened by the aura of religion; rebellion against Abu Bakr became equivalent in their eyes to rebellion against Islam, to apostasy. Hence the term 'wars of the apostasy' — *huroub al-riddah* — used to designate the wars against those who refused to give their allegiance to Abu Bakr. Yet it appears that these rebels were not necessarily all apostates who had lost their faith in God and his Prophet; on the contrary some of them remained committed to Islam but, for one reason or another, would not rally to Abu Bakr's cause and refused to accept that their refusal to do so posed a religious problem. Since these groups were clearly not apostates, the struggle against them should not have been undertaken in the name of religion. If war was inevitable, it was because of politics, the need to defend Arab unity and to preserve the Arab state. In fact some of those who at first refused to recognize Abu Bakr — for instance Ali ibn Abi Taleb and Saad ibn Ibadah — were not treated as apostates.

(5) Others, against whom Abu Bakr went to war when they refused to pay him tribute, never intended that refusal as a rejection or abjuration of their religion; they simply saw no reason to recognize Abu Bakr's authority. For them, as for other great Muslim figures of the age, it was quite natural to refuse to pay tribute, since they did not recognize Abu Bakr's government and were not subject to its power.

(6) Every time one looks closely at the historical evidence concerning those who rebelled against Abu Bakr, the so-called apostates against whom war was waged, one cannot avoid the feeling that distortions abound. Yet there is a ray of light shining through all this darkness. One day, researchers will seize on that ray as their beacon and will perhaps be able to trace it back to the fire of truth.

(7) I have no hesitation whatsoever in asserting that many of the so-called wars of the apostasy in the first days of Abu Bakr's caliphate were not religious wars at all, but entirely political wars which the ordinary people mistook for religious wars . . . . The underlying causes of the rebellion can be deduced from careful study of the descendency and tribal loyalties of those who rebelled against Abu Bakr; to get at the truth, their relations with Quraish, the ancestor of the royal house must be considered; a grasp of the real meaning of God's laws concerning new states and the forms of

solidarity pertaining to the monarchy is necessary, as well as a knowledge of the character and mores of the Arabs.

(8) I tend to think that in fact there was a group of Muslims who recanted their faith after the Prophet's death. Such an outcome would be in keeping with the laws of nature as we know them. It seems even more likely that false prophets arose, both during Muhammad's lifetime and afterwards. We have only to look around ourselves today to see how easy it is for demagogues to find disciples and converts. Ordinary people are all too willing to give credence to the 'prophetic powers' of a man who knows how to charm them and encourage them in their confusion. I am thus inclined to believe that in the early days of Abu Bakr's reign there were indeed some groups who had abjured Islam and others who had fallen prey to false prophets. Abu Bakr immediately went to war against these genuine apostates and false prophets, and fought until he had vanquished them and eradicated their errors.

It is not our purpose here to determine whether or not Abu Bakr was qualified to pass spiritual judgement on those who had abjured Islam; nor are we seeking to establish whether there were any non-religious factors which fanned Abu Bakr's enthusiasm for these wars. What matters is that Abu Bakr's first action within the framework of the new state was to wage war against the apostates. It was at that time that the term *murtaddin* (apostates) was forged to designate genuine apostates; the term was later extended to apply to all those Arabs against whom Abu Bakr went to war, whether they were religious opponents, genuine apostates or non-apostatic political adversaries. All Abu Bakr's wars thus took on a religious coloration and were fought in the name of Islam, so that joining Abu Bakr was taken as equivalent to placing oneself under Islam's banner, and deserting him was seen as equivalent to abjuring and corrupting Islam.

(9) There were perhaps other factors specific to Abu Bakr which confirmed the masses in the mistake they made when they endowed Abu Bakr's principate with the aura of religion.

He had after all held an exceptionally high position alongside God's Prophet, and his name was a landmark in the history of religion. His rank amongst Muslims was correspondingly high. Furthermore, he followed the course laid down by the Prophet very strictly, both in his heart and in his conduct of the affairs of state and other public matters. He did everything in his power to establish policies in keeping with the Prophet's teachings. It is thus hardly surprising that his role as first sovereign of the new state should have been surrounded with all the trappings of religion.

(10) It now seems clear that this title — caliph of God's Prophet — carrying as it does all the overtones we have mentioned and many others we have not, was one of the main causes of misapprehension into which most ordinary Muslims have fallen, namely that the caliphate is a religious role, and that he who holds power over Muslims occupies amongst them the same position as God's Prophet.

(11) It was in the interest of the various sultans to propagate this error

amongst the people, so as to use religion as a shield with which to protect their throne against rebels. Such is their practice to this day. They have used every available means to convince the people that to obey the *Imams* is to obey God, and that to disobey them is to disobey Him. Furthermore, the caliphs did not content themselves with what Abu Bakr had accepted, nor did they refuse what he had refused: they claimed that to be sultan was to be God's caliph on earth, His shadow over all the faithful.

Eventually the caliphate became a subject for theological research, one of the constitutive elements of the dogma of unity, to be studied as such by Muslims on the same level as the attributes of all-powerful God or the qualities of His noble prophets, a dogma to be learnt by heart just like the testimony 'There is no God but Allah and Muhammad is His Prophet'.

This was the great crime of the kings against the Muslims: in their despotism, they turned their subjects away from the true path, they disfigured truth and, in the name of religion, hid the one true light; then, still in the name of religion, they humiliated and tyrannized their subjects and forbade the study of the political sciences. They misled them and imprisoned their reason, thereby denying the Muslims access to anything that lay outside the realm of religion, even in administrative and political matters.

They then imposed upon their subjects a narrow understanding of religion; they restricted their range of enquiry and banned any scientific endeavour which might have had some bearing on the status of the caliphate.

All this led to the suffocation of critical judgement and intellectual speculation amongst the Muslims; political philosophy and all enquiry concerning the caliphate and caliphs were paralysed.

(12) The truth is that this abusive conception of a caliphate imbued with ambition, fear, splendour and force is quite alien to Islam. The caliphate has nothing to do with the divine project, and for that matter neither does the administration of justice and the other functions of government and the state. These are specific political projects with which religion has no concern; Islam has neither recognized, condemned nor forbidden them, leaving us to make up our own minds on the basis of reason, the experience of nations and the rules of politics.

Similarly, religion has nothing to do with the administration of the Muslim armies, civic amenities or other municipal projects: these are all matters for common sense and experimentation, drawing on established ground rules and expert opinion.

There is nothing in the religion which forbids Muslims to compete with the other nations in the social and political sciences. Nothing debars them from overthrowing the decrepit form of organization which has so humiliated them ever since they adopted it. Muslims are free to establish rules of kingship and government fully in keeping with the most recent achievements of the human spirit, and with that which the experience of nations has shown to be the most advantageous in terms of the principles of sound government.

HASSAN AL-BANNA
(1906-1949, Egypt)

The founder and supreme figure of the Muslim Brotherhood (1928), Al Banna had previously studied literature and theology at Dar al-Ulum. Whilst still a teacher at Damanhour, he created a movement which eventually moved its centre of operations to Cairo and was later to flourish throughout the Muslim world.

His teachings and his political activity are natural extensions of the sort of activism preached by Al-Afghani: a return to the wellsprings of Islam will enable Muslims to restore their religion's power and stand firm against all intrusive tendencies, notably Marxism. A period of struggle against the National Democratic Front (1945-48) was rapidly followed by a wave of terrorism, which cost Hassan al-Banna his life.

Main works: **Our Call** (*Dawatuna*); **Towards the Light** (*Nahw al-nur*); **Our Faith** (*Aqidatuna*); **The Muslim Brothers Under the Flag of the Koran** (*Al-Ikhwan al-Muslimun tahta rayat al-Quran*); **Our Problems in the Light of the Muslim Order** (*Mashkilatuna fi daw al-nizam al-Islami*); **Reminders of the Call and He Who issued it** (*Mudhakkirat al-dawah wal-dai*).

The following text constitutes one extreme of Islamic fundamentalism, taken to its logical conclusions; adherence to Islamic law and principle is set up as the one essential precondition for every modern Arab or Muslim state. The force and almost military simplicity of this approach is typical of a man of faith who was, above all, a great mover of crowds.

The Credo of the 'Muslim Brotherhood'[5]

(1) I believe that all things must be rendered unto God, that our master Muhammad — God's blessing be upon Him — was the last of the prophets sent amongst men, that the Qur'an is the book of God, that Islam is a general law regulating the order of this world and the next. I promise to apply the noble Qur'an's teachings in my own life, to adhere to the purifying *Sunnah* and to study the life of the Prophet and the history of his noble disciples.

(2) I believe that rectitude, virtue and science are part of the foundations of Islam. I promise to be upright, to carry out the rites, to shun what is forbidden, to be virtuous, to cultivate good habits and avoid bad ones, to accomplish the rituals of Islam as far as I am able, to prefer love and affection over disputes and contention, to invoke the powers of the judiciary only when it is unavoidable, to be proud of Islam's rites and its language, and to spread science and useful knowledge amongst the various classes of the *Umma*.

(3) I believe that a Muslim must work and earn money, and that any needy person who asks for charity has a right to part of the money I earn. I promise to work to earn my living, to save for the future, to pay the *zakat*, to set aside part of my income for charitable deeds, to encourage any useful economic project, to give preference to the products of my own country and those of other Muslim countries, not to practice usury in any respect and not to lose myself in matters lying beyond my competence.

(4) I believe that a Muslim is responsible for his family, that he has a duty to protect their health, their faith and their morality. I promise to do everything in my power to that end, to propagate the teachings of Islam amongst my family, not to place my sons in any school where their faith and their morality would not be strengthened, to boycott any newspaper, publication, book, organization, group or club which opposes the teachings of Islam.

(5) I believe that a Muslim has a duty to revive the glory of Islam by promoting the renaissance of its peoples and by restoring its legislation. I believe that the flag of Islam should dominate all mankind, and that it is the duty of every Muslim to educate the world in the rules of Islam. I promise to struggle as long as I live to achieve this goal and to sacrifice all I have to this mission.

(6) I believe that all Muslims form a single nation, united by the Islamic faith, and that Islam commands its sons to work for the good of all. I promise to bend my efforts to reinforce the ties of fraternity between all Muslims, and to eradicate the indifference and divergencies which prevail between their communities and brotherhoods.

(7) I believe that the secret of the Muslims' backwardness is their estrangement from the religion, and that the basis of reform should be a return to the precepts and judgements of Islam; I believe that this is possible if the Muslims work towards this goal and if the doctrine of the Muslim Brotherhood is implemented. I promise to hold fast to these principles, to stay loyal to whoever works for them and to remain a soldier in their cause, even if it costs me my life.

(A) The law of the Muslim Brotherhood is inspired by the rules established by Muhammad himself . . . . There is not a single word in the credo of the Muslim Brothers which is not based on the Book of God, the *Sunnah* of his Prophet and the spirit of true Islam. Examine each paragraph as scrupulously as you like: you will find only the Islamic truth laid down by Islam, proclaimed by the religion, recommended by the noble Qur'an and announced by God's Prophet . . . . O sons of our dearly beloved *Umma*, we are Muslims and that is sufficient unto itself. Our faith is drawn from the Book of God, from His Prophet's Sunnah; that is sufficient unto itself. If what we say displeases you, then adopt the doctrines of the foreigners and let nothing bind you to us. Anyone who still doubts the Muslim Brothers after this clear exposition of their position and despite the purity of their faith either has not studied Islam adequately enough to assimilate its spirit and appreciate its objectives, or is simply ill-intentioned and in bad faith.

(B) . . . The religion which satisfies man's spiritual hunger and offers him the necessary tranquillity of conscience and happiness is Islam, the most powerful bond uniting the sources of love within the nation; Islam reinforces understanding between peoples and confidently leads the world towards a general unity, the highest aspiration of reformers and sages and the basis of human welfare. Islam founds the state on principles of justice, establishes government in terms of clearly defined rights and allows each member of the various classes in the nation his due, without frustration, misunderstanding or injustice.

There is a lesson here for those Oriental rulers who in the past have sought or in the future will seek to find some other path than Islam in order to lead their people towards renaissance and to reconstitute the religion, the *Umma* and the state.

(C) The Muslims of today will only succeed by following the same path as their master, Muhammad . . . . In fact, ever since the Oriental nations foresook the teachings of Islam and attempted to substitute others which they believed would help solve their problems, they have been caught in a morass of uncertainty and have suffered bitter defeats; the price for deviation has been high, in dignity, morality, self-respect and administrative efficiency.

The great strength of the Orient is its morality and its faith. If it loses those, it loses everything; but if it returns to them, it regains all it has lost. Unjust force collapses before solid morality, belief and faith. Let the leaders of the Orient, then, take pains to fortify its soul and to restore its lost morality, for such is the only means whereby to bring about a genuine renaissance; they will only succeed in this task by returning to Islam and dedicating themselves exclusively to its teachings.

(D) As for the application of this method to the situation faced by present day Muslims . . . it will take considerable time. The gulf that political and social events have opened up between the Muslims and their faith is wide, and the subjective methods used by the enemies of Islam to draw Muslims away from the religion during the modern area have been effective. Indeed, the Muslims themselves are at war with their faith; they break their own sword and freely hand a dagger to those who would bring them down, by co-operating with those who seek to demolish the religion which is the very foundation of their regimes and the source of their strength.

The Muslim Brothers are deeply aware of all this. We have never believed that effective action would be easy. We have foreseen the obstacles, prepared ourselves and made ready our goods, our faith and our belief.

(E) No one should conclude from the above that action should be renounced. On the contrary, the obstacles will only intensify our energy and the difficulties will only accelerate our march towards the struggle, as the All High insists.

O Muslim Brothers, victory will come if we are patient; our salvation lies in firmness. Those who love God will surely be rewarded.

ABD AL-QADER AUDAH
(?-1954, Egypt)

Having distinguished himself as a lawyer, political theoretician and counsellor to the Cairo Court of Appeal, Abd al-Qader Audah became a member of the Muslim Brotherhood's bureau shortly after the Second World War. He soon became a political figure of stature and was responsible for co-ordinating the activities of the legal organization with those of the underground activist bodies. The military *coup d'etat* on 23 July 1952 raised the Muslim Brotherhood's hopes of gaining greater access to the corridors of power, where they were originally represented by Colonel Abd al-Muneim. The formation of a coalition of dissolved political parties and the swing of public opinion against Gamal Abdel Nasser's monopoly of political power eventually brought Abd al-Qader Audah to the forefront, alongside General Muhammad Neguib. On 26 October 1954, one week after the signature of the troop evacuation agreement with the British, a member of the secret organization attempted to assassinate Abdel Nasser in Alexandria. The event became the trigger for a general wave of repression against the Muslim Brotherhood's underground organization. On 7 December, six Brotherhood leaders, including Abd al-Qader Audah, were executed in Cairo. Audah's prolific writings, although uneven in quality, indicate that political Islam had lost a thinker and a national political leader of some calibre.

   Main Works: Islam and Our Present Political Conditions (*Al-Islam wa awdauna al-siyasiyyah*); Islamic Criminal Law (*Al-tashri al-ginai fil-Islam*); Money and Government in Islam (*Al-mal wal-hukm fil-Islam*); Islam and Our Present Financial Condition (*Al-Islam wa awdauna al-maliyyah*).

   The theses developed below are good examples of the close kinship existing between the political philosophy of a state based on a military regime and the political doctrines of Islamic fundamentalism in its more uncompromising forms.

Authority in the Modern Islamic State[6]

Executive Authority
Executive authority is the exclusive prerogative of the head of state, the *Imam*, whose duty it is to initiate executive measures which will promote Islam and to direct the affairs of state in keeping with Islam. This general formulation covers a variety of functions, notably the appointment, dismissal, guidance and supervision of officials, command of the army, declarations of war; peace or armistice proclamations, the signing of treaties and the delimitation of frontiers; the implementation of the law; responsibility for prayers and pilgrimages; initiation of wars in order to res-

tore the position of the Muslims in the world; codification of rules and regulations to orient Muslims towards true Islam and the power to grant amnesties and pardons for certain sins and crimes. In Islam, the principle is that the *Imam* is the head of state and has overall responsibility for its affairs. The *Imam*'s responsibility is boundless: he lays down state policy, supervises its implementation and has the final say on all affairs of state.

The *Imam* may call on his ministers to deal with matters of state and to orient the course of its affairs, but the ministers remain responsible to him for their actions: their job is to implement his policies and carry out his orders. They are his deputies, their authority derives from his. Each one of them functions as the administrative head of the ministry he supervises: their opinions and their policies only commit the head of state if he explicitly endorses them, but once a policy has been implemented, he carries the responsibility.

Subsequent to this original division of powers between the *Imam* and his ministers, a further differentiation arose between two types of minister. The *Imam* delegates the administration of a ministry to the first kind of minister, who then manages matters according to his own lights and draws on his own interpretation of the facts when making a decision. Although he controls all his ministry's affairs, the minister must keep the *Imam* informed of the measures he has initiated and which the *Imam* is by no means bound to endorse. Correspondingly, it is the *Imam*'s duty to supervise his minister's actions and way of proceeding, so as to ascertain that they are in keeping with the law.

The second type of minister is essentially an executant, who carries out the decisions reached by the *Imam* and serves essentially as an intermediary between the *Imam* and the people of the country: he carries out the *Imam*'s orders, signs his decrees and conveys to him the demands of the people and information as to the turn of events. He has no policy-making role of his own.

Both types of minister are responsible to the Head of State, who can dismiss them if ever they disobey his orders or stray from the policy he has laid down. The Head of State is himself responsible for his policy and for all matters of state to the members of the *Umma* generally, and to the advisory council more specifically.

Legislative Authority

The principle of law in the Islamic *shariah* is that it should serve as a guide to men in every situation, that they may turn to it for judgement in all matters which concern them, both in this world and the next.

The general judgements and principles mentioned by the *shariah* must be taken as the general rules of Islamic legislation; they provide the basic armature which determines the characteristics and forms of control of Islamic legislation.

The *shariah* leaves it to the wise and to public opinion to complete the edifice of legislation, to elaborate its details and interconnections within the framework of principles and fundamental rules laid down in the *sha-riah* . . . .

The restrictions on the right (of the wise) to pass law are to be considered under two headings: *Firstly*, those laws whose purpose is to ensure compliance with the texts of the Islamic *shariah*. Such legislation is equivalent to the rules and regulations laid down by ministers today in their respective fields, so as to ensure that the law is enforced. *Secondly*, laws whose object is the organization and protection of the community whose needs are to be met on the basis of the principles of the *shariah*. Such laws must only be promulgated where the *shariah* itself has nothing to say on the subject in question . . . .

Judicial Authority

. . . As delegate of the *Umma*, the *Imam* will appoint the *gadis* and will be responsible for controlling and dismissing them. But once appointed, the *qadis* should be seen as deputies of the *Umma* rather than of the *Imam*. Hence they are not automatically dismissed whenever an *Imam* dies or retires, and an *Imam* may not dismiss them without some valid reason.

Financial Authority

When the Muslim state was founded, Islam created a new and autonomous form of authority which the world as a whole has only come to recognize during this century. I refer to authority over finance.

The *Imam*, in his quality as delegate of the *Umma* in its entirety, must supervise those who have authority over financial matters . . . even though, once appointed, the latter, like the *qadis*, are to be seen as delegates of the *Umma* rather than of the *Imam*.

Authority to Control and Rectify

The *Umma* as a whole has this authority to control and rectify the course chosen by governments. The wise, the *ulemas*, and those learned in jurisprudence represent the *Umma* in such matters.

This authority is the prerogative of the *Umma* in two respects: (1) The *Umma* must control a government and rectify its course in the light of God's command to the *Umma* to do what is good and shun what is evil. (2) The *Umma* is the source of the rulers' authority, since they are delegates of the *Umma*.

SADEQ JALAL AL-AZM
(1934, Syria)

A Syrian philosopher, born in Damascus, Al-Azm attended secondary school in Lebanon, then the American University of Beirut, finally

taking his doctorate at Yale (1961). He held various academic posts: University of Damascus (1962-63), American University of Beirut (1963-68, 1975-), University of Jordan (1968-69). Since 1969, he has been director of the Arab Studies Review.

Interesting philosophical works precede the author's post-1967 phase during which he began his critical examination of contemporary Arab thought, especially its religious ideology, in an attempt to discover the origins of the collapse. His *Critique of Religious Thought* led to a major political trial in 1969-70, which contributed to a process of radicalization of the political and intellectual movement in Lebanon, despite the fact that until 1967 the country had been very much on the sidelines of the great Arab struggles and heavily influenced by the West.

The extracts quoted here are from the preface of the author's *Critique*. The tone is typical of the kind of fundamental reappraisal which is under way amongst all Arab organic intellectuals today.

Main works: Studies in Modern Western Philosophy; Kant's Theory of Time; The Origins of Kant's Arguments in the Antinomies; *Dirasat fil-falsafah al-gharbiyyah al muasirah* (Studies in Modern Western Philosophy); *Fil-hubb wal-hubb al-udhri* (Of Love and Arab Courtly Love); *Al-naqd al-dhati baad al-hazimah* (Autocritique After the Defeat); *Naqd al-fikr al-dini* (Critique of Religious Thought); *Dirasah yasariyyah hawl al-qadiyyah al-filistiniyyah* (Left Studies on the Palestine Problem); *Dirasah naqdiyyah li fikr al-muqawamah al-filistiniyyah* (Critical Study of the Thought of the Palestinian Resistance).

Critique of Religious Thought[7]

It should be obvious that when I say 'religious thought' I am referring to the higher and more conscious echelons of that integrated and multifaceted block of ideas, representations, aims and attitudes which we call variously 'the religious mentality', 'the backward looking ideology' or the 'historically rooted spiritual mentality'. In this sense the 'religious mentality' is characterized by the hegemony of an implicitly dominant 'backward-looking ideology' which is spontaneously and unconsciously accepted as a framework. What then is the status of this type of thought in contemporary Arab intellectual life?

Following the Arab defeat of June 1967, a number of progressive Arab authors felt impelled to criticize certain aspects of the traditional ideological and social structure of our Arab society, way of life and heritage. In most cases, this critique of the superstructures of Arab society (its thought, its culture, its implicitly backward-looking idealist evolution) remained superficial and hesitant, especially in connection with the 'religious mentality', even though everybody recognized its importance, its all-encompassing character and the extent of its influence. In practice, most critiques in this domain boiled down to a rehash of the vague generalizations and clichés used to denounce a 'passive and backward-looking mentality', a 'faith in mirages, myths and miraculous solutions'; and as usual this denunciation was accompanied by calls for the Arab people to adopt a 'scientific style', a 'rationalist method' in all their dealings, in order to build a modern technocratic state.

Yet not one of these critics and epigones has bothered to criticise the 'backward-looking mentality' in question, on the basis of a rationalist, scientific examination of living concrete examples of this thought, its avowed aims and its interpretation of events . . . .

Furthermore, also after 1967, it emerged that the religious ideology, with its conscious and unconscious elements, explicitly constituted the main 'theoretical' weapon in the hands of the Arab leadership; they used it to conduct both open warfare and underhand manoeuvres against the progressive and revolutionary forces in the Arab nation. Similarly, certain progressive Arab regimes have found in religion a crutch, a means of pacifying the Arab masses and concealing the impotence and failure exposed by the defeat. As we shall show, religious thought serves as a 'theoretical' weapon as much by means of a falsification of reality as by a falsification of the consciousness people have of that reality; a falsification of the real relationship between the Islamic religion and modern science; a falsification of the real relationship between religion and the political realm, whatever its nature (be it Arabism, socialism, scientific socialism, Islamic socialism, revolutionary socialism or whatever); a falsification of the true nature of contemporary states, whether friendly or hostile (as was the case during the recent Islamic summit); a falsification of the realities of the social struggle between the rising revolutionary social forces and the forces of inertia, between the forces of the hegemonic classes and the forces of the exploited in rebellion (for instance, the propaganda for the construction of bridges between the various national classes in the name of reformism, conciliation, love and other spiritual values).

Although religious thought has long been a theoretical weapon in the hands of the reactionaries, the Arab liberation movement has never set out to face up to this weapon, on the intellectual and practical level, by means of a critical scientific analysis which would make it possible to denounce the various forms of falsification and negativity imposed by the religious ideology on Arab people. In fact this conservative attitude was just one element of the generally passive attitude, adopted by the Arab liberation movement and its political and intellectual leadership, towards the need for a critical examination of the Arab social and intellectual heritage, and for a reappraisal of our society's superstructural parameters in keeping with the great material changes which had occurred in its infrastructure. The Arab liberation movement considered this cultural superstructure — with all that it implied in terms of residual intellectual habits, values dating back to the bedouin and feudal eras, deeply archaic human relations, and a passive, stagnant backward looking approach to life — as something worthy of respect and esteem, as somehow surrounded by a halo of holiness which placed it beyond the scope of scientific criticism and historical analysis.

In fact the mistake made by the Arab liberation movement in this area was not so much to have simply fallen into the so-called 'economist deviation', as might appear to be the case, but rather to have been misled by a very distorted form of this 'economist deviation'. Had the Arab liberation movement simply gone along with the 'economist deviation' it would have concentrated its efforts on transforming people's economic and social condition, expecting that this would automatically and without any additional work on the part of the revolutionaries and militants produce a transformation of 'man as he sees himself, his life and the world', to quote Mr Al-Solh.

The reality, however, is that while the Arab liberation movement has indeed transformed some of the economic and social conditions of the Arab people, at the same time it has erected endless obstacles to any change or evolution in their consciousness and understanding, in their vision of 'themselves, their life and the world'. The 'economist deviation' in itself held no attraction for the leaders and intellectuals of the Arab liberation movement, neither as a theory nor as practice. What the Arab liberation movement can be accused of however — that which Mr Solh calls the 'oversimplification' of the idea of the transformation of man — is in fact simply a manifestation of the way the Arab liberation movement has misrepresented the dangers of the economistic deviation. This is exemplified by its failure to bring about any change in the superstructural levels of the social edifice, except such minor transformations essential to the success of a vital economic advance, or those imposed simply by passing time and the accumulation of endless little changes in a clear and distinguishable transformation. In other words the Arab liberation movement has been 'standing on its head' (unlike the economistic deviation, which does at least stand on its feet albeit in a grotesque and unbalanced fashion), in that the revolutionary changes it has brought about in the economic situation, in certain sectors of society, and in the use of technology and modern science have all had to be implemented in such a way as to reinforce existing social relations, class divisions and ideological currents. No attempt has been made to ensure that, with each modification introduced in the infrastructure of society, the corresponding change was instituted on the superstructural level. This method of 'standing things on their head' is particularly noticeable in the cultural policies (just one example amongst many) implemented by the National liberation movement, as well as in its superficial and profoundly conservative approach to our historical heritage, traditions and values, and to religious thought. All of this has delayed the development of desirable changes in the Arab individual, in his vision of 'self, life and the world'. The excuse has been the need to protect the people's traditions, values, art, religion and ethics. The cultural endeavour of the Arab liberation movement has been distorted into an attempt to preserve the 'backward-looking' ideology, along with its different institutions, such as a mediaeval culture and a mediaeval way of thought based on various misapprehensions of reality.

Furthermore, the Arab liberation movement has isolated the 'imperialist relation' from the rest of life in the Arab homeland, and from the complex Arab social phenomena and historical conditions in which it plays a part. As a result, 'imperialism' has become, as it were, the only immediate reality, the only driving force at work in the course of events in the Arab world. There is a fundamental imbalance between the Arab liberation movement's vision of itself and the situation of its society on the one hand, and its vision of its enemies and the outside world in general on the other. This process of abstraction has led to gross oversimplifications, including the presentation of 'imperialism' (or even international Zionism) as the only hegemonic movement at odds with the development of Arab society, yet conditioning its evolution, directly or indirectly. This misunderstanding has led to what has to be recognized as a total neglect of any analysis concerning the status of the ever present forces, institutions, organizations and intellectual endeavours operating within the Arab social structure and influencing its life.

It is essential to appreciate the importance of such factors in the determination of our society's reactions and approaches to things, on both the collective and individual level. The other facet of this progress of isolation of the imperialist relation described above is to encourage a fanatical prejudice in favour of the great ideological illusion that the backward-looking ideology is equivalent to conscious religious thought, and that this ideology, with its aura of values, customs and traditions, is the true expression of the genuine, pure and unchanging essence of Arab identity over the ages, rather than the reflection of an evolving economic situation, a balance between ascending and declining social forces, a changing picture of classes undergoing an historical evolution which only allows a relative fixity.

Notes

1. French translation, *Traite de l'unité divine*, (Paris, 1925), by B. Michel and M. Abd al-Razeq.
2. Article published in *Al-Gamiah al-Uthmaniyyah*, 1st year; reproduced in Muhammad Rashid Ridu, *Tarikh al-astadh al-imam* ... (The Story of the Great Imam M.A.), Vol.II (Cairo), pp.290-391.
3. *Al-Islam wa Usoul al-hukm* (Cairo, 3rd ed., 1925), pp.95-103.
4. Abu Bakr, first caliph of Islam (632-634).
5. *Moudhakkirat al-dawah wal-dai* (Cairo, n.d.), pp.180-185.
6. *Al-Islam wa awdauna al-siyasiyyah* (Cairo, 1951), pp.170-180.
7. *Naad al-fikr al-dini* (Beirut, 1969), pp.7-14.

3. The National Liberation Struggle

MUHAMMAD TALAT-HARB
(1867-1941, Egypt)

After completing his Islamic studies and obtaining a diploma from the School of Administration and Languages, Harb attached himself to Muhammad Farid, leader of the National Party, who obtained a post for him with the 'Daira Saniyyah', the Royal Domains. As the leading lawyer for the estate, and then as director of the Wadi Kom-Ombo Company, Harb was called upon to manage many extensive holdings.

As early as 1908, he drew up the project for an Egyptian Bank, and actively pursued the idea during 1914-18. The 1919 revolution adopted the project as its own and on 7 May 1920 the Misr Bank came into being. From then on the Bank's activities expanded constantly, financing 29 major industrial and commercial companies, and it soon became the biggest asset holder in the Arab world and Africa.

Deeply immersed in Islam, Harb was one of the first apostles of the Arab idea in Egypt, and the first great figurehead of Egyptian national capital.

Main works: A History of the Islamic States (*Tarikh duwal al-Islam*); The Economic Treatment of Egypt and the Project for an Egyptian or National Bank (*Ilag misr al-iqtisadi wa mashrou bank al-misriyyin aw bank al-umma*).

The passage reproduced here is from his speech at the inauguration of the Misr Bank on 7 May 1920. It illustrates adequately the autochthonous 'national' bourgeoisie's desire for independence in economic matters during the 1919-24 revolution.

An Egyptian Bank for Egyptians Only[1]

If our only concern had been to amass the funds necessary to start a bank, without taking the precautions necessary to ensure that it would not eventually become simply one more foreign bank, we would doubtless not have won the support of any of the founders; not one of them would have seen the necessity for yet another foreign bank, given that these already abound in our country.

What Egypt really lacks, however, is a bank with holdings of autochthonous capital, which will work for Egypt and in Egypt's interests. The founders saw that there was only one way to achieve this goal: to issue registered shares which could be held only by Egyptians. In so doing, they drew on the example of what is effected in other countries to prevent foreigners dominating the key sectors of the national economy . . . .

We are accused of being ignorant, incapable of running a bank. It might have been expected that our detractors would be delighted to see us willing to bear the entire consequences of our own incompetence, rather than unloading them on to someone else. Their inconsistency in this matter is puzzling. No. Each country must pursue its own financial policy, must win its economic independence and preserve it. In every country in the world, the task of directing this policy and preserving this economic independence falls to a national bank, whose privilege it is to issue banknotes and to stand above the competition between all other banks, to supervise their activities, to help them with loans when the need arises, to solve and, where possible, prevent crises. Such a bank serves as the criterion of commercial activity and the market in money; it is the barometer which measures the abundance or scarcity of money available for business; it sets the interest rate in the country accordingly and holds gold to meet any eventual needs, allowing it to leave the country only very rarely and then with the aim of improving the exchange rate, or for other urgent measures required by the national interest.

Such a bank is the supreme arbiter of financial credits and business confidence. In a word, it is the banks' bank. Its function is quite distinct from that of the other banks and does not bring it into competition with them; it is the final link in every financial transaction in the country. Every government takes care that no foreign hand can regulate the affairs of the national bank which determines the country's financial policy.

Such was to have been the function of the National Bank of Egypt; it should have been a national bank in the full sense of the term, national both in its capital and in its administration — as is the case in every other country in the world which seeks to preserve its economic independence. In Egypt, however, the shares of this bank are traded on the open market, so that no one knows in whose hands they now rest, or where they will be an hour later; and the shareholders have the final say and decision-making authority in their company's affairs. Again, in Egypt, the National Bank competes with other banks for their normal business. This state of affairs was originally defensible on the grounds that, at the time, the country had no autochthonous banks for which the National Bank could have acted as a central bank, a role it certainly could not fulfil on behalf of the various foreign banks, whose interests generally diverged from its own. Under such conditions, had the National Bank abandoned its traditional banking activities, no benefit would have accrued either to itself or to the country: the main beneficiaries would have been the rival foreign banks. Furthermore, in the days before 1914, the National Bank drew little advantage from the issue of banknotes, since people were still unaccustomed to them. The bank could not be asked to renounce its other activities until it was possible to assure it of a profit equivalent to what it would lose by taking such measures.

Such profit is possible only when autochthonous banks based on national capital exist and use the national bank as a central bank . . . . This is why we sought to set up the Misr Bank alongside the National Bank of Egypt; to recoup the opportunity missed when the National Bank of Egypt was founded.

KHALED BAKDASH
(1912, Syria)

Khaled Bakdash, General Secretary of the Communist Party of Syria, has been the key figure in Arab Communism since 1930. A lawyer, publicist, fine tactician and talented orator, he was eventually elected to the Chamber of Deputies in Damascus. He, more than anybody, defined the attitude of the Arab Marxist left concerning the relationship between unity and democratic progress; his polemic with Gamal Abdel Nasser on this issue (1958-60) was a prelude to a wave of anti-Communism in the Middle East which came to an end, in Egypt at least, in May 1964. Since then, Khaled Bakdash has sided decisively with the Soviet Union and against the China of the Cultural Revolution. Deep-seated differences within the national party led to a split in 1972 which, for a while, significantly reduced the authority of the Secretary-General.

Main works: **Communism and Patriotism** (*Al-shuyouiyah wal-wataniyyah*); **Islam and the National Question** (*Al-Islam wal-qadiyyah al-wataniyyah*); **The Arab Peoples' National Liberation Movement and the Role of the National Bourgeoisie** (*Harakat al-taharir al-watani lil-shuyoub al-arabiyyah wa dawr al-bourjwaziyyah al-wataniyyah*); **The Voice of Independence, Democracy and Unity** (*Tariq al-istiqlal wal-dimoqratiyyah wal-wihdah*).

The Arab Communists and the National Question[2]

It seems clear that the regional, economic, cultural and historical living conditions of a collectivity (or of a nation) create, with passing time, a common feeling amongst its members, which we can call the 'national feeling'. But this national feeling does not remain merely the direct expression and reflection of the material circumstances in which it develops. Over time, it acquires an autonomous existence, a 'pure' existence one might say, so that later on, the direct link between this national feeling and the circumstances surrounding its development may no longer be so obvious. As it develops, this national feeling becomes an immense force capable of overcoming the most dangerous material conditions by penetrating the masses of the people and setting them in motion, thereby itself becoming an active material force. This dynamic force increasingly becomes a form of direct perceptible attachment, akin to what a man feels for his house, his land and his family. Such national feeling is soon transformed into pride, dignity and self-respect . . . .

How then can we ignore or renounce national feeling? Indeed, how can anybody understand the evolution of the international or domestic situation without being aware of the importance of national feeling and its great influence upon the action of the masses, the evolution of the international situation and the state of relations between nations?

We ourselves are not only emotionally sensitive to this national feeling, we are also aware of it as an object of rational and scientific study, through which it becomes deeper, more complete and more perfect. The aim of our whole endeavour is to develop this national feeling in our country, so that it may become an important, invincible force, whose purity, self-awareness and intensity reach the highest levels attainable by human sentiment.

Our Congress is called upon to ratify a National Charter which we will then present to the people and struggle to see implemented. This Charter is a concise scientific outline of the tasks and goals which the national movement in Syria and Lebanon has set itself; in other words, it defines the demands for which our party is fighting in the course of our advance towards our great ideal.

The Charter grasps the national aspirations of our people, and provides an exact reflection of their desire for liberation, national progress, cultural and economic growth, and social development. It is based on four fundamental considerations: (1) The most important problem facing the country is that of its total independence and complete national liberation; (2) Our Syrian/Lebanese homeland is a part of the Arab East; (3) Our people urgently need to enjoy political freedom and constitutional rights in order to complete their cultural and national formation; (4) Our country urgently needs national economic and social reforms in keeping with the degree of evolution it has reached.

On this basis, the articles of the Charter fall into four main sections. The first section concentrates on the most important problem, that of independence and complete national liberation. Of course, this cannot be reduced to the exercise of those rights once enjoyed in our name by foreigners. The fact that we have seized such rights for ourselves certainly constitutes a major step forward towards national sovereignty, but complete national liberation also implies:

(a) freedom from any foreign imperialist influence and from any international considerations which might enable another state to interfere in our affairs or to impose its will upon us by force and violence.

(b) Complete freedom to choose our own path and our own international economic and political relations in accordance with the principles of peace, equality and fraternity between peoples — principles which will provide the foundation stones for the world of tomorrow.

(c) The extension of our national sovereignty to all the key sectors of our country.

The second part of the Charter deals with the problem of co-operation between Arabs, what one might call the problem of Arab unity. It is clear that all the Arab peoples are close to one another, be it geographically, linguistically, economically or historically. Co-operation between them thus becomes a vital and practical aspect of a great many of the issues which concern our respective countries.

In our opinion, the most important aspect of Arab co-operation concerns the solidarity of the Arab peoples in their struggle for independence and national liberation. The various Arab countries are, of course, at different stages in terms of this issue; there are countries still struggling for the most elementary right to independence, for instance Palestine, which still lies under foreign mandate and is embroiled in the Zionist calamity. Others, such as Syria and Lebanon, have won some of their rights and have taken important steps towards national sovereignty. Finally there are countries such as Iraq and Egypt, which are completing the final stages of their progress towards total independence and national sovereignty.

Under such conditions, what other foundations can there be to Arab co-operation than the need for solidarity between Arabs of all countries in the effort to attain the independence and national liberation of each individual country? It is not enough for governments to evince this solidarity; the people themselves must be committed to the idea. Economic, cultural and commercial co-operation is possible to a degree, but it cannot be brought to fruition as long as the great Arab goal — the independence and complete liberation of each Arab country — has not been achieved.

The third section of the Charter bears on political liberty and democratic rights. The government in Syria and Lebanon must be a truly democratic regime, guaranteeing all its citizens such basic civil liberties as freedom of speech, freedom of association, a free press and the right to form trade unions. Freedom of conscience and religious belief must also be respected and protected from any infringement. This same section also deals with the guarantees necessary to ensure equal rights and duties for all citizens, irrespective of race or creed, a point which must not be neglected. Let us not forget that the problem of ethnic or religious minorities has often been used by foreign imperialists as a justification for their domination over us . . . .

The fourth section of the Charter covers the national economic reforms appropriate to the present stage in our country's development . . . .

Our Charter makes no mention of socialism. It contains not a single measure, not a single demand tinged with socialism. It is purely and simply a National and Democratic Charter, nothing more, nothing less. This is our programme during the present stage of national liberation, on which all our efforts and struggles will be concentrated until its successful completion. Our approach represents no backsliding on matters of principle. The question of building socialism in a given country does not depend on the desires or intentions of any one individual, community or political party. It depends rather on the general situation existing in the country, notably its overall level of development.

In everything we decide and set out to do, we draw on science and scientific study. We have our own scientific theory of social development, which is the only scientific theory in this domain. We believe that this theory is correct and has been corroborated by the lessons of history; we will continue to believe in it until somebody produces another scientific theory which will invalidate or supersede our own.

Any scientific theory is, by definition, a general theory . . . . But that does not mean that the results derived from the theory are independent of time or place; on the contrary, the theory itself explicitly states that it will produce different results in different circumstances . . . . In sociology, there are no universal formulae or eternal truths applicable to every country and every period in history. We have no intention of drawing up a list of cliches and prescriptions to be learnt by rote and mechanically applied. We are well aware, for instance, that the immediate tasks facing Yugoslav society are quite different from those facing British, French or Arab society.

It is reasonably obvious that a country suffering the effects of imperialism and economic backwardness cannot set itself the task of building socialism; it can only take on the challenge of its own national liberation, and of the removal of any vestiges of the Middle Ages in its economic and intellectual life. As we have noted, this is one of the lessons of scientific socialism. True, we are a party of sudden change; we want to see a radical transformation of our society and our lives. However, this transformation is not socialist, but national and democratic.

There are those who, for whatever reason, would like to see our party become a party of reform and nothing else. Such people are simply unwilling to face facts: our Communist Party in Syria and Lebanon is, first and foremost the party of national liberation, the party of freedom and independence.

The question of national independence concerns the entire nation. It is thus undeniably possible to achieve unanimity and complete national unity in support of this fundamental aim. National liberation represents the interests of every citizen, irrespective of doctrinal belief, religion or class; it represents the interests of both workers and bosses, peasants and patriotic landowners, small shopkeepers and big merchants.

SHUHDI ATIYYAH AL-SHAFAI
(1911-1960, Egypt)

After completing his studies in philosophy at Cairo University and in English literature at Exeter, al-Shafai became the first Egyptian to serve as English language inspector at the Ministry of Public Education (1945). As the founder of Dar al-Abhath al-Ilmiyyah (1942-46) Cairo's main cultural and political centre, and as the acknowledged counsellor of the National Workers' and Students' Committee (1945-46), he was one of the leading lights of the Egyptian Communist movement, and eventually assumed the editorship of *Al-Gamahir* **(1946-48). Egyptian Communism and the country's Marxist press were profoundly marked by this man, who was a teacher, essayist, political leader, publicist and humanist. He imbued them with a particular openness and a specific national orientation.**

Having already served a heavy term of forced labour (1948-55), he was arrested a second time on 1 January 1959 and killed at the Abu Zabal internment camp on 17 June 1960.
Main works: **Our National Aspirations (***Ahdafuna al-wataniyyah***) in collaboration with Abd al-Maboud al-Giberli; The Evolution of the Egyptian National Movement from 1882 to 1956 (***Tatawwar al-harakah al-wataniyyah al-misriyyah 1882-1956***).**

The author, writing shortly after Suez, draws the lessons from the tacit front between the free officers and the left which came into being during the second half of 1956. The author's theses, which provided the basis for the radical nationalist tendency within Egyptian Communism, were largely taken up in the 1962 'National Action Charter' There was however one main difference: for the author, the Communists were an integral element of the front he envisaged.

'What Is the National United Front?'[3]

We hold that the key to our political renaissance, the precondition for our economic renaissance, lies in the United National Front so often referred to by Abdel Nasser in his speeches.

What do we mean by a United National Front? The first thing which springs to mind is that this Front would be a front of parties, the traditional parties which Egypt has known in the past.

Let us be frank: the return of the old parties, with their traditional structure and orientation, would not be in the interests of the national movement. These parties represent a backward stage of our political and economic development; they would no longer be able to adapt to the economic and political progress achieved by the national movement. All this was highlighted during our latest battle against imperialist aggression.[4]

We do not say that the traditional parties are totally devoid of people who are devoted to their country. But the latter must break out of their isolation and passivity if they are to play a positive role in the construction of a 'United National Front'.

What then do we mean by a 'United National Front'? We have in mind a front which will bring together all the social categories and classes opposed to our enemies abroad — imperialism and Zionism — and to our enemies at home — feudalism and the monopolies; a front which will rally the working class, the *fellahin*, the intellectuals, the students, the small businessmen and manufacturers, the rich country landowners who manage their own estates and pay for hired labour, every category of national capitalist, big or small — in short a front composed of every national element prepared to struggle against imperialism and Zionism, and antagonistic to feudalism and the monopolies. Such a front must bring in all the existing mass organizations; the trade unions and the trade union federation, the professional associations and the farmworkers' unions. It must, in turn, strive to reinforce these organizations, by attracting more members to them and ensuring that their leadership is democratically elected, drawn from the masses themselves, willing to serve the people and able to win their trust.

The Front must strive to organize the Egyptian masses by creating even more farmworkers' unions and peasant co-operatives, enough for the entire countryside; it must help young people, students and women to form unions and leagues of their own; small businessmen and manufacturers must also be encouraged to come together. This Front must have its own mass organizations drawn from the factories, the villages, the neighbourhoods, and from each and every corner of Egypt.

The 'Popular Resistance Committee' and the 'United National Front of Popular Resistance' in Port Said are living examples, born in the heat of battle, of the possible form of the United National Front. We recognize quite openly that today, this is the common front of the people with Abdel Nasser's government, given that Abdel Nasser is not only the President of the Republic but also leader of the national struggle against imperialism and Zionism.

The Front must be the nursery for what Abdel Nasser, in his speech to the 1st Congress on Co-operatives on 1 June 1956, called 'the new leadership the leadership which feels what the people feel'.

The National Front is a political front in the full sense of the term, rather than just an economic, social or cultural front. The leadership which will emerge from each of its sections will, of necessity, be a political leadership, with its own programme, its own goals and its own methods of struggle.

All the different leadership groups are united around the same goals during the present stage of our national struggle; namely, the preservation of our independence, the reinforcement of that independence by the development of our economy, the raising of our people's living standards, and the struggle for world peace. But this unity will certainly not prevent the ineluctable emergence of contradictions between different leadership groups and the growth of class struggle. Nor is it inevitable that this struggle will change into hostility leading, in its turn, to civil war. Such an outcome can be avoided if the country is endowed with a healthy democratic regime under which civil liberties can develop. In this case, the struggle will take place within healthy limits; it will be more akin to competition between the different political leaderships. The latter will each have to show that they serve the interests of the people better than their rivals, and that they are more concerned for the interests of the community as a whole rather than for those of any particular social stratum or minority. They will have to convince the people of the superiority of their judgement and foresight.

The establishment of the kind of front described here, and its participation in government, would make for greater democracy and freedom within the country, rally popular enthusiasm and unite it around the front's goals, break any possible imperialist conspiracy and unmask the manoeuvres of enemies and all prevarication. This kind of front, in a healthy democracy, will provide an effective reinforcement to our political and economic independence; more, it can forge a path for the non-capitalist development of our economy.

RAIF KHOURI
(1911, Lebanon)

Man of letters, theoretician, polymath and Lebanese politician, Khouri was one of the key figures in the progressive and radical wave which swept through the Arab National Movement following the Second World War. From the English School, he moved to the American University of Beirut, where he took his doctorate in 1943. As a lecturer at the Lebanese University of Beirut, he became one of the most widely reputed literary critics in the Arab world, and participated actively in the Movement for Peace.

Main works: **Modern Arab Thought** (*Al-fikr al-arabi al-hadith*); **Does the Moon Hide its Face?** (*Wa hal yakhfa al-qamar?*); **The Myths of the Arabs** (*Asatir al-Arab*); **Characteristics of the National Consciousness** (*Maalem al-way al-qawmi*).

Raif Khouri's theses concerning the national Arab entity provide the starting point for a quarter of a century of Marxist thought on the problem. He stresses the historical transformation of the organic composition of Arab nationalitarianism, as sociological forces gradually took over the spearhead role from purely cultural factors, yet preserved the overall framework of Arab civilization.

The Role of the National Question in the Arab World[5]

On the theoretical level, the following considerations must inform our approach to the problem of nationalities:

(1) The nation forms itself as history unfolds. The emergence of nationalities (in the real sense of the term) runs parallel with the modern world industrial revolution, the collapse of feudalism and the rise to dominance of scientific and materialist thinking.

(2) The various nations fall into two camps: the advanced nations, dominated by hegemonic industrial groups which are impelled by economic forces to seek conquest and expansion, and the vanquished nations which are their prey.

(3) The perpetual competition amongst the advanced nations to extend their zone of influence in the world has led to the great military confrontations, followed by a new division of the world between the victors.

(4) Simultaneously, new ascending forces have emerged to demand that this historical phase in which nationality confronts nationality be brought to an end and replaced by an era of co-operation and solidarity. In the meantime the oppressed nationalities have striven to free themselves and develop their countries.

(5) The ultimate aim of genuine national ideas is the maximum reinforcement of the nation's capacity to produce, in order to promote the material and spiritual well-being of individuals, raise the level of culture and demolish all that hinders the flourishing of the nation's talents.

On this basis, we can sum up the perspective from which the Arab national question should be approached as follows:

(1) The Arabs today are one of the vanquished nationalities; they aspire to recover their freedom and are rallying around this goal, since freedom is the first and most indispensable step towards their advancement and their reunification.

(2) Within the Arab body politic itself, there are many material and spiritual vestiges of the past which oppose the flowering of the nation, vestiges rooted in feudal ills and even in the Bedouin way of life.

(3) However, Arab society also contains rapidly developing positive forces, which vivify our nationality; forces associated with the forefront of industrial and agricultural production; forces which must be encouraged, since they consitute both the armature and the substance from which our national renaissance will be fashioned.

(4) It is not in the interests of the Arabs for the confrontation between nations to drag on, as they are one of the weakened nations and thus likely prey for the nations in conflict. The Arabs' interest is for this stage in the world's history to draw to a close.

(5) In its quest for freedom, Arab nationalitarianism needs a militant vanguard formed and shaped by dint of action itself, endowed with exemplary moral qualities, a sense of self-sacrifice, enthusiasm, a willingness

vanguard formed and shaped by dint of action itself, endowed with exemplary moral qualities, a sense of self-sacrifice, enthusiasm, a willingness to draw its membership and leaders from the popular classes (and not just from the intellectuals, for instance), and a philosophical vision of nature, society and history based on scientific examination of the facts as they present themselves in practice, as part of a process of evolution and turmoil.

(6) Arab nationalitarianism aims to develop Arab economic and cultural potential, to activate cultural creativity and develop talents, ensuring greater individual happiness and the enhanced ability of each to contribute to the happiness of others throughout the world.

HABIB BOURGUIBA
(1903, Tunisia)

A lawyer, journalist and Tunisian politician, Bourguiba studied law and political science in Paris. He left the old Destour in 1934 to create the Neo-Destour, which was set up at the Ksar-Hilal Congress with a view to maximizing pressure on a colonial system already in crisis. He was imprisoned (1934-36, then 1952-54) and exiled on a number of occasions — all of which served to temper this 'Supreme Combatant'.

Bourguiba spent the end of the Second World War in Cairo, where he established new contacts with the Egyptian and Arab national movements. Following the signing of the Franco-Tunisian agreements, he returned to his country in 1955 where he served first as President of the National Assembly and then was elected President of the Republic two years later in 1957. For several years he held a number of portfolios, notably foreign affairs and defence. As President of the Neo-Destour since 1934, he proclaimed the socialist vocation of his party, which became the Destour Socialist Party in 1965. In 1974, he was elected President of the Republic for Life.

His qualities as a statesman became manifest in the creation of modern Tunisia, which willingly complied in the realistic gradualism and *joie de vivre* characteristic of its leader. In foreign affairs, a good neighbour policy towards the great powers, friendship with the West and recurrent hostility towards Nasser's Egypt stand out in a colourful career embellished by a brilliant mastery of language.

Sovereignty and Suppleness[6]

. . . The Destour's egalitarian demands, addressed to France and aimed at obtaining recognition of the Tunisian's rights as an individual, were incapable of liberating Tunisia and bringing France's sovereignty to an end;

indeed, had they been accepted, these demands would probably have achieved the contrary and committed Tunisia irrevocably to the path of assimilation and integration.

When we in our turn joined the struggle, our position was a delicate one; we were naturally opposed to Tridon's ideas, but felt that it was also vital to struggle against Duran-Angliviel by proclaiming unambiguously that Tunisia was a state, that the Tunisians formed a nation with its own past and personality. We were so struck by the rapid advance of assimilationist policy that we sometimes felt that we had arrived on the scene too late; certainly time was not on our side. All the vital forces in the country, from the financiers and the farmers to the administrators and the intellectuals, were moving steadily towards Francization. Even the national movement leaders themselves seemed to recognize this, tacitly at least, by calling on France to grant Tunisians equality with the French and by placing all their demands within the context of a Protectorate.

The Neo-Destour was to change all that.

I would like to conclude with a few words summing up the distinctions between the action of the Neo-Destour and the old Destour, which as you all know is the extension of the movement led by Bash Hamba, who had himself taken over from Al-Hadirah, and so on.

The first point was the fact that the Neo-Destour took the unprecedented step of establishing a plan of action for the national movement, a tactic to be employed with a specific goal in mind, namely the liberation of Tunisia from foreign domination. Our goal was no longer that put forward by the old Destour. This tactic had to be adapted to the circumstances, but at no stage did we allow circumstances to force us into doing or saying anything which might leave the slightest hope that Francization would prevail. On the contrary, we did everything in our power to make the Tunisian personality, the Tunisian nation, the sovereignty of Tunisia stand out against everything which worked towards its obliteration or absorption. This tactic, of course, required a measure of flexibility.

In the early days when we had no clear means of struggle, we could not confront the occupying power's forces directly. But that did not mean that we were prepared to mollify or appease them by accepting a half-French half-Tunisian parliament. That would have been disastrous, since the notion of an inherently temporary Protectorate, leading eventually to the complete independence of the protected state, would have been replaced by the idea of a multinational Franco-Tunisian state in which the French settlement would preponderate.

Our flexibility consisted in telling France that the liberation of Tunisian sovereignty was fully in keeping with both the spirit and letter of the Protectorate. There was no risk attached to recognizing the Protectorate as a regime which would evolve in keeping with the terms set down by those who had established it — in other words an instrument to ensure the advance of a people and its safe conduct towards independence and independent friendship with France. In practice of course, the Protectorate had until then been used as a pretext for the depersonalization of the protected people and as such, it warranted the most resolute opposition. It took a long hard struggle before the protecting power was brought to respect the spirit of the Protectorate and to act in such a way that the natural outcome of its intervention would be independence.

Our situation was comparable to that of a minor lucky enough to have a tutor who loyally watches over the education and blossoming of his charge. Such a pupil will always end up by attaining his majority and freeing himself from tutelage, whilst at the same time creating links of gratitude and friendship with his former tutor.

Thanks to this tactic, we managed to avoid direct confrontation with the regime and to divert it from Francization, so that it could return to its true purpose: to help Tunisia emerge from decadence and build a modern state. Colonna retorted that the essentially provisional regime established by the treaties had ceased to exist and that 'later events' had wrought profound transformations, turning it into a regime of direct administration. Our answer was that, since the Protectorate was a constantly recreated entity, there was no reason why it should not evolve in the opposite direction to that which it had pursued till now and reorient itself towards the emancipation of the protected state, away from the idea of integration into the protecting state.

You will find this new conception of national struggle, based on the idea of an evolving Protectorate, outlined in an article I wrote for one of the very first issues of *La Voix du Tunisien*, at a time when I was studying, to all appearances dispassionately, the history and evolution of such tutelary regimes. The article, which appeared in February 1931, differed fundamentally from everything which had been written previously in all the old Destourian papers, which were mainly full of complaints about injustice and inequality, with endless clamours about certain specific privileges enjoyed by the French.

My article stated that history showed that tutelary regimes could only be transitory. The fact that a people lives under such a regime can be either a simple accident of history, if the people in question retains all its vitality and puts all its efforts into reconquering its lost dignity, in which case the Protectorate will evolve towards independence; or it can be the fate of a broken people who have lost all their spirit, in which case they are doomed to disappear, and the tutelary regime merely provides a respite before their eventual absorption. Tutelage is always a hybrid regime characterized by the presence of two sovereign bodies within a single territory. One of them must disappear, be it the protector state, through the independence of the protected state or the protected state through its final absorption into the protector state. My article ended with a profession of faith which left no doubt as to how the Protectorate would fare in Tunisia.

This was our first essential divergence from the national movements which came before. Nevertheless, we decided not to change the name of the party, not because I was particularly concerned with the Constitution — my main preoccupation was to put an end to French sovereignty — but because I felt that the people had some kind of attachment to the word 'Destour'[7] and I wanted to underline the continuity of our struggle. We saw the Neo-Destour as the continuation of the old one, especially since most of the delegates at the Ksar-Hilal Congress, where the split occurred on 2 March 1934, had also participated in the old Destour's congress held on 12 May 1933 at the party headquarters in Rue de la Montagne in Tunis.

But this new conception of struggle, with its clear objectives, realistic strategy and flexible tactics, was not all that distinguished the Neo-Destour from its predecessor. Our party was also different in that it created for itself a means to bring pressure on France and force her to compromise. It is not enough to mollify and appease the adversary with soothing professions of faith or protestations of friendship; one must also have some means of harassing him repeatedly, to force him to opt for a settlement as the lesser of two evils. But where were we to find such an instrument of struggle; how could we form such an army? There was no point in searching for it in Germany or Turkey. We had to mould it from the Tunisian people itself, for we could rely only on ourselves and could draw only on the capabilities of our own people. At the time, it must be said, the latter were gripped by fear: fear of the police, fear of injustice and oppression. Nonetheless, through repeated contacts, through meetings held in every part of the country, we managed to reach people, to change the way our compatriots thought and to render foreign domination intolerable to them. That was the leverage we needed to win this unequal struggle which lasted a quarter of a century.

Such were the essential characteristics of our movement, and it is these two characteristics you must focus on when you study the history of the national movement in its various stages, each stamped with names such as Jamal al-Din Al-Afghani, Khereddine, Bash Hamba, Ahmad Es-Safi, Abdelaziz Taalbi and . . . Habib Bourguiba.

ABDALLAH AL-TARIQI
(1919, Saudi Arabia)

Following his university studies in Cairo and Texas, Al-Tariqi spent a considerable time with the American oil companies of Western Texas and California (1945-49). When he returned to Saudi Arabia he was appointed Director of the Ministry of Finance Western Provinces Oil Supervision Office (1949-55), then Director General of Oil and Mineral Affairs (1955-60), and finally Minister of Oil and Mineral Resources (1960-62) and Director of the Arabian-American Oil Company (1959-62).

After serving as President of the Saudi delegation to the 1959 and 1960 Arab Oil Congresses, he was forced to leave Saudi Arabia in 1962.

Since then, he has been an adviser on oil matters to the Algerian government and oil adviser in Beirut.

His report on the 4th Arab Oil Congress held in Beirut in November 1963 remains the fundamental document of the Arab world's oil policy. There follow a few extracts in which the precision of the expert is expressed tactfully yet firmly.

Oil and Imperialism[8]

We tend to be dominated by the idea that there are three distinct parties with an interest in the oil industry; namely the producing nations and their inhabitants, the companies which extract the oil, transport it, refine it and market it, and finally the governments of the oil and petrochemical consuming nations and their peoples.

In fact, there are only two parties; the companies do not constitute a distinct third element, since they are just one of the constituents which go to make up the governments and peoples of the consumer nations.

In every major oil company, governments hold a major national stake, sometimes as proprietor, as in the case of British Petroleum where the British government owns 51% of the shares and has the right of veto over all company decisions — a right which it would retain even if its percentage of the equity fell, provided it did not fall below 25%. This company is the biggest presently operating in the Middle East, in terms both of its reserves and of its volume of production; in fact the company holds 28.5% of all reserves and accounts for 28.4% of total production.

It is traditional for the major company in each region to give the lead to all the other companies when it comes to fixing, raising or lowering prices. Given that the British government has right of veto, it has the ultimate decision-making power as to whether to raise or lower prices — and hence, indirectly, to raise or lower production. This power held by the British government is identical to that held by its imperial predecessor, since a colony is by definition an area whose destiny is decided by some other power without consultation or consent.

The same also applies to the American government. The American oil companies account for 56.7% of oil reserves and 56% of production in the Middle East. These companies do their business outside the United States yet they remain bound by American laws, such as the anti-trust law which forbids price-fixing and the tax laws which oblige the 65 American oil companies to pay tax at a rate of 70%, according to these companies' annual reports. This fiscal pressure enables the U.S. government to exercise enormous influence over the companies, which are, for instance, forbidden to trade with states which do not enjoy the favour of the U.S. government and which it does not recognize.

To take one example, the U.S. government banned Middle East oil sales to China, a powerful state of 650 million people whose oil consumption per capita is the lowest in the world. A country thirsty for oil and representing a huge market for Middle East oil is closed to us by the United States government. What gives this government the right to apply its own laws to other peoples, especially in cases where the result is directly damaging to those peoples' interests, as happened in the case of Aramco? This company, at its government's request, refused to sell Saudi asphalt to Yemen on the grounds that the firm that would use the asphalt to pave Yemen's roads was Chinese.

The existing relations between oil consumers and producers are equivalent to relations between colonizers and colonized; the consumers literally suck out the natural resources of the producers and leave them only just enough to keep going. In Saudi Arabia, a country where oil is the seven million inhabitants' main source of income and represents 90% of the country's resources, oil revenues for 1961 were $397 million or $56.7 per head: no one is going to fill empty bellies or improve the towns with sums of that order. And the same applies to all the peoples of the region, with the one exception of Kuwait.

Until recently, in their ignorance and naivete the governments of the Middle East trusted the oil companies in the belief that they would provide for the well-being of the countries concerned; this belief grew when the companies anticipated the wishes of the peoples of the region and accepted a system of profit-sharing between themselves and governments. But the way in which the system has been applied in the Middle East shows to what extent the companies have betrayed the trust placed in them by the impoverished peoples of the underdeveloped world.

For example, when the peoples of the region demanded the application of a system equivalent to that in force in Venezuela, they were told that the Venezuelan government received half of the companies' net profits. In reality, the Venezuelan government enjoys complete freedom in all fiscal matters, whether or not these involve oil companies. This government's income, far from being made up of a certain percentage of the companies' profits, is in fact compounded partly from ground rent, namely the sum due to the Venezuelan government as the landowner, partly from taxes equivalent to those imposed on all businessmen in Venezuela, and partly from customs duties and the like.

The upshot is that the Venezuelan government takes 69% of the oil industry's net profits. In the Middle East, the companies have persuaded the governments of the region that the ground rent due to the landowner should be set against taxes due. Taxes are thus calculated on the basis not of net profits as such, but of net profits minus expenses . . . . In Saudi Arabia, the companies end up paying the government 57.5 cents a barrel, as against the 80 cents which they keep for themselves. The so-called 50/50 split in profits thereby becomes 41.8% to the Saudi government and 58.2% for the companies . . . .

The right of the oil-producing countries to decide amongst themselves the level at which to fix the price of oil is a natural and sacred right. They must never give it up; should the consumer nations ever come to feel that they had been the victims of injustice, an international conference could be convened to resolve the problem or the matter could even be referred to the United Nations.

The oil companies with the full support of the governments of the consumer nations, notably in Western Europe and America, are determined to pump out as much Middle East oil as possible as quickly as possible, irrespective of the national interests of the producers concerned. Since the Second World War, the consumer countries have constantly promoted the construction of oil refineries in the consuming areas, instead of accepting that oil should be refined in the producing areas, which would help the producer countries to industrialize and preserve their right to industrialize on the basis of their own natural resources. The proliferation of refineries and hence of petrochemical industries would lead to real increase in the people's standard of living and increase local labour input to the national industry. Furthermore, the cost of oil refining in the producing countries is moderate compared to what is charged in the consuming countries: the average profit per barrel of oil refined directly in the Middle East producing countries is 80% whereas it is only about 60% on oil refined in the consuming countries, notably in Western Europe.

The policies geared to rebuild and reindustrialize the European countries following the Second World War were premised on preventing the oil-producing countries from building up industries which might compete with those of the oil-consuming countries. Although the countries of the Middle East have oil reserves estimated at 194 million barrels — 61% of world reserves — and currently account for 24.3% of world production, the funds invested in the region represent only 3.3% of total investment in the oil industry.

In conclusion, it should be said that the path we recommend, which involves we ourselves taking charge of the oil industry in our respective countries, is not just a response to nationalist fervour. Throughout the world, it is apparent that oil resources are increasingly being placed within the province of governments. The United States government's share in refineries currently under construction jumped from 25% to 33% in a single year.

France is setting up an official body to control the oil industry throughout the country. Indonesia has empowered a government organization with full authority over the country's oil resources, thereby transforming the companies into mere entrepreneurs. In Britain, the Labour Party is setting up a body to control the refineries. Finally, in Italy, the actions of the ENI speak volumes. When we call for the oil industry in the Middle East to be brought under government control, we are simply reacting to a natural phenomenon imposed by the laws of progress.

But there is more to it than that. The period that the Arab nation is living through today, in terms of the existential possibilities of the Arab individual, is a never to be repeated opportunity. If we do not seize it and strive to use the potential of our oil as a means to fulfil all our other potential, we will have condemned our generation and those that follow to everlasting poverty and backwardness.

CLOVIS MAQSOUD
(1925, Lebanon)

A prominent political theoretician of the Arab National Movement, Maqsoud studied at the American University of Beirut and then at St. Antony's College, Oxford. An extraordinary personal political odyssey took him from the Lebanese Phalange, the party of Maronite fundamentalism, to Kamal Jumblatt's Popular Socialist Party, then on to the Baath and finally, to the Arab Socialist Association set up in 1960 by Kamal Rifat in Egypt to stand in for Egyptian Marxism, which was so bitterly persecuted at the time. Having acted as Arab League representative in India (1961-7) Maqsoud dedicated himself to drawing up an Arab socialist political theory, notably as a member of the Al-Ahram group. In recent years he was the guiding light of the PLO Research Centre in Beirut, alongside Y.A. Dagher, and as itinerant representative and then Bureau Director of the League of Arab States in the US since 1973, he has skilfully pleaded the Palestinian cause.

Main works: **The Crisis of the Arab Left (***Azmat al-yasar al-arabi***); The Nature of Arab Socialism (***Mahiyyat al-ishtirakiyyah al-arabiyyah***); Towards an Arab Socialism (***Nahw ishtirakiyyah arabiyyah***); The Meaning of Positive Neutralism (***Mana al-hiyad al-ijabi***).**

When it comes to elaborating a theory to account for a world torn by crisis, the balance of power on a world scale is more central than any ideological considerations, as is illustrated by the following analysis, even though events have overtaken it.

Positive Neutralism[9]

Positive neutralism is the essential characteristic of contemporary Arab foreign relations. It will come to an end when the needs in response to which it developed are no longer felt; when peaceful coexistence is complete and the rules of international conduct are firmly established on the basis of mutual respect and a policy aimed at definitive disarmament. It will end when trust has replaced suspicion and fear, when the reins of political power have been torn from those who exploit, monopolize and traffic in war. Only then will there be no longer a need for positive neutralism. One of the most striking characteristics of modern history is that the unity of mankind and the solution of humanity's problems can only be achieved through the socialist vanguard and its liberated popular bastions. This vanguard itself constitutes the most appropriate instrument to ensure the success of positive neutralist policies both in terms of their own ends and as a means of building an ideal socialist society. The Arabs have endless potential in this respect.. . . .

Sceptics have been known to ask what sources of strength a policy of positive neutralism would be able to draw on . . . .

(1) Firstly there is the moral strength of the policy, given that it expresses both the aspirations of the Arab, Asian and African peoples and the reality of their situation in the context of the present world confrontation. It is a policy fully in keeping with their national and popular goals and inspiration . . . . The various peoples of the world understand that a healthy and complete solution to their multifarious problems can only be envisaged in the context of establishing the appropriate international atmosphere, characterized by permanent and tension-free interaction between the main power blocs. The peoples' desire to build new healthy and progressive societies thus leads them to concentrate their efforts in the international sphere on the reinforcement of those factors which promote peace, trust and liberation. This involves a permanent quest for any areas of agreement and flickers of understanding between the contending powers, as well as an effort to enlarge the domains within which peaceful solutions to problems can be found. In the course of these efforts, ideological meeting points will be discovered, to which it will be possible to draw the attention of the contending power blocs; these points could then be enlarged upon, to cover more and more aspects of life, in such a way as to ensure that the remaining differences are no longer sufficient to justify confrontation and tension . . . .

(2) . . . The theory of mutual deterrence leads to an equilibrium in terms of strategic nuclear weapons . . . . The resulting moderation of concrete international aggression and the corresponding diminution in pressure on states not aligned with either of the two blocs allow new factors to emerge, notably the far greater room for manoeuvre and freedom of initiative of the neutral states in their efforts to preserve their neutrality and strengthen the peace . . . . The main advantages drawn by the neutral countries from the equilibrium between the two blocs are as follows:

(a) Diplomatic action to maintain this equilibrium by means of disarmament and to deprive the most dangerous militarists of their efficacity and political hegemony.

(b) Encouragement of any early manifestations of economic and commercial competition and cultural interrelation between the two blocs.

(c) The quest for the guarantees necessary in order to enable an international organization committed to arms limitation to monitor military production in the two camps.

(d) The reinforcement of the UNO as an instrument to settle differences, and action aimed at securing the participation of the neutral states in institutions charged with the resolution and prevention of conflict.

(e) A complete rejection of summit conferences which limit the neutral countries' influence and raise false hopes in the peoples of the world — hopes that the great powers have no way of satisfying.

(3) The contradictions within each of the two blocs, resulting from the nature and background of the two existing structures . . . . One of the main sources of the strength of positive neutralism is the fact that neither of the camps forms a completely united bloc in terms of interests, aims and regime. The attitudes adopted by each of the two camps are the outcome of a confluence of many different interests and specific circumstances. It is therefore possible to readjust this nexus towards some greater correlation with the interests of positive neutralism, providing one knows where and how to intervene. The positions adopted by the Western and Communist camps are, generally speaking, not the logical outcome of a coherent set of goals or a monolithic ideology: rather, they are the product of the harmonization of divergent ideological and political factors. Naturally, such harmonization implies a constant effort to ensure that differences are not allowed to turn into contradictions. And although there are indeed some important and growing contradictions within each of the two camps, these contradictions are rarely antagonistic contradictions of the sort that exist between the two camps . . . .

It would thus be wrong for us to take up a position on international problems in terms of the existing power blocs as total units, since the fundamental differences between the various countries of each bloc are in fact the crucial factor which determines the reality of the situation . . . .

The solution to the crisis of modern man is a renewed commitment to truth; knowledge of truth and commitment to it are, after all, the two keys of constructive peace. Truth is eternal, and in the present phase, it is through socialism that it finds expression. Let us therefore strive to understand truth, to move closer to its radiance and to bring it to bear upon our national and individual personalities.

That is what we mean by positivity, and that is the message of our neutrality.

GAMAL ABDEL NASSER
(1918-1970, Egypt)

Born in Alexandria on the eve of the revolution of 1919, Nasser began by studying law, but dropped it to enter the Military Academy and rose to the rank of lieutenant-colonel attached to the General Staff. He served first as an instructor at the Military Academy and then at the Staff College, distinguished himself during the 1948 Palestine War, and soon after founded the secret organization of Free Officers which seized power on 23 July 1952, overthrowing the monarchy and instituting the republic. President of the Revolutionary Guidance Council (1952)

of the Republic of Egypt (1956) and then of the United Arab Republic (1958), Nasser successfully set out to dismantle the old regime and uproot the political, economic and ideological imperialism which was keeping Egypt in servitude. In this sense Gamal Abdel Nasser is the true creator of modern, independent industrial Egypt.

An autocrat, but above all a pragmatist, he emerges through his writings as dedicated to the historic task of winning back the power of decision making for the Egyptian and Arab peoples, as a prelude to the reconquest of identity.

Main works: Philosophy of the Revolution (*Falsafat al-thawra*); Our Social Revolution (*Thawratuna al-igtimaiyyah*); National Action Charter (*Mithaq al-amal al-watani*); The Great Change (*Al-tahawwul al-azim*); Socialism (*Al-ishtirakiyyah*).

In 1962, ten years after seizing power, President Abdel Nasser drew up a balance sheet of his first decade in office. In this he emphasises the Charter and the problems of building the nation once independence has been achieved. It is worth noting the great stress he places on the importance of regaining decision-making power (the national 'will') and the link he establishes between independence, statism and socialism.

The Morrow of Independence[10]

The depth of the Egyptian people's revolutionary understanding, the clear vision of their aims and the honesty of their insight have enabled them to re-evaluate the possibilities before them, following the great victory of the battle of Suez. Even as they celebrate their victory, the Egyptian people have grasped that what they won in the battle of Suez was not yet freedom, but only the will to forge that freedom through revolution. Glorious battle enabled them to discover their own capacities and potential, and thus to discover the revolutionary path to freedom.

For our noble people, the triumph against imperialism was the beginning of the struggle, not the end. What has been won is simply a better position from which to pursue the battle which must be fought if real freedom and national fulfilment are to be achieved.

The question which sprang up spontaneously following the resounding victory of Suez was as follows: 'To whom it did belong, this free will that the Egyptian people had won for themselves in the course of that terrible battle?' And history answered quite unambiguously: 'That free will can belong only to the people and necessarily serves only their goals and objectives.'

A people do not win back their resolution from the hands of their despoilers only to tuck it away in the museum of history. They hold it close and reinforce it with all their national potential, to transform it into a power capable of realizing their aspirations.

This phase of the struggle is undoubtedly the most serious in the series of challenges the nation must face. It is at this juncture that many popular movements which had aroused great hopes faltered and regressed. They made the mistake of believing that they had achieved their revolutionary aims the moment they won their first victory over external pressures. They thus left the situation unchanged, forgetting that the exploitative elements at home were intimately linked with the forces exercising pressure from abroad — a form of co-operation based on mutual advantage, all at the expense of the popular masses.

The popular movements in question then fell back behind deceptive constitutional façades, believing that freedom had secured their rights. But these movements were eventually to discover — usually too late — that their failure to pursue revolutionary change in the economic domain had stripped political freedom of its substance, leaving only the fragile façade which soon crumbled under the strain of its contradiction with the real state of affairs.

Another factor which has caused popular movements to falter during this bitter phase of national struggle is the failure of these movements to base their actions on a theory inspired by the national experience. To recognize the objective norms relevant to the social task at hand by no means implies that one has to accept ready-made theories and reject the national experience. Real solutions to a people's problems cannot be carbon copies of the experience of other peoples. No popular movement which assumes responsibility for the social task can afford not to recognize the value of experience.

Acceptance of national experience does not, however, entail the condemnation of all previous theories and the refutation of every other solution. Such fanaticism would prove costly, especially when the people are in the throes of that mental puberty which demands some spiritual element. On the contrary, the national experience must assimilate every kind of food and digest it in the living cells of the nation. It has to know what is happening all around it — but even more crucially, it has to live in its own lands.

Experience of truth and falsity is the path to maturity in the life of nations as in that of individuals. Consequently, political freedom, in other words democracy, cannot be reduced to the adoption of constitutional façades. The same applies to social freedom: socialism cannot be reduced to conformity with immutable theories devoid of roots in the national experience.

Following the popular revolutionary movement of 1919, Egypt fell prey to the great masquerade of phoney democracy. As soon as colonialism had recognized Egypt's independence, the revolutionary leadership allowed itself to be misled by the democratic appearance of constitutional façades with no economic foundations . . . .

Colonialism ignored these paper guarantees of independence, and had no hesitation in trampling all over them the moment its interests required it to do so. This was entirely to be expected. The façade of false democracy represented only the democracy of the reactionaries, who were not about to break their links with colonialism or cease all collaboration with it. It was thus inevitable that in the era of reactionary democracy and mock national independence, governments were incapable of acting without a prompt from colonialism's official representative in Egypt. In fact in many cases such governments existed only with the concurrence of this representative. On one occasion, a government was even hoisted into power by his tanks.[11]

The artificiality of this façade and the mockery of reactionary democracy are thus exposed. Political democracy and Political freedom alone are seen to be meaningless without economic democracy and social freedom.

It is obvious that the political regime of a country directly reflects the country's economic situation and faithfully represents the interests that dominate it. If feudalism is the dominant economic power in a country, then political freedom in that country can only be the political freedom of feudalism. Feudalists will dominate economic affairs, define the political stance of the state and use it to defend their own interests. The same is correspondingly true of exploitative capitalism.

In Egypt, before the revolution, economic power was in the hands of a coalition between feudalism and exploitative capitalism. It was thus inevitable that political life and the parties reflect this power and serve as the façade for this coalition.

It is astonishing to note that during this period certain political parties had no qualms about proclaiming that power should only be conferred on those who held assets. Given that feudalists and exploitative capitalists were the only real asset-holders at the time, this recommendation was not just a tacit acknowledgement of the comedy imposed by the dominant forces upon the Egyptian people in the name of democracy. It was in fact a frank and sincere statement of the painful truth.

Socialism is the road to social freedom. Social freedom can only be achieved if each citizen is given the opportunity of acquiring a fair share of the national wealth. This is not just a question of a redistribution of the national wealth amongst the citizens; above all, it requires the broadening out of the foundations of this national fortune, so that we can satisfy the legitimate rights of the popular masses.

Socialism, based as it is on justice and the satisfaction of needs, is the road to social freedom. The solution socialism offers for social and economic underdevelopment in Egypt is a revolutionary march towards progress. It is not an hypothesis selected amongst many, but an unavoidable fact of history imposed by reality, the broadest hopes of the people and the instability of the world in this second half of the 20th Century.

Capitalist experience has gone hand in hand with imperialism. The economic momentum of the capitalist countries originates from the investments made in the colonies. The treasures of India, most of which were absorbed by British imperialism, constituted the basis for the economic activity which led to the development of British agriculture and industry. Just as Britain's economic development was started off by the Lancashire textile industry, so Egypt's conversion into a vast field of cotton provided the British economy with its life blood, at the expense of the starving

Egyptian peasant.

The days when colonialist piracy could despoil the resources of one people to the benefit of another, without any moral or legal restraints whatsoever, are well and truly past. It is high time we cleared away all the subsisting vestiges of this situation, especially in Africa.

There were also other experiences of progress, in which the goal was attained at the expense of a committed population, miserably exploited either in the interests of capital, or to further doctrinal ambitions which went so far as to sacrifice the living generations in the name of those yet unborn.

That state of affairs is simply no longer admissible. Progress by means of spoliation or forced labour is intolerable in the framework of the new human values. It is human values which have done away with colonialism, just as they have eliminated forced labour. These human values have gone beyond the destruction of the two old forms of progress. They have illuminated the spirit and ideals of a new era, using science to inaugurate a different kind of work towards progress.

Scientific socialism is the form most suited to the implementation of a real plan of action towards progress. Any other form of plan will be unable to bring about the desired progress; those who demand that capital be allowed to operate freely and imagine that progress will ensue are gravely deluded.

Capital, left to its own ends in a country forcibly reduced to underdevelopment, is incapable of developing an economic momentum of its own. The great capitalist monopolies implanted in the advanced countries benefitted enormously from the resources drawn from the colonies. The subsequent development of these world monopolies left local capitalism in countries aspiring to progress with only two alternatives.

The first of these was for local capitalism, incapable of coping with world competition, to withdraw behind protectionist barriers paid for by the masses. The second was to accept that its only hope of development was to link up with the global monopolies, to follow in their tracks, to become their tail and thereby drag the nation towards a dangerous precipice

It is increasingly apparent that in a world where the gap between the advanced countries and those hoping to catch them up is growing, one can no longer leave progress to fortuitous individual efforts motivated only by a desire for selfish profit. Such efforts are no longer capable of meeting the challenge. This can only be done by: (a) uniting the national economy; (b) putting the experience of modern science at the service of investment in the economy; (c) drawing up a general plan of the process of production.

Along with the problem of increasing production, that of equitable distribution must also be tackled. This demands that programmes be set up in every domain of social activity to ensure that the workers benefit from the positive results and goods produced by their labour. In this way a society will be built in which the well-being the masses have aspired to and for which they have struggled so hard is achieved. The task of broadening the foundations of national wealth cannot be left to the whims of a naturally exploitative and abusive private capital. Similarly, the equitable distribution of the surplus profit from national production cannot be left a matter for free choice and good faith, however well intentioned these may be.

The spirit of the national revolution thus leads to a specific and concrete conclusion: the need for the people to own all the means of production and to orient the surplus produced according to a plan drawn up in advance. If one does not act on this conclusion, the goals of the revolution remain unattainable. This socialist solution is the only path to economic and social progress. It is the path of democracy, in all its political and social forms.

The fact that the people control all the means of production implies neither the nationalization of all the means of production, nor the abolition of private property, nor any infringement of legitimate right to inheritance.

The two main ways of achieving it are: firstly, the creation of a competent public sector, charged with directing the various stages of progress in every domain and with the ultimate responsibility for the development plan; secondly, the existence of a private sector which has rejected exploitation and contributes to development in the context of the plan as a whole.

Both sectors must be controlled and dominated by the people. This socialist solution is the only way to bring together all the different elements of productive work. The latter will be carried out according to scientific and humane rules, in such a way as to provide society with the energies it needs to reorganize its life according to a predetermined and well thought-out general plan.

Successful socialist planning is the only means to realize the full potential of all the nation's material, natural and human resources. Practical, scientific and humane implementation of the plan will provide for the well-being and prosperity of the popular masses. Planning will guarantee the proper exploitation of existing, potential and eventual resources. It also guarantees the continuous availability of the main services, improvement of existing services and their extension to regions previously allowed to fall into neglect and ruin by the arrogant selfishness of the ruling classes, who for so long imposed deprivation upon the struggling masses.

The implication of all this is that planification must be a creative, scientific and organized operation capable of meeting all the challenges to be faced by our society. Therefore it cannot be merely a simple attempt to evaluate the possible; it must be a means to give our hopes concrete expression. Planification in our society will have to find a solution which ensures the material and human success of the national endeavour, a solution to the following difficult equation: How is one to increase production and at the same time increase consumption of both goods and services, whilst continually increasing the funds available for new investments.

This complicated equation, with its three unknown quantities, demands strong effective organization capable of mobilizing the productive forces, harmonizing them with production itself and raising them to a higher level, both materially and intellectually. During this phase the revolutionary endeavour will need to draw upon all the experience of the Arab nation, the fruit of a long and glorious past and a source not only of profound wisdom but also of a revolutionary spirit capable of effecting radical change.

Unity cannot and should not be imposed. The means which nations use to attain their noble ends should be as noble as the ends themselves. Coercion, in all its forms, is thus incompatible with unity. It stands condemned both as immoral and as a danger to the national unity of each Arab people, and hence of the unity of the Arab nation as a whole. Arab unity is by no means a uniform constitutional mould: rather, it is a long path along which there will be an unknown number of staging posts before the final destination is reached.

In the Arab world, any national government which reflects the will of the people and their struggle for national independence is a step towards unity, in the sense that such a government cannot be opposed to the ultimate aspiration to unity. Any partial state of unity between at least two of the peoples of the Arab nation constitutes a progressive step in the march towards unity and brings us closer to complete unity, by making it easier for others to follow in the same path and by rooting the idea of unity even more firmly in Arab soil.

If the United Arab Republic believes that its message implies an obligation on its part to act so as to promote Arab unity, achievement of the ultimate goal will be made easier by the clear and precise delimitation of the means appropriate to this particular stage of the Arab struggle.

The preamble is the peaceful rallying call. Next comes the scientific application to specific ends of all the progressive concepts of unity implicit in such a call. Experience has shown that as the different stages of the movement towards unity follow one upon the other, certain economic and social rifts will appear and will be exploited by elements hostile to unity in their efforts to prevent it.

The evolution of the task of unification towards its final goal must in any case be accompanied by practical efforts to bridge all the economic and social gaps which are due to the uneven progress made by the different Arab peoples along this path — a differentiation imposed by the isolationist forces of reaction and imperialism.

Intense and deliberate efforts must also be made to open the way for new attitudes of mind, which will prevent dissension gaining a hold, overcome the last vestiges of the cultural incoherence of the 19th and early 20th centuries, and do away with the plots and manoeuverings which sometimes cloud people's vision.

The United Arab Republic, acting in the complete conviction that it is an integral part of the Arab nation, must place its appeal and the principles it embodies at the service of every Arab citizen, without pausing an instant to consider the outdated notion that it might thereby be interfering in the affairs of others. In this context the United Arab Republic must take care not to become embroiled in the local quarrels of parties in any specific Arab state; to do so would be to demean the appeal of unity and its principles. Whilst the United Arab Republic believes that it has a duty to support any nationalitarian movement, this support must nonetheless confine itself to matters of fundamental principle, allowing the various local elements to work out for themselves specific tactics and opportunities for progress in the light of the local situation.

The United Arab Republic must also open up avenues for co-operation between all the progressive nationalitarian movements in the Arab world. It must seek to form a spiritual association so that all may benefit from the common experience. But it cannot impose upon them a formula and lay down how this progress is to be achieved. The creation of a federation of popular nationalitarian and progressive movements in the Arab world will impose itself at some later stage in the struggle.

None of this should be taken as critical of the Arab League; although the latter is incapable of leading the Arab world towards its noble and distant goal, it is at least capable of moving a few steps forward along the path. The people wish to see the complete realization of their hopes, and the Arab League, as an association of governments, is inherently limited in what it can achieve. But any contribution advances the date when the final goal can be reached. Given this reservation, the Arab League deserves our support and our understanding that its capabilities are limited by the circumstances attendant upon its creation and by its very nature. The Arab League is capable of co-ordinating certain aspects of contemporary Arab activity. But it must not, under any pretext whatsoever, become a means of blocking the present and undermining the future.

MAHDI BEN BARKA
(1920-1967, Morocco)

Ben Barka was Professor of Mathematics at the Rabat Faculty of Science. After completing both Koranic and modern studies, he organized the first Moroccan programme of modern science teaching in Arabic. Right from 1934, he was active in the national movement. As one of the 30 signatories of the Independence Manifesto which set up the Istiqlal Party in 1944, he suffered the consequences in the ensuing repression. Co-ordination with the Trade Union movement was one of his particular concerns. Following independence, he became President of the Consultative Assembly and leader of the National Union of Popular Forces, created in 1959 after a split with the Istiqlal.

He played a major role in the Afro-Asian movement, notably as one of the leading lights of the Tricontinental which, following the Havana

Congress (January 1966) set out to amplify the struggles of the African, Asian and Latin American peoples against imperialism. Mahdi Ben Barka was ideally suited to the task. Kidnapped in Paris on 29 October 1967, he disappeared under mysterious circumstances.

Main works: **Towards the Construction of a New Society** (*Nahwa bina mujtama jadid*); *Option Révolutionaire au Maroc: écrits politiques*.

The Needs of the African Liberation Movements[12]

It is clear that a proclamation of independence, which is a purely political, not to say juridical event, cannot change the fundamental structures of an ex-colony. Independence is the precondition and the promise of liberation, it is not the liberation itself.

During the first three years of its independence, Morocco has witnessed the perpetuation and in some cases the accentuation of its economic dependence and its administrative and technical backwardness . . . .

In all the African countries, we must be on our guard against neo-colonialism, from the moment independence is proclaimed; for as long as the colonial structures persist, the way will be open for imperialist exploitation. Independence which contents itself with sticking new labels on the old colonial domination is quite simply a joke and a trick.

It is on the basis of these specific considerations that one should analyse the problem of the presence of foreign military bases and the various efforts to have us participate in the cold war.

It is their economic preponderance which allows the ex-colonial powers to maintain substantial military forces on our territory. Capitalist investments and the existence of a settler community constitute both a reason and an alibi for a military presence which serves as one element in a global cold war strategy. The alibi that the proclamation of national independence might lead to major instability has been exposed by the example of all the new African states. The atmosphere of national discipline established following independence has guaranteed the foreign communities the peace and prosperity that the militaristic and repressive colonial administration was incapable of providing.

Far from being a factor of stability, the presence of foreign troops constitutes a constant threat to the very existence of young sovereign states. These forces are not averse to using liberated territory as a base for aggression aimed at supporting colonial wars against neighbouring peoples. To take just one example, there was the case of the Moroccan Provincial Governor (Addi or Bihi) whose revolt, organized in the very first year of independence by reactionary and anti-national elements, was armed by the French forces stationed on our soil who hoped to involve southern Morocco in their colonial war against Algeria.

This is why, ever since independence, we have made the evacuation of all foreign armed forces one of our national priorities. It is not just a matter of eliminating the vestiges of colonial occupation. Our major concern is to get our country working towards its own economic, political and social advancement. That long-term project requires a lasting peace and the ability to keep our country out of military alliances and quarrels between alien blocs.

Our efforts along these lines have recently culminated in the evacuation of the American bases in our country. We will continue to work for the evacuation of the other foreign troops, the French and the Spanish, in order to ensure the success of our foreign policy based on non-dependence. This policy should be adopted systematically in every African country concerned, like ourselves, to build in peace and fruitful collaboration with all friendly countries.

This policy of non-dependence is especially important in the light of the new conceptions current in neo-colonialist circles in Europe, where Africa is seen as part of the stakes in a world-wide political confrontation. Africa is cast simply as a reservoir of mineral and energy resources necessary to the economies of the industrialized Western countries. All the projects aiming to associate Africa with the European Common Market, to set up a Eurafrica or to establish joint investment funds are likely to be geared towards the interests of foreign capital and can only hinder the harmonious and speedy development of the African economy.

It should not be forgotten that, for a quarter of a century, the prices of the manufactured products imported from Europe have risen steadily and the price of raw materials taken out of our continent has fallen unremittingly. The stability and economic growth of the industrialized countries of Europe has thus been achieved at the expense of the underdeveloped countries which provide the raw materials.

Faced with an accelerating liberation movement in Africa, these same imperialist interests strive to perpetuate this economically exploitative relationship under the guise of co-operation. More and more of our countries find themselves confronted by organized blocs which aim to impose a new colonial order.

The duty of our African countries, and of the other developing countries of Asia and Latin America, is to achieve an equivalent level of organization and a common approach leading to effective co-operation and some safeguard against the worst forms of exploitation. This approach must inform all the UN-sponsored economic conferences on Africa such as the one currently being held in Tangiers. African popular organizations must work to make these conferences into occasions when real co-operation enables African countries to build their economies and increase the well-being of their people, instead of perpetuating unequal relations and outdated privileges.

Our analysis of the manifestations of neo-colonialism in Africa would be incomplete without some mention of the danger represented by reactionary national forces. Imperialism cannot survive in Africa without the cover provided by the interests of certain retrograde elements.

We have underlined the popular and national character of the national liberation movements in Africa. It is worth adding that the conquest of political power changes the import of certain positions; sections of the population who remained neutral or supported the liberation movement during the period of direct struggle may adopt a quite different course once independence has been proclaimed. Rural or pseudo-religious feudal land-owners may grow stronger and seek to take over from the displaced colonial power. If they are not curbed, they will use the new power provided by democratic and parliamentary organizations to establish their privileges on a new juridical basis.

European models of political organization, based on a pluralism which reflects quite different economic and ideological realities from those that prevail in our countries, can be used by these anti-national elements as a base from which to canker the body politic. Empty polemic and demagogy will then plant the seeds of doubt and scepticism amongst the popular masses, paving the way for every form of disguised colonial exploitation.

These reactionary elements, the instruments of neo-imperialism, often go so far as to attack the working classes, whose unity has been cemented in the course of the national struggle. Spurious attempts to create an artificial trade unionism are thus just another form of neo-colonialism.

Alongside these reactionary and anti-national elements, imperialism has found a second ally. As soon as the immediate disadvantages of imperialism's political preponderance are removed, the big mercantile bourgeoisie, whose power derives entirely from economic liberalism, suddenly becomes aware of the benefits of the colonial presence. It then fiercely opposes any attempts to direct economic and commercial policy towards real independence, which would force it to either enter the production cycle or disappear altogether.

Finally, having never participated in the liberation movement, the many intellectual cadres and administrators left over from the colonial period are often unable to rid themselves of the habit of servility: they remain marked by a lack of enthusiasm, imagination or honesty which makes them peculiarly inapt to serve the people's aspirations efficiently. Before long they become the servants of whoever holds power.

The danger hanging over all newly independent states is that the conjunction of these evil forces may perpetuate economic dependency and underdevelopment, thereby making a mockery of political independence. The alliance between a powerful and reactionary feudalism, a servile and gutless bourgeoisie and an inefficient and corrupt bureaucracy can easily lead to a condition several degrees worse than that prevailing under certain forms of imperialism.

If we draw on the experiences of India, China, the Central European countries, the Middle East and Latin America, we arrive at a model of economic growth based on scientific necessity. In this domain we are long past the stage of scholastic argument. We now know that liberal capitalism offers no way forward for our countries. Liberalism has thus become the alibi of the reactionary forces, and nothing else. We now know that the pre-conditions for breaking out of underdevelopment are a thorough reform of the agrarian structure, rapid real industrialization and an efficient and coherent investment policy, all organized according to a plan which sets itself specific monetary targets and eliminates the risks inherent in liberalism. We now know that the main means of arriving at these results are, domestically, intellectual investment and the mobilization of the population's ability to work, and internationally, the quest for economic and technical co-operation.

But real international co-operation can no longer rely solely on the whims of private interests. It must also be promoted on the state-to-state level. That is one reason why we must do everything in our power to further the change which is beginning to appear in the competition between the great powers. The arms race might just turn into a race to help under-developed countries.

In this process of building a new economic and social Africa, we must stress the preponderant role of the organized peasantry and working class. These forces are the only guarantors and real backbone of our policies. These policies will be attacked both by foreign imperialism and by its agents at home. Only a conscious union of patriotic, popular and progressive forces will be able to establish the basis for the real democracy which will give independence its meaning. We now know that the march towards independence and real democracy is a long and difficult one, full of pitfalls. Imperialism also knows it and no longer fights so fiercely against political independence, feeling secure in the belief that time will preserve its economic domination.

We must take care that political independence, the independence granted to us by another, does not become a weapon in the hands of imperialism, a way of ensuring that others defend imperialism's main economic privileges. Faced with the alliance between imperialism and domestic reaction, we must seek out an alliance with the liberal and progressive forces in the ex-colonizing countries and establish a union of patriotic national forces in all the African countries.

It is in this context that the various movements towards African unity should be understood. These unions will be based on an economic and political necessity; they will be a defensive reaction against the union of imperialist interests in Africa.

The tendencies towards the unification of Africa, based as they are on the need to defend independent economic policies against the alliance between imperialism and local reaction, will be the fundamental factor determining the success of our efforts to build up our continent. Co-operation, mutual aid and the search for the peace that will change the nature of East-West competition are integral aspects of that policy. Only by becoming aware of these needs can we forestall the disappointments and discouragements that can ensue when a dearly won independence fails to live up to its early promise.

To respond to the solidarity of the colonizers, we must promote the kind of solidarity between African peoples which will reinforce our struggle both against domestic reaction at home and against imperialist manoeuverings abroad.

Thorough and serious study of our problems, our experiences, our successes as well as our failures, requires that we encourage every form of cultural co-operation; this is essential if the idea of African unity is ever to become second nature. In this respect the present regularly maintained contacts between the various trade union organizations in Africa constitute a very welcome step forward, and we have every reason to believe that further progress will be made at the African Trade Union Conference shortly to be held in Casablanca.

Finally, this solidarity must be broadened out to encompass all the liberation movements in the world, especially the genuinely progressive movements in the West, whose fundamental goals are the same as ours: the dignity and physical well-being of humanity. Colonialism was not a curse upon the colonized peoples alone. By the struggles for influence, dissensions and wars it provoked, it was also disastrous for the peoples of the colonizing countries. We believe that as Africa works to free itself today, it is also working for a world in which peace and justice reign and from which the causes of conflict and exploitation have been uprooted.

There are vague glimmers, from both the East and the West, announcing a change of orientation towards co-operation and peaceful competition instead of the arms race and the drive for hegemony we have seen until now. We dare to hope that Africa will first benefit from this change, and then help to consolidate it. The union of the progressive forces within each of our countries, in Africa and throughout the world, will be the guarantee of this future of co-operation, peace and mutual aid we so devoutly seek.

Notes

1. *Muhammad Talat Harb fi bad kutabihi* . . . (Cairo, 1957), pp.17-21.
2. *Al hizb al-shuyoui fil-nidal liaj al-istiqlal wal siyadah al-wataniyyah* (The Communist Party in the Struggle for Independence and National Soveriegnty), (Beirut, 1964), pp.60-74.
3. *Tatawwar* . . . (Cairo, 1957), pp.238-241.
4. The Suez affair, in October-November 1956.
5. *Maalem al way al qawmi* (Beirut, 1941), pp.88-90.
6. *Introduction à l'histoire du mouvement national* (Tunis, 1962), pp.26-31.
7. Constitution.
8. *Nahw taawun afdal bayn al-duwal al-musaddirah wal-douwal al-mustahlakah lil-betrol* (Towards a Better Co-operation Between Oil Exporting and Oil Importing States), Beirut, c.1964, pp.1-23.
9. *Mana al-hiyad al ijabi* (Beirut, 1960), pp.113-151.
10. *Mithaq al-amal al-watani* (Cairo, 1962).

11. On 4 February 1942, Britain forced the king to accept the return to power of the Wafd, the only party capable of leading Egypt into the war against the Axis powers.
12. Rapport de l'UNFP à la 2e Conférence des Peuples Africains (Tunis, January 1960).

4. The Reconquest of Identity

ABDALLAH AL-NADIM
(1843-1896, Egypt)

Al-Nadim was one of the key figures of the 1882 Egyptian revolution. His remarkable and, for that time, unique life was later to become a source of inspiration for the revolutionary younger generations of Egypt. Born in Alexandria to a humble family, he completed traditional religious studies there, took a course in telegraphy, then established himself in Cairo where he joined the entourage of the great poet Mahmoud Sami al-Baroudi. Palace intrigues forced him to leave the capital and he returned to Alexandria, where he joined the 'Misr al-Fatat' (Young Egypt) group and founded the Islamic Benevolent Society (1879), whose school he directed.

In 1881 he founded the satirical journal, *Al-Tankit wal Tabkit*, then, after the outbreak of the 1882 revolution, he became the country's official orator. Thanks to him, a new journal, *Al-Taif*, became the voice of the revolution. For nine years after the defeat, Abdallah al-Nadim managed to evade police detection. Under various disguises, he travelled the towns and villages of Egypt, writing profusely all the while. In 1891 he was arrested and exiled to Jaffa. The following year, he was pardoned by the new khedive, Abbas II, and returned to Cairo, where he started the satirical journal *Al-Ustadh*. The journal soon became the main avenue for critical social comment, with Nadim as the apostle of a popular and libertarian patriotism which made the journal the most important Egyptian publication of the period. He was once again forcibly silenced on 13 June 1893, this time at London's insistence; only ten years after the defeat of Tal al-Kebir the national movement was already reviving.

The sultan invited him to Istanbul, in order to neutralize his influence. His last years, marked by his friendship with Jamal al-Din al-Afghani, and his polemic against the all-powerful Abul-Huda al-Sayyadi, were spent in frustration and exile, far from his native Egypt for which he was prepared to sacrifice everything and which today recognizes her debt.

Main works: **What Has Been and What Will Be** (*Kana wa yakounou*); **The Lineage of Al-Nadim** (*Sulafat al-nadim*); **The Motherland and the Rise of Tawfiq** (*Al-Watan wa tali al-tawfiq*); **The Nails** (*Al-masamir*).

The text presented below broaches the three main themes of Egyptian national existence: the struggle against the occupier, the national community and relations with the Arab brothers.

How Can the East be True to Itself?[1]

'If you were like us, you would have done as we do' — Europe falls back on this formula every time it launches a new form of civil imperialism or religious expansionism against the East.

Once the Europeans had achieved their goals in their own countries, they surged forth, inspired by the twin visions of science and industry and driven by the twin forces of religion and monarchy; they penetrated the countries of the East, first as tourists and traders, then as observers and eventually as dominators.

The Press dupes the Orientals, mocks their spirit, misleads their great men, vilifies their religion, their traditions, their way of life, their national sentiment, their industry and their agriculture. It proclaims that the West is the fount of law, the well-spring of science, the criterion of virtue. It insists that only by borrowing from the West can a nation exist, that worth is reserved for those who have studied in the West, glory the exclusive privilege of those born there and honour the prerogative of those who speak Western languages, follow Western religious rites and wear Western dress . . . .

Europe has told us unambiguously: you are savages because you do not know how to make clothes and furniture and because you need our manufactured goods which you will only be allowed to receive if you sign the relevant economic treaty. This is how Europe ensured the penetration of her products into the East, that she might seize its wealth; she destroyed all the Eastern industries and grabbed the products necessary to them . . . . Everything produced in India, China, Persia, Anatolia and elsewhere is sold by Europeans who profit therefrom as much as by the sale of the products of their own industry. The Orientals have been reduced to mere employees, planting, harvesting and manufacturing in order that Europe's trade should grow, her fortune increase and the power of her royal houses be swelled by the resulting flow of wealth. For the Orientals: no chance to better themselves, no possible aspiration to power; it is as if their race had been created to serve the Europeans they are so obviously incapable of imitating.

To keep the Orientals at an even greater distance from industry and all its fruits, intrusive so-called counsellors appeared, to stifle Eastern energies, accusing Easterners of weakness and convincing them that their countries are unsuitable for industry and totally lacking in the necessary infrastructure and machinery. Yet these counsellors are fully aware that many kingdoms which lacked machines have simply bought them from abroad, built up a national industry, forced their population to buy the industry's products in order to ensure its prosperity, and protected the population's wealth by banning the import of foreign goods. These men tell such lies in order to keep the Oriental under the Western yoke and maintain the East as the commercial battlefield for Europe . . . . The feeble-minded allow themselves to be duped by these false counsellors, believing them to be sincere; when the Europeans see this, they are astonished at such passivity and say: 'If you were like us, you would have done as we do.'

For thirteen centuries the Muslims and the Copts lived as members of a single household and treated each other as part of the same community. They were united, as a family. There were never any aggressive clashes between them over religion, nothing to parallel what has happened to the Jews in the West, where they have been expelled from their own countries, tortured, robbed of their property, loaded with chains, and made to choose between renunciation of their religion or exile and forced labour in the hell of Siberia. The Muslims have never acted towards the Copts as the French did towards the Jesuits — their brothers in religion if not in doctrine —, nor like the Bulgars who burnt mosques and murdered anyone found praying on a Friday, nor like the Russians who forced the Circassians to abandon their homeland, their hearths and their cattle and make for Turkey, stripped of all possessions.

The fusion between Muslims and Copts has been the dyke which has preserved Egypt from the flood of European propaganda aimed at confusing the people and sowing the seeds of dissension between creeds . . . .

Let the Muslim amongst you, O Egyptians, turn to his brother Muslim and strengthen the religious bond between them. Let them both then turn to the Copt and the Israelite and strengthen the patriotic union that binds them all together as one man with a single goal: to keep Egypt for the Egyptians . . . .

When will slumbering energies be aroused? When will new trading houses open, as well as new national companies which require only a little share capital to start making big profits? When will we be able to re-open the old firms that have been forced to shut their doors? Are we really incapable of rising to the level of other nations, even in the domain of illiterate boors, forced by the necessities of life to join in trade? Is it not possible to form companies for the purchase of state domains or khedival estates and put them to use, employing your brother the fellah and making up for some of what has been wasted in the fleshpots and given away to foreigners? It is not worthwhile to open schools that your sons may be educated and in order to erect a barrier against the European influence being inculcated by European schools. Go to your sons before you lose them! Teach them that you are their fathers before they renounce you! Transmit your religion to them before they turn against you! Teach them to study the history of your country and your forefathers before they forget you! Win them back to patriotism before they become your enemies and spill your blood in order to better resemble those who have educated them and made them their sons . . . !

Accursed condition to which these phantoms called 'knowledge' and 'civilized ways' have reduced us! We have planted hatreds in our now starving and aggressive hearts. We have exhausted ourselves in pointless enmities through ignorance and stupidity. We have exposed our innermost selves to the scorn of others, through folly and idiocy. We have sold our soul to foreigners for a pittance, through imbecile misjudgement.

If we had spoken with one voice, if our souls had come together, if our innermost beings had been cleansed, if we had used all these energies to preserve the people of our homeland and speak clearly for our two races,[2] the mighty would have envied us and Europe would have looked upon us with admiration and respect. But the folly of the Orientals has made them like the logs devoured in a fire so that others may forge metal, cook or otherwise profit from the flame . . . .

Woe, that men whose forefathers throughout the ages exchanged the benefits of civilization and travelled freely in each other's lands, indivisible and inseparable by any outsider, have now fallen so low; the tradition has been forsaken and those who came after allied themselves with strangers, served the foreigner and helped him to intervene, or even to seize the other nation's country; and not because of any hatred between the two nations or war between their patriots, but for the wages of a roadsweeper, for the price of rags worn by a beggar!

To those using their religion as an excuse, we say that the nation's independence is far more worthwhile than humiliation by foreigners of the same religion. The foreigner dupes our people and then, having used them to attain his ends, casts them back into the ranks of the totally enslaved, granting them no rights other than that of serving him, recognizing no distinctions between them and their countrymen of other religions, exploiting and enslaving all alike.

Shall we thus say, 'Our hour has come', and satisfy our animal natures, turning our backs on the honours or indignities the future may hold for our compatriots and brothers? Accursed is he who opts to save himself by soaking his bread in the blood of his brothers and of his race! The animal defends his neighbour, irrespective of species: can man accept to be less virtuous than the animals?

If you have faith in heaven and hell, then come closer to God, that He may open the gates of heaven to you; come closer to Him by refusing to help the foreigner against your brothers. Whether you believe in the existence of God and the immortal soul, or that there is neither God nor Allah, as the insolent secular party proclaims, illustrate the pages of history with an eternal glory and the enduring quality of a fine thought. But if you hold that all faith is illusion and that everything is reducible to the blind push and pull of animal nature, taking us where reason has no will to go, then you can despair.

In a word, the strongest medicine is cauterization by fire. We are at a climax. If we manage to mend this motheaten cloth, if we support each other and speak with a single Eastern Egyptian, Syrian, Arab and Turkish voice,

91

then we will be able to say to Europe: 'We are ourselves and you are who you are.' But if we stay as we are, riven with contradictions and capitulations, constantly turning to the foreigners for aid, then the Europeans will be entitled to chase us out of our countries, down to the last mountain cranny, and then, having parked us amongst the wild beasts they will rightly turn to us and say, 'If you were like us, you would do as we do'.

TAHA HUSSAIN
(1889-1974, Egypt)

The uncontested grand old man of Arab letters, Hussain was trained in the national tradition at Al-Azhar, at the Egyptian University, where he became the university's first D.Litt. (1914), and in the school led by Muhammad Abduh and Lufti al-Sayyed. He also made advanced studies of European culture, notably in Paris where he obtained another D.Litt. (1917).

On his return to Egypt, Hussain became the first Egyptian to occupy the chair of Arabic literature at the Cairo Faculty of Letters, where he subsequently served as dean on several occasions. He became literary director of *Al-Siyassah al-Usbouiyyah*, founded the journal, *Al-Kateb al-Misri* (1945-48), and joined the Wafd, becoming technical adviser to the Ministry of Public Education in 1936 and then Minister in 1950.

Taha Hussain was a doctor *honoris causa* of the universities of Rome, Athens, Lyons, Madrid, Oxford and Palermo, President of the Egyptian Institute and the Arabic Language Academy in Cairo (1963) and a member of the Academies of Damascus, Baghdad, Paris, Rome, Mayence, Teheran and Madrid.

His main contribution is to have introduced the historical conception into cultural history and literary criticism, notably during his famous polemic with the Azharist school over pre-Islamic literature. He also had a considerable influence over Egyptian education policy and philosophy, setting it on a liberal, national and rationalist course which avoided the twin pitfalls of excessive traditionalism and Americanization. From 1939 onwards, during the final phase of his development, Taha Hussain became the epigone of the Mediterranean and liberal vision of Egypt, at a time when Arabism was in the ascendant and Gamal Abdel Nasser had defined the three spheres — Arab, African and Islamic — of Egyptian national thought.

Main works: On pre-Islamic Poetry (*Fil shair al-gahili*); On pre-Islamic Literature (*Fil-adab al-gahili*); The New Evocation of Abil-Ala (*Tagdid dhikra Abil-Ala*); The Book of Days (*Al-Ayyam*); On the Margins of the Life of the Prophet (*Ala hamesh al-sirrah*); The Future of

Culture in Egypt (*Mustaqbal al-thaqafah fi Misr*); **Invocation of the Partridge** (*Doua al-karawan*); **Those who Suffer on Earth** (*Al-muadhaboun fil-ard*); **Memoirs** (*Mudhakkirat*).

When the Wafd emerged as the leading party of the Egyptian bourgeoisie between the wars, there was an urgent need for a corresponding philosophy of culture. Taha Hussain outlines his position, shortly after the revolutionary upsurge of 1935-1936.[3]

The Mediterranean Vocation of Egyptian Culture[4]

Is the Egyptian mentality, imagination, perception, understanding and judgement Oriental or European? To put it more precisely: is it easier for an Egyptian to understand a Chinaman or a Japanese than a Frenchman or an Englishman? That is the question we must decide before we can investigate the basis on which we shall build our culture and our educational system. The best method would be to trace the history of Egyptian thought back to the earliest days, and then to follow its long tortuous and complicated evolution towards modern times.

The first thing we notice about the history of Egyptian life is that we do not know whether in ancient times there existed the kind of regular and constant links with the Far East which might have influenced its politics, its economic institutions and its thought.

The specialists in ancient Egyptian history are unable to point to any specific vestiges or texts that would testify to the existence of such regular contacts. At most, they can show that towards the end of the Pharaonic era, the Egyptians were cautiously exploring the Red Sea, never venturing far from the shoreline without considerable reticence and apprehension. I do not believe that their motivation in doing so amounted to much more than a desire to lay their hands on the harvests of India and the southern Arabian countries . . . . But they did not persevere, and never went very far; certainly they never set up the kind of communications system that would have had a profound influence on thought, politics and the economy.

It seems unlikely that the Ancient Egyptians' contacts with the East went much farther than what we now call Palestine, Syria and Iraq, in other words the Eastern Mediterranean. Three links, however, were undoubtedly both important and continuous and they were organized on such a vast scale as to have a considerable influence on the intellectual, political and economic life of all the countries concerned.

The result of these historical indications is plain: the Egyptian mentality has not entertained important links with the Far East; it has not co-existed peacefully and benevolently with the Persian mentality, with whom its relations have indeed tended more towards enmity and war. On the other hand the Egyptian mentality has been in constant contact with the countries of the Near East, has influenced them and has been influenced by them;

furthermore it has entertained relations of co-operation and understanding with the Greek mentality, relations leading to fruitful, continuous and mutually beneficial exchange of political and economic ideas.

This all seems reasonably obvious; a listening European would no doubt smile at our efforts to establish what he takes absolutely for granted. But according to his level of knowledge, the Egyptian and the Oriental will either explicitly deny or refuse to accept that the Egyptian mentality has been exposed to Mediterranean influence from its earliest days, and that it has been cross-fertilized in every domain by the peoples of the Mediterranean . . . .

I will never forget how, a few years ago, I was baffled and confused by the attitudes of a group who then called themselves *Al-Rabitah al-Sharqiyyah* (The Oriental Association). Their strange line of thought and activity was based entirely on their preference for solidarity with the Far East to solidarity with the Near East. For my part, it strikes me as transparently obvious that we feel a certain kinship with the Near East, not only because we share a language and a religion with those countries, but also because of our geographical proximity and the similarities in our origins and historical evolution. If we are to go beyond this Near East, then I fail to see that we can do so on the basis of considerations such as a shared mentality or historical proximity; unity of religion or the mutual provision of temporary political and economic advantage would seem more relevant.

But history has long established that the unity of religion or language cannot constitute a valid basis for political unity or for the creation of a state. The Muslims themselves abandoned the idea of taking religious or linguistic unity as the foundation on which to build a kingdom long ago. I doubt that anybody would seriously deny that they based their policy on practical advantage, rather than on religious, political or ethnic unity, right from the end of the 2nd Century (H) . . . . The Muslims continued whenever possible, to base their policy on practical advantage alone, to the extent that by the 4th Century (H), the Muslim world had already replaced the Muslim state; nationalities appeared and states proliferated in the Muslim countries . . . .

Of all the Muslim states, Egypt was the one that recovered its ancient personality the fastest — indeed that personality had never been forgotten. History teaches that Egypt put up a fierce resistance to the Persians, only came to trust the Macedonians when they had become fully assimilated, . . . and was made to submit to the power of Imperial Rome only by dint of constant coercion. In fact Egypt's resistance to Rome was such that the Caesars were forced to use violence repeatedly to impose the yoke of martial law.

History also shows that Egypt's acceptance of Arab domination following the conquest was not completely free of resentment, not to say resistance and revolt. The country only really settled down and regained its self-confidence once it had reasserted its independent personality under Ibn Tultoun and the various governments that succeeded him.

ANTOUN SAADAH
(1909-1949, Lebanon)

Born in Lebanon, where his father was a doctor, Antoun Saadah emigrated to Egypt and then to Latin America, settling in Brazil. It was there, under the influence of Philip Hitti and Henri Lammens, that his ideas on the Syrian nation ripened. After his return to Lebanon in 1929, in 1932 Saadah founded the Syrian National Party, which he turned into a secret organization geared to a militant activism and drawing its first members from his own students at the American University of Beirut.

Syria had been chopped to pieces by the San Remo, Sevres and Lausanne treaties. Saadah set out to reunite the country. He argued that the Arab defeat in the first Palestine War (1948) was due to the attitude of the Arabs themselves; hence his apologias for the Syrian nation couched in terms of Caananites and Phoenicians.

His party aroused violent passions. Saadah, who was himself imprisoned several times, strove to rally the Lebanese abroad, notably in Latin America, and to elaborate a particular total ideology, social-nationalism. On the 9 June 1949 there was a bloody confrontation between the Lebanese Phalange and Saadah's party; the latter fled to Syria, where it was welcomed by Colonel Husni al-Zaim who looked with favour on the attempt to establish a 'Greater Syria'. Saadah then personally declared war on Lebanon and started training his commandos. In July, he was extradited by the Syrian government, condemned to death in Lebanon and executed on the 8 July 1949.

Main works: **The Constitution of Nations (*Nushou al-umam*); Commentaries on the Doctrine (*Shurouh fil-aqidah*); The Principles of the Syrian Social Nationalist Party.**

Syria, Mother of Nations[5]

Unity of language does not make a nation but it is necessary if one is to maintain its cohesion. Whenever language is taken as a basis for nationality, it is usually a way of expressing a need for national expansion and enlargement, as in the case of Germany . . . . The Arabic speaking world no more constitutes a nation than the English or Spanish speaking worlds. Each of the nations within these worlds elaborates its own particular literature exploring its specific problems and expressing a kind of psyche and taste, all in a language which acts as a bridge between specific nations. Some communities do not even need a common language to constitute a nation, Switzerland, for instance . . . .

Where religion represents a unity of belief amongst a people it becomes one of the factors reinforcing the international spiritual cohesion of that people. Also, the more a people is backwards in terms of its grasp of new philosophical ideas, the more religion acts as a dominant factor in that people's mentality. In fact, religion, by its very nature and origin, is non-national, opposed to nationalitarianism and the formation of nations; it is necessarily humanitarian, with a universal connotation. Religion is a single whole but there are many nations. And in the clash of nations, each clings grimly to any belief, religious or non-religious, which may help to preserve some kind of spiritual independence.

The religious league sought to prevent the growth of nations, but as the nations developed, they changed religion to make it better suited to national conditions. In this sense religion is still in the process of becoming one of the elements of nationalitarianism . . . .

The nation is a society of men who live in a given territory, sharing interests, psychic and material concerns and a unique destiny. These interactions with their nation throughout its long evolution endow it with the characteristics and qualities that distinguish it from other communities.

Let us now turn to the specific social religion from which the Canaanites drew their essential vision of the world, and which has sometimes been called the Canaanite fallacy . . . . It is important that social scientists should be aware of the reasons which lead us to say that the Syrian Canaanites were the first to establish the national relation on the basis of an idea of nationhood . . . .

Of all the peoples of the ancient world, the Canaanites were the first to embrace love of their nation, on the basis of social cohesion in keeping with a national sensibility and a feeling for the unity of life and of destiny. A group of them started out north-westwards from the area around the Dead Sea, came down towards Lebanon and entered history as the Phoenicians . . . . The Canaanite Phoenicians founded the civil state which became the model for the Greeks and Romans. Despite the states that were founded on their territory, the Canaanites did not make war and retained their unity as a people who faced life together . . . .

Long ago the Phoenicians established an electoral system of monarchy, with a sovereign elected for life. In this domain and in the creation of a historic state they preceded all other peoples. They created the first democratic state, the state of the people, of the nation, the national state with its roots in the will of a society conscious of its own existence and purpose . . . . Although the Canaanite Phoenicians created a maritime empire, their expansion remained national expansion; they founded imperial colonies which remained tied to the mother country, for better or worse. It was more akin to the expansion of a nation than to the expansion of a state.

ALAL AL-FASI
(1910-1974, Morocco)

**Founder and president (1946) of the Istiqlal, and leader of the struggle
for the unity of Morocco from 1930 onwards, Al-Fasi was exposed to
repeated persecutions, and twice exiled. From Cairo (1948-1953) he
organized the resistance movement and launched the historic call to
arms on 20 August 1953. On his return to Morocco in 1956, he was
appointed professor at the Rabat Faculty of Law, and then Minister of
State for Islamic Affairs (1961-1963). He later served as a deputy and
was director of the journal** *Al-Bayyinah.*

**The core of his theoretical work, strongly inspired by Muhammad
Abduh, consisted in defining the kind of intellectual and social renewal
of the national tradition which could stand as a rampart against that
kind of modernity which is mere imitation of the West.**

Main works: **Autocritique** (*Al-naqd al-dhati*); **The Great Arab
Maghrib** (*Al-Maghrib al-arabi al-kabir*).

**The text presented below was written in Cairo in 1952, and marked a
turning point in the evolution of the Arab National Movement. The
reader will note the careful distinction drawn between two modes or
levels through which the Arab world can gain access to contemporary
civilization.**

The Problems of a Contemporary Approach[6]

One aspect of the intellectual weakness which has afflicted most people
today is the division of society into two camps: those who hold that
whatever the Ancients did or thought constitutes the truth, to be adhered to
at all cost, even if this means distrusting everything that has not been passed
by their forefathers and is not part of the traditions into which they were
born; and those who are so dominated by their desire for novelty and inven-
tion that they come to believe that everything inherited from the past should
be swept away.

Life is movement; and movement demands two things: continuity of dis-
placement and transition from one point to another . . . .

The root of the mistake some people make is that they confuse the contemporary with contemporaneity, what is contemporary with what is happening contemporaneously; they forget that it is quite possible for there to
be nothing in our epoch which is in keeping with the true 'contemporary
spirit', whilst what happened during the Middle Ages or before may be
essentially contemporary. We can find living examples of this thesis simply
by looking around our own countries; some of our institutions still take as
their reference point a model which dates back to the era of the Thousand
and One Nights, yet certain periods of our past provide examples of
organization and civilization worthy of the most modern epoch in its most

97

advanced aspects. Take for instance the Benevolence Bank at Fez, which attained a level of organization surpassing that of any of the contemporary aid and co-operation bodies. If the system once implemented at Fez were adopted today, it would eliminate all the abuses by loan-mongering banks, including the accumulation and monopolization of money and the ruination of families and consciences. Similarly the various forms of black market which have emerged alongside certain aspects of the contemporary economy befit the most backward and benighted of past eras . . . .

The truth is that the contemporary spirit came to an end with the outbreak of the Great War, in other words the moment 20th Century man discovered that the ideals of the revolutionary democrats — who had put their faith in science and believed that world progress was the ineluctable consequence of scientific advance — were grossly over-optimistic. The Western camp then split into three groups. The first of these turned back to Christianity . . . and can now be called conservative; in effect, it represents little more than a class trying to hold on to what it grabbed long ago.

The second group is composed of those who, having despaired of democratic ways of thinking and operating, turned away from the Church and endorsed its condemnation by the French Revolution. This group then rallied to the Communist doctrine . . . .

Finally, there is a third group, people whom Christianity and Communism have not been able to satisfy — people who are looking for a solution to that which the church has disdained and the Cominform has left unanswered. In the West, some of them are awaiting a magician who will provide what neither Hitler nor Mussolini could give them. Others turn to existentialism, which, in the end, is no solution, since it is in effect more corrupting than uplifting . . . and is ultimately merely another determinism.

Doubtless, the West still possesses considerable intellectual and spiritual resources; but I defy anybody to prove that these resources were not modern in nature before the Great War, or to deny that there is, in the West today, an attempt to go back to first principles in order to make a stand against the prevailing intellectual and moral chaos. Therefore let us not shun our own fundamental origins, made up of faith in freedom, pride in reason and unchanging values.

Above all, we owe it to ourselves to keep before our eyes the goal we are working towards; namely, to serve our society, elevate it, promote its self-awareness and infuse it with the determination to defend its rights and do its duty. The core of all this is the continuity of the Moroccan nation's existence and the endurance of the intellectual and spiritual values which have shaped it and made its life one of the successes of human civilization in the highest sense.

Now although the preservation of the nation in precisely the form it had in the past is not essential to this kind of continuity, it is vital that the transformation should take place within the framework of an established identity and on the basis of a progressive methodology which will open new vistas, without either diverting our society from its fundamental course or disfiguring its sense of self. For us, Morocco is only worth something as the homeland of the people who united Arab civilization and Islamic culture; Morocco, swollen with immigrants and foreigners and forced into an alien mould, would no longer be the Morocco for which we are prepared to die and to which we are so devoted . . . .

Consequently, the first criterion of true thought is that it should help this nation and further its progress. Any thought which seeks to divide it, to disrupt its unity and extinguish it as a national entity with its own specific and particular characteristics is inadmissible. Since ideas do not appear out of the blue but rather work their way into a society with the help of specific phenomena, our duty requires us to investigate whether particular phenomena meet this primary criterion. If they do, well and good; if they do not, then we must have no hesitation about opposing and eliminating them, even if they appear to be the most seductive and brilliant developments of our epoch.

The second precondition is that ideas should answer the needs and desires of the nation, since the purpose of any national movement is to realize the hopes of the people, the hopes which reformers and men of action can sometimes express, albeit usually according to their own interpretation . . . .

The right approach is to try to interpret the people's actions and the form of organization they adopt as a way of discovering the central idea which they are working for and striving to defend. This is an extremely difficult problem, given that the people do not always act in their own best interest, that they are susceptible to spontaneous error and open to the misleading counsel of the ill-intentioned and the profiteers; the people thus need men who are concerned to understand the popular aspirations as the people experience them themselves and not just as they may appear from actions and errors.

The third precondition is that ideas should be progressive. Any thought which is not geared to turn the nation towards evolution and progress is sterile and should be rejected and condemned . . . . It sometimes happens that some human groups become mixed with others without really knowing what to do about it. They then undergo a change in the process of which they may become a more civilized and cultured nation than before, but at the price of losing touch with their own being.

The new nation may become great, but — it will be a different nation. The old nation will annihilate itself that a new nation may arise . . . . Any major change not in accord with the desires or purposes of those that suffer it can only be a catastrophe for them. The only way to avoid such an outcome is to direct the nation towards progress, to blend the nation's past, present and future into a harmonious melody, held together by the high ideals it has always set itself as it moved ever forward through the stages of its existence.

The fourth precondition is universality, in other words the idea must encompass reform in every aspect of the country's life in which progress can be furthered . . . .

The experience of the past must remain in our minds every time we consider the present and work towards the future . . . . Freedom will only be achieved if the people are truly self-aware, fully conscious of their own goals and choose the form of human experience which will help them preserve the viability of their own experience as independent human beings, not as mere copies of some model. Just as the multiplicity of shapes which make up a living thing all come together as parts of a single individual, so the multiplicity of forms taken by human experience are in no way contradictory to the fact that each nation belongs to a single world, the world of humanity, with its own specific goals. The independence of the individual and of the nation is the embodiment of a true thought which guarantees popular responses, continuity, progress and universality.

MAHMOUD AMIN AL-ALAM
(1922 - Egypt)

Sacked from his post as tutor in Philosophy of Science at the Cairo Faculty of Arts in 1954, Al-Alam nonetheless remained, until 1958, Egyptian Marxism's leading authority on aesthetic and literary matters and one of the most widely reputed young masters in the Arab Middle East. His many writings, which have still not been brought together in a single collection, bear witness both to his deep roots in the Egyptian and Islamic tradition and to his broad awareness of culture. Imprisoned along with his fellows in the 1959 wave of repression, he later became Director of Publications at the Ministry of Culture (1967), President of the Akhbar al-Yawm group of journals (1967-1969) and a member of the Central Committee of the Arab Socialist Union. In May 1972 he shared the fate of the Ali Sabri group and was sacked from his post as Director of the Theatre (1970-1972). Since that time he has dedicated himself to his cultural and philosophical writings. He has also been one of the key figures of the Egyptian and Arab left abroad opposed to President Sadat's policies.

Main works: On Egyptian Culture (*Fil-thaqafah al-misriyyah*) (in collaboration with Abd al-Azim Anis); Ideological Struggle (*Maarak fikriyyah*); Philosophy of Chance (*Falsafat al-musadafah*); Culture and Revolution (*Al-Thaqafah wal-thawrah*); Considerations on the Literary Works of Nagib Mahfouz (*Taammulat fi adab N.M.*); Song of Man (*Ughniyat al-insan*); Marcuse or the Philosophy of the Blind Alley (*Marcuse aw falsafat al-tariq al-masdoud*).

The text that follows is a refutation of the thesis developed by T.S. Eliot in *Towards a Definition of Culture*. It was written just before the Suez affair.

Towards an Egyptian National Culture[7]

It would appear that culture does not rest on a single, solid and clearly defined foundation; rather, it is the outcome of a process in which many factors are brought into play — the process of society, involving all the categories that go to make up a society and all the means it has at its disposal. The relationship between culture and this process of interaction is no simple matter of unifactorial causality; on the contrary it brings into play new interactions which make culture one of the guiding forces within the social process itself.

If such is indeed the meaning of culture, what then are the constitutive factors, characteristics and modalities of our Egyptian culture? Despite the central importance of this question, it has to be recognized that till now it has not been the subject of any serious studies. True, Dr Taha Hussain touched on the matter in a few lines at the end of his *Mustaqbal al-thaqafah fi Misr* (The Future of Egyptian Culture) but he did so in obscure and nebulous terms and restricted himself to noting that 'Egypt has its own specific course in expression, just as it has its own specific course in thought'.

When we ask the following question: 'What is the personality of our Egyptian culture?' . . . we must specify the modalities of the vast social process which we have identified within our Egyptian reality. Without going into a detailed study of the economic and sociological factors whose interaction constitutes the social process in which all our popular classes participate, we can evoke the general social substratum which is itself fairly clear and evident.

Imperialism continues to occupy a crucial part of our country, puts obstacles in the way of our national economic renaissance and brings harmful influences to bear on our cultural sensibility and our system of education.

That is our sociological infrastructure. It is impossible to underestimate or ignore its objective implications for every aspect of our national life. Our social process entails adoption of an unambiguous stance *vis-à-vis* imperialism and an unremitting and tenacious effort to liberate ourselves from all its political, military and cultural aspects. Every Egyptian citizen, consciously or not, is an integral part of this general infrastructure. Similarly, our private life, with all its emotions, affections, efforts and achievements, is more or less directly linked to this infrastructure, whether we like it or not. The *fellah* who is unaware of the connection between poverty and the New Orleans Stock Market, the state employee who is unaware of the link between the rising cost of living and the preparations for war, the itinerant peddlar who knows nothing of the laws of the market, and all the other social categories make up the fabric of our social life. They all struggle for a better life and hence to free themselves from imperialist domination, whether they know it or not. Similarly our problems, from the little insignificant ones to the big central ones — unemployment, love, religion, corruption, freedom, marriage, vice and virtue, sickness and health — are all the fruits of this infrastructure.

Adoption of a specific stance *vis-à-vis* imperialism and foreign domination over various aspects of our social life is thus an essential element of our social process. Similarly, there can be no doubt that one of the attitudes towards imperialism which is expressed as part of that social process is treason, the collaboration and collusion with imperialism by its agents and creatures whose local interests demand that its plans succeed. The social process can thus be differentiated into two tendencies: the one expressing the effort to elevate our Egyptian reality and eliminate all the forces blocking its growth and development, the other expressing precisely those forces which block such evolution.

On the basis of these considerations, it becomes possible to elaborate the real meaning of our culture, to discover its laws and observe its tendencies. Of course I would not claim that it is for Egyptian intellectuals to work out a specific plan for armed struggle, just as it is not the writer's job to feed his reader with accounts of heroic deeds or the musician's job to compose inflammatory hymns. I simply mean that when they express themselves, the thinker, the artist and the writer choose their raw material from amongst the interpenetrating elements of our society, whether consciously and willingly or not. I also mean that these elements and relations reveal a specific attitude towards the imperialist octopus which weighs upon our national sensibility and blocks our process of original creation. The upshot is that our artists and thinkers' choice of raw materials and their treatment of it will determine just how sincere they are when they face our social reality, work out its dynamic and express it.

Awdat al-ruh[8] (The Return of the Soul) did not play an active part in the 1919 revolution, but it did express a decisive stage in our national growth. *Pygmalion*[9] rebelled against active and productive life, preferring the impassiveness of the statue; the play thus represented a new stage in Tawfiq al-Hakim's attitude towards our national history. The Egyptian existentialists do not say openly: 'We are traitors, we do not believe in Egyptian patriotism, since patriotism is an abstraction, nor do we believe in the struggle against imperialism, since we are free to act or not to act, *mutatis mutandis*'; but their propaganda in favour of individualism and absolute freedom amounts to a retrograde position *vis-a-vis* imperialism and our revivified social process. The heroic music of Abd al-Wahab[10] does not always express a genuine national sentiment; on the contrary, it is a manifestation of artistic poverty and insincerity. By contrast, the non-heroic popular songs of Sayyed Darwish, such as *Ya amm Hamzah, Al-dik bi yeddann kou-kou-kou-kou, Al-shayyalin* (Uncle Hamzah!; The Cock Crows at Dawn, The Porters), crystallize the Egyptian sensibility and express its growing tendencies.

Since culture is the reflection of the process of social reality, and since our social reality is the struggle for liberation, we can only determine the meaning of Egyptian culture by going to the heart of Egyptian reality. For instance, what relation is there between Tawfiq al-Hakim's theory of time and predestination, and our natural history? What is the relation between Bishr Fares' poetic symbolism and the contours of our society? What are the sociological implications of the morality in Shawqi's[11] poems? It is by exploring these and other notions, by striving to understand meanings in the light of our social reality, that we will be able to define an overall sense of our Egyptian culture and water its various roots.

This sociological study of cultural expression in all its forms in no way detracts from the artistic value of literary or other works; on the contrary it could help us to understand many complex artistic problems. To take a simple example: Tawfiq al-Hakim's attitude towards life determines the way static characters and ideological dialogues are given artistic expression in his plays. It is Tahu Hussain's non-assimilation of our day-to-day reality in all its details and complexity of interaction, in both town and country, which has stripped his novel *Doua al-karawan* of life and made it such a collection of high-sounding abstractions.

MUTA SAFADI
(1929, Syria)

Born to an intellectual Damascus family, Safadi studied philosophy at Damascus University and taught in various *lycées*. In 1961 he was invited to give a course at the Faculty of Letters. The rapid development of his cultural activities soon led him to give up teaching altogether and devote himself entirely to writing.

Safadi started out as a poet; indeed he was the Laureate of the journal *Al-Adab* in 1954, but he later turned to philosophy and politics. A Baath supporter of long standing, he gradually moved away from Baathism and, from 1963 onwards, put his hope in socialism, which he saw as one element in the national renaissance of the Arab world. Since 1977, he has been director of the Arab Development Institute in Beirut and editor of the journal *Al-Fikr al-Arabi*.

***Main works*: The Generation of Destiny (*Jil al-qadar*); The Revolutionary and the Arab Revolutionary (*Al-Thawri wal-Arabi al-thawri*); Philosophy of Anguish (*Falsafat al-qalaq*); The Baath Party, the Tragedy of its Birth and Demise (*Hizb al-Baath, masat al-mawlud, masat al-nihayah*).**

Muta Safadi's poems, plays, novels and philosophical works represent an attempt to give greater theoretical depth to the Arab revolutionary wave. His phenomenological and then socialist analysis is notable for its rigour and its opposition to traditional formulations; at the centre of this process lies the problem of the Arab hero for our time, as the following text explains.

The Crisis of the Contemporary Arab Hero[12]

I am a revolutionary! Why did I revolt? How can I revolt?

I am a revolutionary, an individual revolutionary. Individualism in itself marked the first stage of a separation which developed within the body of anxieties through which Arab life proceeded until the experience of resurgence enveloped it in its mobility and upheaval.

The particular preoccupation in question has no exact equivalent in the West; the relevant experiences are lacking even for a Heidegger. This difference emerges clearly when we consider the absolute specificity of Arab experience. It is of course undeniable that preoccupations and anxieties exercise a kind of despotic domination over individuals who try to break away from them. But whilst the endeavour of Heidegerrian Existentialism is to confront individual freedom, which is then realized in passive isolation, the Arab revolutionary cannot be content with freeing himself from the grip of such anxiety; he must turn and fight against it, both in the depths of his individual being and in the others who surround him. The point is that, whilst the Arab revolutionary remains an individual, he also carries within himself a being which incites others to establish their own true individuality by recognizing the one precondition for the projected Arab selfhood, namely, to be an Arab revolutionary. This Arab preoccupation is thus a particular form of anxiety; it shares the same existential roots, but it differs from anxiety in that this Arab preoccupation can always be overcome whenever some genuine revolutionary spark comes along to disperse its troubled homogeneity. It also differs in that its despotism is even heavier to bear, and finally, in that it appears to us as a material thing stripped of its human elements. Whilst anxiety is an inescapable feature of man's extra-legal existence, in the Arab case it is weighted with all the negativities opposed to revolution in national life. This preoccupation thus becomes rooted in time, despite its materiality, and is seen by revolutionaries as the product of the past; not the human past, but rather the past of a specific nation, with all the characteristics it has acquired in the course of its history as a national subjectivity. The preoccupation is the product of the preoccupation of past 'others', and present 'others' are those who continue to bear what has been forged for them. They live cut off from their being, in a present where time ticks by mechanically; yet the time they live by is simple repetition . . . .

The task of the Arab revolutionary is thus a double one. First he must free himself from anxiety as a human being, and then from this Arab preoccupation, as a member of the nation . . . .

This preoccupation . . . is not a dimension of the outside world; it sits here, inside, in one's chest, a featureless weight. It was this weight which Michel Aflaq expressed, in a sociological formula, when he developed the (Baathist) ideology of resurgence; 'a corrupted reality sits on the breast of the *Umma*' . . . . It sits there, hanging with its undetermined weight across the palpitating vessels of our breath. The revolutionary finds himself at the heart of this preoccupation; a circumstantial condition directs him towards an existential absolute, or to put it differently, he moves from being an individual in revolt against something specific to a more generalized position of rebellion . . . .

Every time he defines a particular aspect of this preoccupation, he defines his commitment to revolution in an everyday framework which constantly collapses into its constituent elements. The subject of his preoccupation can be described in a variety of ways — reactionary traditions, political fragmentation, imperialism, feudalism, etc. — ; all these terms come readily to hand and have a lasting offensive potential as part of the revolutionary effort as a whole; but they do not describe that comprehensive, independent and existential concern which is a commitment to revolution . . . .

Only heroes can assume the responsibility of victory, with its immense sadness and equally immense joy . . . . The deep and sincere feeling involved in the perpetual revolutionary movement leads the revolutionary to deride any partial revolution. He is caught in one of the most troublesome binds there are: his belief that everything leads to its own opposite. Hence the moment the goal is attained, the greatness of the victory is lessened by an exhausting and growing feeling of powerlessness . . . . Freedom is an unremitting burden, a never-ending anxiety, a contradiction which tears one apart; it makes a broken man of every victor . . . . The revolutionary is forced to fight on several levels, against a variety of factors differing in terms of seriousness, importance and worth. He or she stands against them all.

There is one particular level of anxiety that the young Arab will begin to feel even before his revolutionary consciousness comes to the fore. Before coming into contact with the symbols of 'corrupted reality within society', he lives in a kind of isolation, amongst his peers and congeners. He feels his individuation not as the consequence of a negative normative judgement on a society deemed an unworthy opponent, but as an individuation through a sense of loss, as experienced by those who find themselves plunged into frightening and mysterious circumstances.

This leads to contradictory attitudes; he rejects 'this society' in favour of 'the other society' he will build. He thus comes to approach society as an abstract idea rather than as a tangible reality. He presupposes that this society does not exist, and that even if it did, it would be only a very secondary and marginal aspect of his experience; he then comes to designate society by a term which implies both an absence and a presence; he calls it 'them'.

When a revolutionary refuses to talk in such terms, he also refuses to approach his own existence in this way, . . . and for two complementary reasons; firstly, because he seeks to free himself of his isolated existence and the accompanying fiercely negative sense of being; secondly, because the revolutionary needs the feeling of collectivity, not as a personal matter but as the core of his experience as a militant, endowing every aspect of that experience with its positive or negative value.

The moment the young man sets out in life, he adopts, be it deliberately or unconsciously, the type of anxiety chosen for him amongst an infinite variety of possible forms. This is what we rationalize when we describe the influence of an education. The reality is that in an environment such as the decadent Arab milieu, education can only be a way of ensuring the endurance of the old within the new, thereby draining the new generation of its revolutionary spirit. The form of education in question is not formulated as an end in itself; the community conveys it unconsciously, as if it were some form of instinctive self-defence mechanism to protect its undermined existence from any surprises the new revolutionary generation might bring . . . .

The first glimmers of the revolution thus impinge upon the young man's subjectivity as a cultural issue, as a rejection of the pedagogic mould he has unconsciously sunk into . . . He is against his house, because in it, there is only 'them' . . . . The house is a little nook of anxiety, a dark cave in the city; its odour is replusive; its shadow is immutable; its contents are scattered about tastelessly; everything in it is weighed down by laws — laws of purity, laws against pollution, laws of material purity affecting one's body, one's clothes. As a field of meanings, the house is the abode of various repressed instinctive feelings, where hatred conspires against simplicity, calculation conspires against spontaneity and habit conspires against innovation. The young man thus evolves through a forest of restrictions, all ensconced in the name of the gods and of his elder brother and of his mother, of the dervishes and of the mighty, of the local madmen and the old women haunted by *djinns* and demons, of the turbans and the rosaries and of the policeman, the delator and the foreign soldier.

Naturally, he is a frightened man, and all those around him are frightened. This shared fear, within the community, is itself a kind of security, provided one does not step outside, where one has to be frightened alone . . . .

You are being watched!

The eyes of all the secret forces are upon you, piercing your very soul, you can feel them all around, lurking in every shadow. Every one of them is stronger than you are; your father, the *djinn*[13], the schoolmaster, the foreign soldiers, God . . . .

Our man is under surveillance. He can never escape the secret eyes, nor the ineluctable punishment, on earth as in heaven, whether he tries to hide or not. This way of being — being watched — will always dog our man, like a darkness within, a black core which will follow him through all the vicissitudes of his revolutionary or antagonistic action . . . . The world demands that he value the concepts laid upon him; he can thus either bow under the pressure of a habit, the habit of servitude, humiliation and capitulation, or he can secretly reject all these values as the product of constraint and obligation; what he cannot do is apply his revolutionary consciousness to gain some detached appreciation of their true worth. The result is that deep within himself he becomes a hate-filled anarchist who does exactly the opposite of what his values demand the moment he feels that he is no longer under surveillance.

Such formal virtue is the outcome of a morality based on anxiety. It has nothing to do with what the man himself is about; its power does not extend to the dark caves and corners, to the pools of inner shadow always fleeing before the light, dreading boldness.

Such is the bastardized man who has lost touch with the meaning of both good and evil.

MUHI AL-DIN SABER
(1920, Sudan)

After studying literature at the Universities of Cairo and Paris, Saber took his doctorate at Bordeaux in 1949. He subsequently became editor-in-chief of the journals *Sawt al-Sudan*, *Al-Istiqlal* **and** *Al-Zaman*, **tutor at the University of Khartoum, Under-Secretary of State at the Sudanese Ministry of Social Affairs (1954-55), then Director of the Department of Social Science at UNESCO's Fundamental Education Centre at Sirs al-Layan (Egypt).**

A sociologist, publicist and poet, he played a major role in the cultural renewal of the Sudan and was thrice appointed to the presidency of the Sudanese delegation to the Congress of Arab (Cairo 1957) and Afro-Asian (Tashkent 1959, Cairo 1962) Writers. Following the progressive military coup of May 1969, he was entrusted with the Public Education and Culture portfolio, which he held until 1973. In 1976 he was appointed Director-General of ALESCO (the Arab League's UNESCO).

Main works: **Cultural Change and Community Development (***Al-Taghayyir al-hadari wa tanmiyat al-mujtama***); Local Government and Social Development (***Al-Hukm al-mahalli was tanmiyat al-mujtama***); The Bedouins and Bedouinism, an Introduction to the Sociology of Bedouinism (***Al-Badu wal-badawah, muqaddimah fi ilm al-ijtima al-badawi***).**

The theoretical work from which the following text is taken marks a turning point in Arab sociological thought. Its central theme is that the culture of industrial societies, the inevitable accompaniment to the adoption of modern technology, must in the long term prevail over local specificities.

National Specificity and Universalism[14]

The interaction between the types of behaviour pursued by the different civilizations whenever they come into direct contact and confrontation, we shall call 'the cultural illusion',[15] in order to express the nature of the relationship that people imagine exists in such cases.

When two cultures meet, the victorious culture imposes its concepts, values, archetypes and characteristics upon the defeated culture, whose role is at that stage the purely passive one of giving its consent to what is happening. It allows itself to be beguiled by the appearance of strength and by the novelty of the victorious culture, yet remains ignorant of the latter's truly specific traits, of the influence it will bring to bear and the role it will play.

This is precisely what happened during the European expansion throughout the last four centuries, as European modes of government, methods of production and military strategies spread to the other continents.

A second phase in the life of the vanquished cultures then ensues, a positive phase in which these cultures turn to the (victorious) cultural modalities and adopt their appearance, in the belief that these modalities are the basis of that culture's strength; by adopting them the vanquished cultures are expected to attain equality and become able to shake off the yoke and power of the victorious culture.

During this phase, the victorious culture is seen to stand opposed to this tendency and to act in such a way as to prevent the vanquished culture from adopting values which would unite the two cultures.

For example, the creation of trade unions and recourse to the legal right to withdraw one's labour — both integral elements of the European approach — were banned and liable to prosecution in the colonies. Similarly, the constitution of democratic parties and the demand for independence were met with opposition extending to war . . . . Even though the democratic system itself — and the idea of national independence as it is practised today — are fundamental aspects of European culture, that same culture resolutely resisted them the moment they were employed as a means whereby to promote the equality and similarity of the vanquished cultures with European culture.

A third phase of the cultural illusion begins immediately after this second phase which was characterized by the victor's resistance to change. It is based on the idea of a 'golden age', on a return to the past and on the national pride of the emergent societies. This is the phase we are currently going through, marked as it is by vacillation between the vital needs of the nascent nationalities for economic progress, scientific knowledge and technological capabilities on the one hand, ancient cultural values and archetypes representing the national heritage and the cultureal manifestations associated with past glories, elevated into holy ideals, on the other. No nation feels short of high ideals specifically enshrined in its own past history.

The national and patriotic tendencies which arise in such [developing] societies constitute a rejection of and resistance to the value judgements passed by Western culture upon the [vanquished] cultures and the lifestyle of their peoples. During this third phase the victorious culture is itself afflicted with a sense of ambiguity and reduced to a troubled confusion similar to that prevailing in the developing societies.

While the developing societies seek to make progress while looking backwards, to build a glorious present based on principles drawn from the past, to use modern techniques yet reject the corresponding values and mores, the advanced societies face an equivalent dilemma. The export of technology as a merchandize is an indispensable economic process given that the market is a constituent element of technology's very existence. But the moment they seek to realize such material profits, these cultures become wary of the resulting reinforcement of the [developing] societies and of the possibility that the latter might one day attain parity and become competitors.

The outcome is military aggression, economic blockade, arms embargoes, racial discrimination and all the other methods of putting pressure on developing societies or on cultural minorities within a particular culture.

This approach manifests itself in other guises as well, notably ethical, moral and ideological self-justification. But in the final analysis, it can all be reduced to one culture's efforts to defend its own privileges, assert its superiority and underline its specificity and ability to determine its own character.

This is what we mean by the 'cultural illusion'; a non-objective form of self-justification, a purely subjective approach based on a culture's appreciation and evaluation of itself. In the case of the developing societies, this involves a refusal to look at concrete realities and a retreat into the past so as to compensate for this refusal, even though the societies in question no longer actually live by their ancient values.

Nonetheless these societies envisage their present values as an extension and complement to their history. This is particularly true concerning past glory, which can hardly be considered glorious in the modern sense or in terms of the new values. It becomes mixed in with the new values embodied in the society's national vision, since it thereby increases the possibility of evoking similar glories in the new context, given that the culture of today is cast on the continuation of that which gave rise to the glories of the past.

This is in fact largely an illusion. Present-day culture is in no way the ancient culture, even though some of the old culture's traits and patterns survive. The new culture adopts new values, in the light of the cultural structure as a whole. The language evolves and the religion is reintegrated and expounded anew, broadening its scope and relevance to encompass new needs.

In the case of the more evolved societies, the cultural illusion consists in the affirmation of the present, rejection of the past and fear of the future . . . . This too is illusion: the culture of these societies incorporates its own auto-diffusion. Merchandize must be sold in order to reproduce itself. It cannot be stocked or monopolized precisely because of its economic nature.

All aspects of this kind of behaviour, be it in the developing countries or in the advanced countries — are essentially based on illusion. They are subjective in that they negate a fundamental truth, namely cultural complementarity. The developing societies which seek to implement industrial technology, accept scientific ideas and engage in an industrial economy whilst preserving their traditional values are the victims of a serious misapprehension. These phenomena encompass an approach and values that they impose on all who come into contact with them: the idea of the role of microorganisms in disease is incompatible with the notion that disease is brought about by evil spirits, just as the perception that banks and credits are necessary to stimulate industrial activity makes nonsense of a ban on interest, and the drive to build factories and establish a hierarchy of professional skills cannot accommodate the practice of giving the highest salaries to the most pious and virtuous workers . . . .

The same appliles to the advanced societies: it is foolish to sell spinning and weaving factories to a given country and still hope to be able to sell that country textiles, or to sell a country an arms and munitions factory and expect to keep it weak and humiliated. Such illusions are dangerous. Machines function wherever they are, provided the relevant mechanical and technical conditions are fulfilled: their productivity is the same, whatever the geographical or cultural context.

It is equally impossible to contain scientific ideas and technological knowledge within a closed circle, or to turn them into the appurtenance of a single given society; they constantly break out and propagate themselves, and people are always waiting to understand and apply them; the very nature of scientific ideas, of of humankind, makes it so.

True, a period of cultural transition is necessary before the manifestations of world culture are organically integrated into the various national cultures and penetrate their structure, a phase during which the culture of the future elaborates its own forms of harmony, contact and conditioning. But this is only a phase and will pass with time.

The 'cultural whole' of a particular nationality does endure, with its own specific character. But that does not mean that there can be no similarity in the general framework and the cultural elements and models. Amongst the latter, there are some which are universal and which we have chosen to refer to as a 'civilization'. It is the unique pattern of interaction between these models and characteristics of a civilization on the one hand and specific cultural traits on the other, which maintain the national character of each society. But the latter is more of an historical vestige than a premonition of the culture of the future. Man dreams of cultural and social unity, similar to the biological unity which unites our race throughout the world of the living.

Notes

1. *Sulafat al-Nadim*, selected works edited by Abd al-Fattah al-Nadim, and published by Amin Hindiyyah, Vol.II, (Cairo, 1901), pp.64-83.

2.   The reference is to Syria and Egypt.
3.   On Taha Hussain see also R. and L. Makarius, *Anthologie de la Littérature Arabe Contemporaine*, t.I, (Paris: Le Seuil, 1964), pp.127-133.
4.   *Moustaqbal al-thaqafah fi misr*, (Cairo, 1936), (ed. 1944), pp.13-21.
5.   *Nushou al-umam*, Vol.I, 2nd edition, (Beirut, 1959), pp.154-161.
6.   *Al naqd al-dhati*, (Cairo, 1952), pp.81-91.
7.   *Fil-thaqafah al-misriyyah*, (Beirut, 1955), pp.21-25.
8.   Famous novel by Tawfiq al-Hakim.
9.   Play by the same author.
10.   A famous composer of popular and romantic music. Abd al-Wahab was also the most renowned modern Arab singer.
11.   The 'prince of poets', Ahmad Shawqi (1888-1932).
12.   *Azmat al-batal al-arabi, Al-Adab*, Vol.VII, No.12, 1959, pp.13-16, 28-32.
13.   Spirits.
14.   *Al-taghayyir al-hadari wa tanmiyat al-mujtama*, (Sirs al-Layan, 1962), pp.310-316.
15.   The author himself translates *hadarah* as 'culture'. He reserves the term 'civilization' for *madaniyyah*. Culture is thus to be taken in the sense defined in German philosophical terminology as *Kultur*, the material manifestations of civilization.

5. The Problem of Power: The Popular Masses, the Intellectuals and the Army

AHMAD LUTFI AL-SAYYED
(1872-1963,Egypt)

After completing studies in law, Al-Sayyed was introduced by Saad Zaghloul to the group centred round Muhammad Abduh and Al-Afghani in Cairo. He founded *Al-Garidah*, which became the mouthpiece of the moderate Al-Umma party, and was its editor from 1907 to 1914. From 1908 onwards he was one of the key promoters of the Egyptian University, where he was later Rector for many years. Dissensions within the Wafd alienated him from politics after 1919.

One of the leading intellectual figures of contemporary Egypt, A. Lutfi al-Sayyed is remembered as the theoretician of the Egyptian national personality, the apostle of liberalism and the man who reintroduced Aristotleianism to Egypt. When he retired from the University in 1942, he became President of the Cairo Academy of Arabic.

Main works: Forgotten Pages from the History of the Independence Movement (*Safhat matwiyyah min tarikh al-harakah al-istiqlaliyyah*); Meditations on Philosophy, Literature, Politics and Sociology (*Taammoulat fil-falsafah wal-adab wal-siyassah wal-igtama*); Selected Works (*Al-Muntakhabat*); The Story of My Life (*Qussat hayati*).

The ideas developed below formed the starting point for the modern constitutional and democratic movement led by the Wafd from 1919 to 1952. The piece reflects the author's rage against the traditionalist formations of the Egyptian renaissance.

In Praise of Liberty[1]

Every time I try to write about what for me is the fundamental problem and root of all my concerns, I run up against the attitude of my readers, who react as if I were talking about something superfluous, whereas the reality is that man needs freedom no less than the soul needs a body . . . . It has occurred to me that the distance our milieu has recently taken from demands for liberty . . . does not stem from any absence of desire or loss of hope for change, but rather from our situation; the prevalent love of speechifying on the subject of reconquering freedom calls to mind a person of high rank who is insecure about his position; in other words someone who craves but cannot act . . . .

People may say that all this is foreign teaching which Egyptian writers have plagiarized, copying their European masters to meet Egypt's needs rather than listening to their own hearts. But they would be wrong: these Egyptian writers have set out to explicate the feelings and hopes they see beating in the hearts of our people. Even if you deny us everything else, you cannot take away the fact that we are human beings, that we too thirst for liberty and hope one day to recover a fitting place in the concert of nations; in any case, no nation has a higher claim to be called civilized than the Egyptian nation, given all the factors that make up its unity. Even assuming that you can deny us everything, you cannot rob us of our right to live — and life and liberty are one and the same.

Our liberty suffers from our deficiencies in juridical affairs and even more from our lack of action. This obvious absence of liberty can be seen in the way a citizen approaches a petty official, as if he were his government's subject; the humiliation of it blows in his face like dust every time a government representative, rightly or not, treats him harshly. This capitulation, this passivity before the *mamour*[2] or the governor, can all be traced back to the established laws and the despotism of the rulers.

Any lacunae in our liberty stem not only from the law, be it ancient or modern, but also from the general behaviour of the rulers which is now so widespread that it has come to constitute a kind of law. We have had little say in the drawing-up of these laws; they reflect the wishes of the rulers rather than of the nation. Any restriction on our liberty, in theory or in practice, is an artificial and temporary obstacle imposed by law. We are, by our very nature, human beings with an immense thirst for liberty, and place little value on a life which does not unfold within its ambit . . . .

Honourable deputies: the good that will result from land improvement, bridge building, canal digging, irrigation and the pursuit of perfection in frivolity is as nothing compared to the harm that will be brought about by restrictions on our liberty or even by any delay in the liberation of our souls. Put your political theories aside. Spare us the brilliance of socialist doctrines. It is, above all else, liberty that we need.

The doctrine espoused by those who believe in liberty is based on the principle that public opinion in the free countries and the Egyptian government must not sacrifice the liberty and the interests of individuals to the liberty of the collectivity or of the government in matters of state. This doctrine demands that the government be endowed only with those powers it needs, and that it confine itself to three domains: the police, justice and national defence. All other domains and interests must be left within the jurisdiction of individuals and free collectivities . . . .

Even if we grant that a socialist government, or one that concerns itself with domains other than the three mentioned above, can be useful and beneficial in the democratic countries, that is to say those which are governed by the nation, does that mean that intervention by the government in areas lying outside its normal realm will be advantageous in Egypt? Common sense tells us that we have no interest in seizing the rights of the individual and turning them over to a government in which we have no share and over which we can exercise no control!

The deplorable condition in which we find ourselves, and which is blighting our mores, economy and political life, can be traced back to one basic cause, namely a formidable lack of liberty in our make-up — a lack produced by the ancestral despotism, the socialism turned on its head, which we have lived with era after era . . . .[3] Above all else, we Egyptians need to provide more scope for the exercise of individual liberty, that we may rediscover the lost qualities which are so essential to civil progress and competition in the arena of life. Only in this way will we rid ourselves of this attitude which makes us turn to the government whenever anything serious or delicate arises. Only in this way will we bury this concept, so widespread in the East, that the nation is a flock and the state its shepherd who does with it as he pleases.

Despotism is the most characteristic attribute of governments, be they monarchist or republican; only the fear of falling makes them hesitate. Throughout history and in every country, only weakness or death are shown to have put an end to the despotism of monarchs and governments. Injustice lurks within the soul; strength allows it to unfold, whilst weakness afrights it. It is thus vital to put strict and clearly defined limits upon government action, limits which cannot be sidestepped or misrepresented and which cannot be breached, whatever the situation. If we have such limits, the people will be equipped to cope with governmental injustice. Without them, living in society means living as serfs; it would be more dignified to live in isolation, like the beasts.

MUHAMMAD MANDOUR
(1907-1965, Egypt)

A Doctor of Law (Cairo, 1934) and of Letters (Paris, 1946), Muhammad Mandour was also a professor at the Cairo University Faculty of Letters (sacked 1945). He later became a professor at the Institute of Arab Studies and editor-in-chief of *Al-Sharq*.

Born a *fellah*, he always retained a deep sense of the sensibility of the Egyptian peasant, despite a ten-year stay in Paris. On his return to Egypt, he was elected to the Chamber of Deputies, became editor-in-chief of *Sawt al-Umma* and emerged as one of the main figures of the Wafdist left, alongside Aziz Fahmi, who was assassinated in 1951. In 1946 Mandour became a victim of the first wave of repression against

the left. From 1954 onwards, he developed a critical realist aesthetic, in keeping with his political radicalism.

Main works: **The New Criterion** (*Al-mizan al-gadid*); **Arab Critical Method** (*Al-naqd al-manhagi ind al-Arab*); **Literature and Criticism** (*Al-adab wal Haqd*); **The Act of Poetry** (*Fann al-shair*); **New Problems in Modern Literature** (*Qadaya gadida fil adab al-hadith*); **Unpublished Works** (*Kitabat lam tunshur*).

World opinion is almost completely unaware of the major role played by the Egyptian student movement in the aftermath of the Second World War. Spring 1946 saw the constitution of the National Workers and Students Committee which, until the July 1946 repression, was to become a real national centre of political decision-making.

The huge national demonstrations on 21 February, 1946 are now commemorated on International Youth Day. The NWSC slogans still inspire the new generation in Egypt, who since 1968 have worked to give the country's politics a radical turn.

The National Workers and Students Committee[4]

A phenomenon has occurred in Egypt in the last few days which marks a crucial turning point in our modern history. We can see how far we have come when we compare the national movement in 1919 to the national movement of today. In 1919 the nation began to move only when told to do so by its leaders . . . . Nowadays the process of political thought is much more mature; our youth, 'students and workers', choose their own forms of concrete struggle, put them into practice, and the nation responds to their rallying cry.

In 1919 the movement was entirely political; it had only one goal: the abolition of the protectorate and the independence of the country. Today, on the other hand, it is clear that the contemporary movement does not see national independence as the final goal of the struggle. Everybody realizes that there is no point in abolishing servitude to foreigners if we are still weighed down by domestic servitude; that it is not enough for the homeland to be dear to everyone's heart if so many individuals remain humiliated; that the elimination of imperialism is itself only a means to raise the standard of living of all classes of people, by preventing the foreigners' appropriation of our country's sources of wealth.

It is not enough to defend our means of subsistence and those of our sons and fellow citizens from the foreigners. If justice is to prevail, if all talents are to be given a fair chance, if the road is to be cleared for every productive human activity, then we must also defend these things against the Egyptian exploiters, the rich who still thirst after greater riches.

These ideas embody our highest aspirations. The whole country is espousing them and they have recently had a resounding impact. Nothing will stop them reaching their goals now — goals which can be summarized as political democracy, social justice and the independence of the Nile Valley. Such ideas are no longer mere thoughts and theories; they have been translated into organized action. The first step in this direction was taken by the educated youth of the university, anxious both for their own and their country's future. They took the first step towards the workers, of their own free will and not because of any secret influences, as some have claimed in an attempt to discredit this handsome gesture.

Is it quite clear that there can be no shilly-shallying. The masses of the nation are determined to change the present social situation and bridge the gulf which separates the rich from the poor in Egypt. Never again will be people be content with hollow promises and derisory reforms smacking of charity. What is now required is a daring policy aimed not simply at fighting poverty, illness and ignorance — the natural task of any government, whatever its nature — but at creating working conditions in keeping with the dignity of man, so that people see the fruits of their labour and find no artificial barriers or unjust inequitable obstacles blocking the development of their talents.

We have not pulled these ideas out of a hat; we have heard them from all the youth of the university, and even from their professors. We have heard them from the million and a half state employees; in the factories and private companies these ideas have become the workers' constant refrain.

There is still one important class within the nation, the peasant class, which has not yet grasped the extent of its own misery and taken steps to end it — but that situation cannot last for long. The movement of ideas we have described is no longer restricted to the big cities, it has spread to the *markas* (districts) and is beginning to filter down to the villages. There is not a village in the country where students and intellectuals on leave are not mixing with the *fellahin*, opposing their parents' ideas and spreading the new approach everywhere.

KHALED MUHAMMAD KHALED
(1920, Egypt)

A graduate of Al-Azhar, Khaled won the torch of Al-Afghani and Abduh back from the reactionary and clerical right-wing. In the aftermath of the Second World War his participation in the second wave of the Egyptian national movement, alongside the Wafd and the left, led him to denounce the theocracy preached by the Muslim Brotherhood and to underline the absolute necessity of giving parliamentarism a social and economic content relevant to the people. His first book, *Min hunna nabda* (We Start From Here) appeared in 1950 and was followed by a dozen more as well as by copious newspaper articles. The corpus of

his work amounts to a call for democratic socialism which attempts to make Islam the heart of populism; with its generous and impassioned tone, it has had a profound influence on Egypt's contemporary socially-oriented Islam. Following the Iranian revolution, Khaled declared his conversion to the theses of political Islam in an autocritique through which he also distanced himself from fundamentalism and theocracy.

Main works: **We Start From Here** (*Min hunna Nabda*); **Citizens, Not Subjects** (*Muwatinoun, la raaya*); **This or the Deluge** (*Hadha, aw al-tufan*); **Democracy Forever** (*Al-Dimaqratiyyah abadan*); **We, the Humans** (*Nahnou al-bashar*); **The Ten Commandments** (*Al-Wasaya al-ashr*).

The central concern of K.M. Khaled's thought — democracy — is well summarized in the text below. The author was to plead the same case, brilliantly, before the Preparatory Committee of the 1962 National Congress of Popular Forces. His theme: no renaissance without freedom.

Democracy, the Precondition for Renaissance[5]

Can a government be both despotic and just? . . . .

If we say that a single person can hold a monopoly on truth and justice, the implication is that both truth and justice are of so mean a nature that they can be encompassed by a single mind, perhaps even by a sick or wandering mind. Religion rejects government by one individual, and the world is even firmer in its rejection. The same applies to the one party state, another form of evil and despotism.

There are in Egypt many people who demand that parties be done away with each time something irritating occurs. Such people are making an enormous mistake. The reality is that the source of evil is the weakness of the parties, not their plurality. And if it is argued that the plurality of parties is the cause of their weakness and corruption, because of the divisions and divergences entailed, we can only answer that it is to the plurality of parties that many countries owe their strength and supremacy . . . . The causes of weakness and decadence must lie elsewhere. All this is worth stressing, particuarly given the national psychological tendencies mentioned earlier, the result of too many years spent bowed before a single master and a single party.

The one-party state destroyed Germany, broke Italy's back and brought ridicule upon Japan; in the same period, events swept despotism aside in Turkey and re-established the plurality of parties there . . . .

A democratic government is forced to act with some moderation, thanks to the separation of powers and the control exercised by parliament. Such a regime embodies the sovereignty of the people, and their safeguard. The laws do not express the aims of some absolute ruler but rather aspects of the will of the nation and the guarantees necessary if that will is to prevail.[6]

The speed with which absolute power can bring about reform is bought at too dear a price if it is at the expense of the will of the people. Furthermore, even if such reforms are in keeping with the popular will, the fact remains that excluding the people from the choice, discussion and formulation of the relevant laws also deprives them of an essential aspect of progress and development, namely political education. This is precisely why dictatorships may carry out reforms but can never bring about a renaissance. And there is a difference between reform and renaissance.

Renaissance is the upward progress of our human, political, economic, literary and intellectual life: in all its various forms it is a laborious permanent liberation. In politics it is a liberation from aggression and fear; in economics, a liberation from exploitation and need; in cultural life, a liberation from ignorance and oppression. Renaissance is both liberation from regimes which have lost all legitimacy and the creation of new institutions based on the present needs of the nation and its vision of the future.

Reform is a new building, the flow of a river, the opening of a school. But the *Nahda* has a deeper meaning: it is a way of life which refreshes the soul of the entire community and harmonizes with the people's natural right to life, liberty, prosperity, science and peace. It is an absolute and generalized wealth, the wealth of knowledge, morality and production.

It is stupid to carry out reform in a harsh and brutal manner when it could be effected just as easily in an atmosphere of freedom and calm. The history of Athens and Sparta has an important lesson for us here . . . .

So I ask myself, why should the renaissance need a dictator when it can be carried through just as well under a democracy? Some people will answer that the renaissance needs to be protected against subversive plots, to which I can only reply that dictatorship is itself the most dangerous of all such plots. As we have seen, it implies a subordination of the collective personality and robs the renaissance of the most important sources of permanence and success, namely the participation of the people and the parliamentary control they can exert . . . .

A new factor has come into play, ensuring that the people are unlikely ever to lack enthusiasm for renaissance and reform. Renaissance, in the real sense of the word, is no longer just some political, religious or legal reform; rather it is an economic restructuring which is indissociable from the problems of production and distribution; it thus has a very close bearing on the people's way of life. In this new sense, renaissance means that a society assures its people of the right to work, provides them with a sufficient share of what is produced and enables them to satisfy their intellectual and spiritual needs . . . . When people discover the renaissance which offers them all this, they will pursue it of their own free will, eagerly, without any help from a dictatorship which would impose happiness and force abundance upon them.

Democracy is the natural rampart of the renaissance, even if the protection it affords may sometimes seem slight. But the harm which may come from such weaknesses can never be so great as that which flows from dictatorship in any form. The fact that the nation rises up in revolt to defend its dignity is no justification for suspending all parliamentary activity, under the pretext of ensuring protection from possible reactionary plots. How much truer this is when the revolution unfolds peacefully and without impediment, as happened recently in Egypt, and when its goals and tendencies are deeply popular.

IBRAHIM AMER
(1922-1976, Egypt)

A journalist and essayist with a working-class background, Amer became editor of *Al-Misri* and after 1954, of *Al-Gumhouriyyah*. He published several works in which he sought to provide a Marxist interpretation of Egyptian history, concentrating notably on the modern national movement and the agrarian question. He was the first to apply Marx's ideas on the 'oriental mode of production' and K. Wittfögel's concept of the 'hydraulic society' to the specific conditions of Egypt. His work developed steadily in this vein until it was brutally interrrupted by the wave of repression against the left in 1959. He re-emerged in 1964, notably with articles in *Al-Hilal* and *Al-Musawwar*, and continued working as a political journalist in Beirut until he was assassinated in 1976.

Main works: The Nationalization of the Canal (*Tamim al-qanat*); The Egyptian National Revolution (*Thawrat Misr al-qawmiyyah*); Land and the Fellah, the Agrarian Question in Egypt (*Al-ard wal-fellah al-masalah al-ziraiyyah fi Misr*).

The notion of a Misr al-iqtaiyyah (Feudal Egypt) is often used haphazardly in political essays as the basis for rather vague analyses. Amer was the first to provide a fundamental critique of the period, defining the reign of Muhammad Ali as a transitional stage between feudalism and capitalism, and showing to what extent Egypt had become a backward capitalist-type country during the last third of the 19th Century.

Theory of 'Oriental Feudalism'[7]

The existence of certain aspects of the corvée system in the agricultural economic system at any one time does not necessarily mean that the dominant system is feudal, especially in countries enslaved by the most intense form of capitalist system, namely imperialism. Imperialism has, in effect, created capitalist regimes in America, Africa and Asia, whilst nonetheless conserving forms of agricultural production based on corvée labour and even on some forms of slavery.

The political aspects of a feudal regime are based on the relationship between the rulers and the ruled, the relationship being that of master to slave rather than that of state to citizen . . . . Given that personal links play such an important part in feudal government, it is at the local and regional level that maximum efficacity is attained . . . . Since political power is personal rather than public, that is, since it is vested in individuals rather than in organizations, there is little differentiation between the various political tasks: a military chief often doubles as regional administrator, the latter doubles as judge, etc. In most feudal societies, military duties are seen as the main task of those who hold political power . . . and military tradition often remains a powerful force in society. Nonetheless, the role of personal links alone is not enough to show the existence of a feudal regime.

The mistake of considering feudalism as a purely political regime becomes manifest when we try to define the specifically feudal characteristics of the relationship between landowners and tenants. Most dominant classes have always lived off the labour of the agricultural *fellahin*, by arrogating the power to impose taxes and enforce laws upon them. The presence of this characteristic is thus not, by itself, diagnostic of feudalism.

We therefore reject the argument that feudalism is simply a method of government and a political system. As we see it, the essence of any real understanding of feudalism must be an appreciation of its political and social aspects as reflections of a specific economic regime.

It cannot be denied that until the end of the 18th Century, agricultural land was owned entirely by the state, and Islam did not interfere in this, either way. The phenomenon in question existed in Egypt long before the penetration of Islam, and can also be found in certain non-Islamic countries.

The real reason for the absence of the phenomenon of private landownership in Egypt during the period is precisely that which explains its generalization throughout the area extending roughly from the Sahara in the west to the Asiatic plateau of central China in the east. Agriculture in Egypt was based on large scale artificial irrigation. This state of affairs led to the emergence of a specific type of society in Ancient Egypt, Western Asia, India and China.

To obtain an exceptionally high level of productivity from artificially irrigated land, the state was forced to carry out irrigation projects such as drilling wells, creating ponds, digging canals, etc., as well as regulating the level of rivers and protecting crops against floods. All this required centralized state power over agricultural land, which could only be achieved by state appropriation of these lands and the creation of a central authority which could allocate water for irrigation and mobilize the inhabitants to carry out the necessary tasks; agriculture thus became a government matter . . . .

This system of state control over agricultural land meant that it was the king and his officals rather than private landowners who benefited from any surplus value.

What then is the basis for the argument that the dominant regime in the days of Muhammad Ali[8] was a 'feudal' one? At first sight, the very existence of the Mamelukes[9], regarded as the princes of specific territories, could indeed lead to the belief that feudalism on the European model was in force in Egypt, at least in the period immediately before Muhammad Ali. But as we have seen, Egypt's system of artificial irrigation had always necessitated the existence of a central authority with overall responsibility for administration and, simultaneously, for all military tasks. The outcome was a type of centralized power based on state officials rather than on autonomous governors, a centralized power much greater than that exercized by any Mameluke. To ensure their domination, the Mamelukes were thus forced either to assume the central authority themselves or to go to war against it, which course often led to their destruction or subordination. At best, they could effect the removal of one viceroy and ask the Sultan to designate a successor . . . .

It is true that the Mamelukes managed to seize lands, bequeath tenure to their descendants and sometimes even achieve some independence from the central authority; however, they never managed to win for themselves the ownership of the land, the legal right to exercise the power they held in practice. The proof is that Egypt, whether in the days of the governors of the Caid[10], in the Pharaonic era or in the days of the Mamelukes under the Sultan, has always remained a single political entity and has never gone through the kind of internecine strife which rent Germany, Italy, France and England during the feudal era in Europe.

The *multazim* were not landowners, merely tax-collectors, similar to other financial officials and state functionaries . . . .

Under Muhammad Ali, despite the general distribution of agricultural land, only Muhammad Ali himself had the right to dispose of land: he forbade all land sales and legacies; those who inherited land inherited only its usufruct. Under Muhammad Ali, land was state property; the agricultural lands of each village were a source of collective profit. In many cases, these lands were distributed each year amongst the agricultural workers, even though taxes were set for the village as a whole; it fell to the *sheikh al-balad* to determine what was due from each worker.

Nonetheless, there was a major difference between the type of landownership under Muhammad Ali and that under the Ottoman Sultans. Under the Ottomans, the state monopolized both the use of the land and the profits derived from it, whilst under Muhammad Ali, although the state continued to monopolize the use of the land, the profits tended to stay in private hands. This represented the first major step in the gradual emergence of private landownership in Egypt, alongside the old form of state ownership which was disintegrating under the increasing pressure of world capitalism and as a result of specific internal factors . . . .

Furthermore, the state monopolized both domestic and foreign trade . . . and used agricultural produce as the basis for profit from market operations. The land on which this produce was grown thus itself became a form of merchandize. The foundations for capitalist exploitation of the land in Egypt were laid. Nonetheless, the state preserved some elements of the old corvée labour system.

The system of agricultural exploitation under Muhammad Ali can thus be described as marking the transition between feudalism and capitalism, during which time Egypt underwent an ambivalent transformation. The regime turned into a form of oriental feudalism in a stage of advanced decay containing within itself the elements of a capitalist regime, based on the market economy and geared towards the development of private land ownership. The domestic tendency towards capitalism was reinforced by the intervention of international capital in the last years of Muhammad Ali's reign . . . . This was eventually to lead to direct intervention and the 1840 Treaty of London, when the European powers banded together against Muhammad Ali and did away with his system of agricultural and commercial monopoly.

To those who argue that capitalism om Egypt was created and imposed from the outside, we would suggest that the internal factors warrant closer examination. The causes of capitalism's emergence in Egypt antedate any foreign intervention. The main factors were the passage of Egypt's agricultural economy from a natural economy to a market economy, along with the steady growth of industrial and commercial cities, and the corresponding urban demand for agricultural produce.

It is a mistake to employ purely sociological criteria, to the exclusion of any economic considerations, when assessing these factors. To ignore relevant local factors and argue that the Egyptian 'bourgeoisie' had no desire to make a revolution against 'feudalism' is to put the cart before the horse; the basis of change is the development of new economic factors and not the desire of this or that class to make a revolution.

FATHI RADWAN
(1912, Egypt)

Lawyer, diplomat and publicist, in 1933, along with Ahmad Hussain, Radwan founded the Misr al-Fatat party which based its ideology on national socialism, Islam and nationalism. Following the Second World War, he assumed the leadership of the radical wing of the old National Party and provoked a split, drawing on the support of the more militant members, especially the young.

Radwan's close links with the Free Officers won him the portfolio of the Minister of National Orientation and Culture (1953-59); the programmes he launched during his years in office have had a major impact. More recently, he has concentrated on novels and plays, as well as contributing to *Al-Ahram.*

When the late President Anwar Sadat developed his policy of rapprochement with the West and became involved in the Camp David initiative, Ahmad Fathi Radwan emerged as the figurehead of the Egyptian political class. He expounded the theses of the national movement and of the 1952 revolution firmly and somewhat haughtily, notably in his editorials in *Al-Shaab*, the weekly journal of the Socialist Labour Party; he was consequently caught up in the wave of repression encompassing the whole Egyptian political class and every school of thought within the opposition during the summer of 1981, which led up to President Sadat's assassination on 6 October 1981. In the renewal of political life under President Husni Mubarak, Fathi Radwan now stands as the doyen and moderator of Egypt's national political class.

Main works: Citizen, My Brother (*Akhi al-muwatin*); This People (*Hatha al-shaab*); The Devil's Tears (*Dumou Iblis*); An Era and Some Men (*Asr wa rigal*); Mustafa Kamal.

From the time of the British occupation in 1882, the historical role of the then leader of the Egyptian revolution — Ahmad Arabi — had remained obscure. With the seizure of power by the Free Officers on 23 July 1952, the spotlight swung back onto his contribution, in the perspective defined by F. Radwan in the following text.

Ahmad Arabi[11]

Ahmad Arabi's promotion to the rank of army colonel was really a promotion for the entire Egyptian people. The entire Egyptian people were, till then, mere privates, both in international affairs and domestic politics, second class conscripts who could see and feel but never spoke; they were the objects but never the subjects of action.

Arabi in the army was the symbol of the *fellah* within the state. Whether Arabi did or did not effectively assume the leadership of the revolution, the fact remains that he and his brothers were the emblem of one particular class within the Egyptian nation. It was thus inevitable that Arabi and his brothers should feel as strangers within the army and be aware that they held their rank despite their sovereign's wishes. When humiliation was heaped upon them, it created in them an intense awareness of the rights of the community they represented. Books and scholars have taken to speaking of Arabi's revolution in all its various aspects without even mentioning the role played by the Egyptian people. They talk of the revolution's causes and premises, of the day of Abdine when the army rallied round, with the backing of the entire Egyptian people, and supported Arabi's proclamation that the people were neither a legacy nor an estate, that the Egyptians would no longer allow themselves to be handed down from father to son — all this following the bombing and burning of Alexandria and the defeat of Tal al-Kebir. But what was the people's role in this, what did they contribute? Were they simply bystanders? Or did they enlist, provide help, raise funds?

Both Arabi himself and various foreigners have answered these questions. Foreigners, such as the Swiss, John Ninet, and the Englishman, Blunt, have painted a moving picture of a people with an unyielding will and a strong faith who struggled under the most unhappy and miserable of conditions, without arms, equipment, or advance planning — yet endured and won through. Arabi himself said:

> This war was declared when there was not a single dirham[12] in the state's coffers . . . When the public, the nation as a whole — every tendency and every faction — learnt of this, they gave money, cereals, horses, camels, cows, sheep, fruit and vegetables, even pigeons. Some gave half of all they had; some gave it all; others offered their children for the defence of the nation, not being able to go themselves. In short the entire Egyptian nation profered gifts and evinced a nobility and pride which had not been seen for centuries. I ask all-powerful and all-merciful God to reward the nation as it deserves, by returning its independence and its freedom.

In his book on *Arabi, al-zaim muftara alayhi*, Muhammad al-Khafif mentions a letter sent from exile by Arabi to Sabonghi, a friend of the English writer Blunt, who had close links with Arabi and his friends. Here are a few extracts:

> Please remind our friend Mister Blunt that, on top of what I described in my letter to him on the 15th of this month (July 1883), all the expenses incurred during the war — some £E100,000 — were met with donations from the entire Egyptian nation, irrespective of confessional distinctions. When the war broke out, we had only 10,000 soldiers and 1,200 uniforms, incomplete ones at that; we had only 1,500 *adl*[13] of grain. But by the end of the war, the army's quartermasters held agricultural produce, cows, flocks of sheep, cloth and money to a value of over a million pounds. It had all been donated by the nation to the army that was defending its homeland. During the hostilities, not a single *dirham* came from the government's coffers to meet the army's needs.

Consider that last sentence and you will see Arabi's revolution and the war which broke out between Britain and Egypt in 1882 from a new angle. The revolution belonged to the people, with all that that implies; a people with all its classes and individuals, its diversity, its various beliefs, tendencies and positions, freely and willingly united behind a single ideal in which it has faith and which it will labour to realize.

The people that acted thus was a people weighed down by the debts of the reigning dynasty and entrapped by the concerted plots of the great powers; a people within which several races intermingled, each seeking their own interest; a people whose life had consisted entirely of corvée and the wars into which they were cast like wood into a furnace, without any idea of their aims or the cause of the conflict; a people whose king stood opposed to their leader, a people whose virtues had been so exploited that they would have been forced to abjure them had it not been for their ancestral sense of continuity and their fortitude in the face of catastrophe; a people who fought a war whilst their enemies denied them the means of subsistence and ransacked the treasury into which so much blood and sweat had been poured.

This people is the conclave of our fathers, whom a falsified history has depicted as weak, cowardly and vacillating. This people is us! Let us have faith in it and in ourselves.

. . . The officers whom neither the Ottoman sultan's proclamations nor Muhammad Sultan's[14] manifestos nor Muhammad Tawfiq's[15] money could sway then wrote one of the most honourable pages in the history of the defence of the homeland throughout the ages; Muhammad Ebeid, Ahmad Farag, Abd al-Qader, Abd al-Samad and Hassan Radwan managed to inflict grave wounds upon the enemy and cast out the spectre of shame from their country.

Egypt has a right *vis-à-vis* Arabi and a duty to its own history . . . to say that Ahmad Arabi made an inexcusable mistake concerning world public opinion — even allowing for the fact that it was his own honesty which led him to give credence to promises and signed agreements. Arabi had not grasped the realities of international politics, with its mire and its cunning, and believed that Britain would not dare infringe the neutrality of the canal and that de Lesseps could protect him.

The descendants of Arabi and the sons of Egypt must realize that international law is not enough if it is not backed by physical force and the people's preparations for defence.

MUHAMMAD HASSANEIN HEIKAL
(1923, Egypt)

An influential journalist and publicist, Heikal became editor of the *Akhbar al-Yawm* press group after completing his studies at the American University of Cairo. In 1957, he was appointed editor of *Al-Ahram*, the Arab world's major daily newspaper, and transformed it into the flagship of the most important press and publishing group in the Arab world. In April 1970, he assumed the key function of Minister of National Orientation.

Heikal was the friend and trusted adviser of President Abdel Nasser, whose thoughts he was generally taken to express. His theses and his manner made him the representative spokesman of the new state bourgeoisie which came to power in Egypt on 23 July 1952.

Following a first confrontation in Spring 1954, the army and the intellectuals were to clash head-on year after year. The climax came in

1961, when a wave of repression against the Marxist left led, in turn, to the disaffection of the majority of the Egyptian intelligentsia. It fell to Heikal to find a plausible justification for bringing the intellectuals and the left under the rule of the military regime. The text below presents the official thesis according to which the army, before the June 1967 defeat, constituted the entire vanguard cadre of the country as a whole.

After Nasser's death, Heikal acted as his trusted heir, his epigone and the spokesman of the National United Front whose course he sought to plot through a rapidly changing world. He was dismissed in 1974 because of his disagreement with the post-October 1973 war realignment towards the West. Since then, having turned down the offer of a post as presidential adviser, he has concentrated on elaborating a journalistic-political opus whose controversial theses have found a considerable echo in the Arab world and the world audience.

Main works: The Psychological Complexes which Dominate the Middle East (*Al-Uqad al-nafsiyyah allati tahkum al-Sharq al-Awsat*); The Crisis of the Intellectuals (*Azmat al-muthaqqafin*); What Happened in Syria? (*Mahda alladhi gara fi Suriya?*); *Abdel Nasser wal-alam* (Nasser and the World); The Road to Ramadan; The Sphinx and the Commissar; The Autumn of Anger.

The Military and the 'Crisis of the Intellectuals'[16]

To begin with, let us define a few terms:
(1) By 'revolutionary driving force' I mean the revolutionary vanguard which went into action on the night of 23 July to bring about a fundamental and general change in the structure of Egyptian society.
(2) By 'intellectuals', I mean those who have had the advantage of education and the opportunity of assuming leadership in various realms of thought; I am not referring to any specific individuals but rather to a general tendency amongst these intellectuals or, more precisely, to an apparent majority.
(3) The crisis in question has emerged in the context of Egypt, of the United Arab Republic; that is where I have experienced this problem myself and have been able to follow its course both as a journalist and as a citizen sensitive to the atmosphere of the country whose air he breathes.

As I see it, relations between the 'revolutionary driving force' and the 'intellectuals' have gone through various successive crises . . . .
(1) The first crisis was provoked by the demand that the army return to barracks following the successful execution of the 23 July revolution. There were those who argued that the army was not a governing body and that once it had accomplished the revolution, it ought to withdraw and leave power to the experts whose rightful prerogative it was.
(2) The second crisis was provoked by the demand for a return to parliamentary life and party political activity, considered as the basis and immutable form of democracy.

(3) The third crisis was provoked by what was seen at the time as the replacement of 'men of experience' by 'men of trust', a crisis which broke out over the appointment of certain military officers to technical positions in various companies, government bodies and institutions which had until then always been filled by the relevant experts.

The army movement was formed as a force for revolution in the context of the appalling vacuum created by the failure of intellectuals to assume the genuine leadership of the people . . . .

Several factors . . . combined to make of most intellectuals in Egypt a class whose real interests differed from those of the people and who had close links with the ruling classes whose specific privileges they protected.

Imperialism, royal power and the big landowners structured party political life in the period before the revolution, and worked to widen the gap between the masses and most intellectuals, primarily by constantly encouraging the latter to have nothing to do with popular demands and to concentrate all their energies on reinforcing the established order, participating in its development and strengthening its assizes . . . .

'Where were the intellectuals in all these struggles? What vanguard role did they ever play in leading the masses? The truth is that, with a few exceptions, they kept well away from the fray. Some of them sided with the enemies of the people because of their class links; others preferred to save their skins, withdraw from unpredictable public affairs and mind their own business . . . .

What we called the 'Bahout incident' — in which the *fellahin* rose up against the local landowners and set fire to the *daira*[17] of a feudal lord — was not just an ordinary village incident; it was the spark that set off the tinder of revolt against land shortage. If the revolution — and the ensuing land reform — had been delayed, there would have been a 'Bahout incident' in every village where the land was held by feudalists.

The same applies to the 'Cairo fire'.[18] Arsonists may well have been responsible for the original blaze, but that is secondary. What matters is that masses of people expressed their true feelings by rushing out to fan the flames, to loot and pillage. The Cairo fire was thus no simple police matter, as it might appear. It was a genuine explosion of resentment by those who had nothing against those who monopolized the means of subsistence. It is surprising that the anger of the masses was vented upon cinemas, hotels and elegant down-town shops; it was all part of a natural outburst of anger against deprivation. Yet all these warnings were wasted on the ruling class, who ignored their real meaning and sought to cope with them by proclaiming a state of seige, imposing a curfew and using the army in an attempt to terrorize the population.

The 23 July 1952 can be seen as the inevitable outcome and culmination of all these warnings . . . . The army did not go into action under the command of its general staff, its generals and the heads of the different services; it was led by a youthful vanguard whose links with the masses were still strong, who had no class loyalties to overcome and who ignored the blandishments of opportunism and passivity; they went into action with a measure of hope and boundless faith.

The attitude of the masses demarcates success from failure. As it turned out, the masses poured into the streets to give their unmitigated support to the young vanguard, who had by then left the army in response to the call of the masses with whom they were interacting; meanwhile every other social category manifested a complete incapacity to meet the challenge of events.

In other countries, we have seen the army as such go into action as an instrument of petrification rather than revolution. In many countries, the army has left its barracks at the instigation of the wealthy, the powerful, the right-wing, to bar the path of popular struggle and block its natural leftwards drift; the army is, after all, usually the servant of those who really hold power in a country. But it was the left who triggered off the events of the night of 23 July and assumed the responsibility of forcing a change, thereby responding directly to the wishes of the people and pursuing their demands with great probity . . . .

Most intellectuals failed to appreciate the clearly defined issues of the moment, either because of their class links which distanced them from the genuine demands of the popular struggle, or simply because of their isolation from that struggle.

Furthermore, these intellectuals began to be plagued by pangs of conscience. The emergence of a revolutionary leadership from amongst the ranks of the youthful vanguard who had set the army moving, the living contact between that leadership and the masses, and its success in formulating the demands of the masses was a constant reminder to most intellectuals of their own incapacity to fulfil the role which should have been theirs. As for the calls for the army to return to barracks, they amounted to a sure recipe for exposing revolutionary action to two types of danger.

Firstly, if the army had responded by returning to barracks, it would have done so in appearance only, not in practice. In the frightening political vacuum that would then have prevailed, it would have been difficult to find any group capable of carrying through the revolution without the support of the army; the army would have remained lurking in the background as the supreme authority in the country, a most dangerous outcome. Furthermore, if at any time something occurred which ran counter to the army's view, the only way the latter could impose its will would be by force of arms, which would bring us down to the level of Latin America with its recurrent *pronunciamentos*. It would then be quite natural for any group seeking power to work to divide the army, with all the possible disastrously violent consequences.

We have a second possibility: that of the army refusing to return to barracks and taking power, as an army. This would pave the way for military fascism and the inevitable drift away from the demands of the popular revolution, since the masses would be forced to take orders from on high . . . .

What was the answer? Gamal Abdel Nasser's point of view was as follows . . . . The vanguard which took action from within the army did so not because they were soldiers but because of their feelings and their interaction with the masses. It was thus vital for this vanguard to leave the army, join the masses and continue to express their demands while embarking on revolutionary action to meet those demands. And what about the army? The army *qua* army will be reorganized on a new basis, allowing it to be the guardian of national aspirations and the servant of the people it protects.

. . . What was the reaction of the majority of intellectuals? Some fell back into passivity, like crabs withdrawing into their shells. Others proclaimed their political allegiance to the new situation, recognizing the *de facto* ruling regime whilst continuing to have doubts and scruples about it. They all waited expectantly for what the future would bring . . . .

I would like to make a distinction between two things; on the one hand loyalty to the revolution as a governmental regime, and, on the other, revolutionary loyalty, which is participation and equitable interaction with the revolution itself.

It is indisputable that the revolution met with the political loyalism it needed from the intellectuals. They co-operated fully, working hard for the realization of the projects the revolution had launched; but all this was the result of their political loyalty. The point is that the revolution is more than just a collection of projects. It runs much deeper, in that it is a fundamental transformation of the structure of society. This is where mere 'improvement of the situation' — the natural goal of every good government under normal circumstances — differs from 'revolution' . . . which is a process of restructuring society on a basis which gives each citizen an equal chance to develop his potentialities and a right to [benefit from] the national revolution in keeping with those potentialities.

It is thus not enough that many intellectuals collaborated with the revolutionary driving force following 23 July. That was simply political loyalty. The natural and necessary role of intellectuals is not to be content with 'co-operating' with the revolution, it is to interact with it, to sponsor its cause, to don its mantle, to endow it with a revolutionary theory, to forge its revolutionary faith from the depths of their knowledge and understanding, the faith with which it will fray the revolution's path towards a fundamental and radical modification of Egyptian society.

Collaboration with state projects does of course constitute an important and fundamental part of the intellectuals' role in the service of national development. But during the present period of popular struggle, revolutionary work, work to promote and implement the revolution, consists in rebuilding the social edifice and requires us to contribute all our knowledge, experience and understanding to that endeavour.

AHMAD TALEB-IBRAHIMI
(1932, Algeria)

Ahmad Taleb-Ibrahimi was the son of Sheikh Bashir Taleb-Ibrahimi and the most prominent figure in the Islamic revival in Algeria alongside Ben Badis. After taking a medical degree in Paris, he became president of the General Union of Algerian Muslim Students in France, then of the French Federation of the National Liberation Front. He was imprisoned first in France (1959-1963), then in Algeria (1964).

For a while, Ibrahimi practised medicine at the Moustapha hospital in Algiers, later becoming Minister of National Education (1965-1970) then Minister of Information and Culture (1970), in which capacity he launched a broad variety of projects aimed at renovating the Algerian national project, taking the Algerian revolution as a starting point and the *Nahda* of the Arab world as the target. He is currently Minister of Foreign Affairs and State and a member of the political bureau of the FLN.

Main works: **Prison Letters; Speeches (3 vols.); From Decolonization to Cultural Revolution (1962-1972).**

Two extracts, the second dealing specifically with 'Aspects of the Cultural Revolution', drawn from the Conference of Trade Union Officials held in Algiers (February 1972) illustrate the courage and lucidity of Ibrahimi's cultural policy and philosophy.

Renaissance and 'Cultural Revolution'[19]

When we say that salvation lies in a renewal of Arab thought, it is because we do not forget the first renaissance which began in the last century, even though its motivations and goals are no longer applicable. In those days, it was a question of standing up to an all-powerful West by calling for self-assertion and a return to the wellsprings; in fact, it was a strategy for defence, a withdrawal into oneself which allowed one to take a stance as an opponent. But today, now that we have recovered our independence, endless evocation of past glories is not enough if we are to build a modern state. Such a flight into the past amounts to a rejection of the present. It is a weakness.

Let us remember Afghani's words: The East will only find salvation by reconciling itself to reason and science. To reconcile oneself to reason and science is, amongst other things, not being content with belief, learning to reason, learning to predict, learning to organize. It is also, or so it would appear, having a clearer idea of development.

It was said on several occasions during the recent conference of 77 that if liberty was the great idea of the 19th Century, then development is the great myth of the 20th. But do we all endow this word with the same references, the same hopes? Are there not those who see development as a simple accumulation of technical means? Yet in practice, the mere acquisition of technical equipment is not enough if we are ever to accede to that industrial society towards which any efficacious policy of social, cultural and economic progress ought to lead; the equipment has to be integrated into one's own civilization, it has to be assimilated. Otherwise technology will only be a shell and may, at times, impede more than it protects. It is a mistake to think that progress can be achieved by a kind of juxtaposition of modern techniques and traditional values. We must avoid false alternatives: either cut yourself off from the past or give up on social progress; renounce the fundamental spiritual values or abandon all hope of economic progress; or even this phrase, from an African writer: 'The stink of the furnace is better than the scent of the rosebud'. True synthesis is to declare oneself in favour of both furnaces and roses, of science become culture! It is not enough for our students to acquire knowledge, as many of us were content to do in the past; we must also acquire know-how and, above all, a rational way of thought. Transmitting knowledge is insufficient; we must form minds which, I repeat, realize the harmony between what is rooted in the depths of their hearts, namely the legacy of the past, and this world of machines which they must dominate if it is not to crush them.

There can be no cultural revolution without revolution, without a transformation of the economic, political and social system . . . . On the historical level, the concept of cultural revolution is inseparable from the struggle to build a socialist society. It is only where the exploitation and alienation of the workers in the name of a system based essentially on profit has been eliminated, where the state has taken over the nation's assets and the workers are allowed to participate effectively in the management of firms and in the democratic life of the country, and where the general interest prevails over personal interests that one can say of a cultural revolution that it has some chance of success . . . .

In simple terms, one could say that cultural revolution, over and beyond the specific characteristics of a given people and a given time, consists primarily in: (1) making knowledge and know-how available to the popular masses; (2) promoting cultural development and the democratization of culture; (3) forming a new man in a new society; (4) a constant effort to lead and explain . . . .

Moving from the general to the specific, we see that Algeria disposes of important advantages which increase the chances of such a cultural revolution's success, and suggest that it will not run counter to our traditions. . . .

The first point, concerning the battle against ignorance, for a democratization of education and the development of scientific and technical training poses little problem given the qualitatively and quantitavely massive efforts our country has made in this domain.

It is nonetheless worth stressing that this Algerian effort is made in the context of decolonization. The Algerian revolution did not stem from a struggle between the social classes of a single country; it resulted from the struggle of an entire people against foreign occupation and for the recovery of its land, its language, its history, its culture, in short for the affirmation of its genuine personality which had for so long been repressed, denied and stifled. This does not mean that once independence had been achieved, classes did not form — but that is another story. We are thus confronted with a major problem which faces every cultural revolution; what attitude should be adopted towards the legacy of the past, since no revolution which is not purely theoretical starts off with a clean slate. To a greater or lesser extent, the past survives in structures, behaviour, ways of thought and in our whole system of social relations. One of the infantile diseases of every revolution is a temptation to indulge in nihilism, the illusion that the past can be wiped away at the stroke of a pen. In practice, the past can be neither denied nor annihilated by waving a magic wand. It must be subjected to careful critical analysis, so as to preserve those elements which can be of service in the country's fundamental endeavours, whilst sifting out that which is reducible to mere mythology.

As we see it, the problem arises differently according to whether we are talking of the colonial legacy or of the Arab-Islamic legacy. Concerning the colonial legacy, we can say that we have avoided both the temptations of nihilism and any slavish imitation of the past. This is particularly true in the case of the French language. After ten years of independence, the Algerian school is an accomplished fact, with its own structures, curricula and orientations. True it is based on a *de facto* bilingualism, but one must be clear as to what this means. There has never been any question of accepting some doctrinaire bilingualism which would make Arabic the language of the humanities and French the language of the scientific disciplines, still less a policy relegating Arabic to the status of the language of the street and the masses, whilst French remained the language of the laboratory and the elite. Our bilingualism is a matter of circumstance and what is best for the nation.

For a long time yet, we will need French as an open window onto technological civilization, until Arabic adapts to the modern world and Algeria trains its own Arabic-speaking cadres. French will enjoy a privileged status amongst the foreign languages taught in our schools, but that will not prevent our children from studying other living languages right from the secondary level. I would like to add a few words on the subject of Francophony. Algeria has always refused to associate itself with this movement because Arabic, which is our national and official language, also has a world vocation. A Francophone grouping cannot approach the major problems of our time with any sort of economic, political, still less geographical unity. Also, it objectively incorporates neo-colonialist tendencies. Rather than promote the crystallization of blocs, we believe it is better to encourage the interpenetration of cultures. Algeria hopes that peoples and culture can meet despite the barrier of language.

The Arab-Islamic legacy, on the other hand, belongs to us; it is part of our life, even if for more than a century we had little opportunity to benefit from it or to enrich it. In the context of decolonization, a cultural revolution largely means a return to the wellsprings, to authenticity, so as to re-establish the link with a past which was obscured, hidden or deformed during the foreign occupation. But here, too, critical examination is essential if we are not to get bogged down in slavish imitation of the past, as if everything had already been said and there was nothing new or better under the sun!

Let us make a distinction between the problems of an immutable and eternal faith and the problems of the social relations between men, which change with each era. 'Each era has its book' says the Qu'ran. This verse should give us pause, since, if I understand it correctly, it implies that each generation has a vision of the world that corresponds to its degree of evolution and thus each generation should engage in an *ijtihad*, an effort to adapt its social relations. The day the gates of *ijtihad* were closed to make way for *taqlid* (imitation) was the day the decadence of the Muslim world began. I believe that our young people today have a duty to highlight this idea of *ijtihad* in both word and deed; the salvation of the Muslim world depends on it. I would add that the problem of Islam must be posed lucidly on the ideological level if one is to make the necessary distinctions between what is truly integral to Islam on the one hand and the superstitions, attitudes and intellectual clutter which have accumulated over the centuries of decadence on the other. One final point is worth making about this dialectic between *ijtihad* and *taqlid*: when we express our admiration for any particular era of the past (the 10th Century for example), we should understand that that century was great not because it imitated the past but because of its creativity. Cultural revolution is precisely a way of developing creative initiative amongst the masses. As the philosopher says, 'The river stays true to its source by going towards the sea.'

All this helps us broach the second major aspect of the cultural revolution, which concerns, as we have seen, cultural development, including the conservation and preservation of our cultural patrimony, the creation of new spiritual works and the diffusion of both ancient and modern works to the widest possible audience. Free Algeria's efforts in this domain have not really matched what has been achieved in education and training . . . . During the colonial period, work on recovering Algeria's patrimony focused mainly on the Roman period; there was a clear ideological reason for this, namely to convince young Algerians that whilst the present and future of their country were French, its past was Roman (cf. the well known theses of Louis Bertrand on Latin America). But it is obviously futile to seek to cover up several centuries of the past. History always manages to bury those who attempt to distort it. It is thus quite natural that our young researchers should now concentrate particularly on investigating the Muslim period.

We also have a duty to inspire respect and love for the works of those who came before us and to grasp the importance of history as a source of cohesion and stability.

There can be no doubt whatsoever that for over a century of colonial rule, the Algerian people were exposed to one of the most intense attempts at depersonalization any people has ever faced. An attempt was made to destroy the Algerian's own culture and substitute a foreign culture, an alien way of life and of thinking. No level of cultural life was spared this assault, from the most humble everyday customs to the most elevated considerations of morality and aesthetics. This is why every Algerian must be aware that he constitutes a link in a long chain going back to the most ancient times. A worthwhile future cannot be built divorced from a deep sense of the past.

Certain distortions of our country's history, and in particular those that we were inculcated with as basic truths, must be exposed once and for all. When one reads everything that has been written on the Arabs and the Berbers in Algeria, for instance, one realizes just how much work has gone into undermining the unity of the Algerian people. To begin with, it is historically false that the Algerian population is made up of Arabs and Berbers. The first Arabs who settled in Algeria in the 8th Century took autochthonous wives. The religion and the language they and their descendants introduced were to become a binding force, a fermenting agent and a defensive rampart. Ethnically speaking, Algeria is thus not a juxtaposition of Arabs and Berbers (as is so often said) but an Arab-Berber mixture of peoples who have embraced the same faith, the same system of values and who share a deep love of the same land.

Similarly, when we speak of Arabism, the concept has an essentially cultural content. We certainly cannot subscribe to any racial interpretation of the nation of Arabism; from a racial interpretation to a racialist theory is only one short step, which some people might well be tempted to take. By giving Arabism a cultural content, we eliminate the seeds of disunity and provide the Arab world with an indestructible foundation.

If I have insisted on the importance of history as a source of rootedness and cohesion, it is because Algerian culture must inscribe itself within the historical continuity of our people, even as it faces resolutely towards the future . . . .

There remains the third aspect of cultural revolution: the adoption of a lifestyle and way of being which harmonizes with the spirit and goals of the revolution. In practice, this means eliminating what we have designated the negative factors. Economic development can itself bring on certain ailments, and cases in which the national patrimony has been put at risk have already been brought to the public's attention. The spirit of lucre and greed which animates a money-mad civilization must be resisted wherever it manifests itself. A society in which profit constitutes the main motivation cannot call itself socialist. Since our future lies above all in the hands of the workers, the trade unions can and must have a considerable role to play in doing away with negative behaviour and finding new stimulants other than the quest for profit, such as devotion to one's people and country, love of work and respect for the principles of justice and equality. Trade unionism, freed of its spirit of revendication by the invitation to participate in management, should dedicate much of its efforts to the unremitting struggle to create a new man. It is both useful and necessary to train new trade union officials, but it is the training of all the workers that really demands attention. The strength of a revolution depends on the support of the masses. Working to reinforce, enliven and maintain that support by constant exhortation is one of the best ways of serving the Algerian revolution. And of course, to win people over to a new way of life one must adopt it oneself. Credibility is vital: to gain the support of the masses, it is not enough to spread ideas, there must also be complete harmony between word and deed.

In conclusion, the cultural revolution is more than the fact that the revolution has a cultural aspect just as it has industrial and agricultural aspects. It is the cultural revolution which provides the creative impetus to achieve all the transformations essential to our country and our society, such as industrialization and land reform.

All the great liberation struggles, all the revolutions, including our own, were won with spiritual weapons rather than material ones. The cultural revolution is ultimately the mobilization of the dormant energy of the masses. 'Nothing is more prodigious than man' said the ancients. It is particularly true of man animated with the energy and supported by the moral strength which flow from a cultural revolution by and for the people.

Notes

1. In *Al-Garidah*, 18, 20 and 31 December 1913, reproduced in *Al-Muntakhabat*, (Cairo, 1945), pp.60-93.
2. The head of an administrative region.
3. The ancestral tendency to centralism in every aspect of national life which has persisted in Egypt from the days of the Pharaohs right up to today.
4. *'Ittisal al-muthaqqafin bil ummal'*, *Sawt al-ummah*, 1 March 1946.
5. *Al-dimuqratiyyah abadan*, 3rd edition, (Cairo, 1958), pp.39-47.
6. *Muwatinoun, la raaya*, (1st edition, 1951), 6th edition, (Cairo, 1958), pp.152-153.
7. *Al-ard wal fallah . . .* , (Cairo, 1958), pp.32-36, 61-82.
8. Viceroy of Egypt (1805-1849), of Albanian origin, born in Cavalla (1769), the creator of modern Egypt. His descendants occupied the throne till 1952.
9. Special military formations originally made up of slaves; having become a feudal military force, they held power in Egypt from 1250 to 1517.
10. Upper Egypt.
11. *Akhi al-muwatin*, (Cairo, 1956), pp.30-91.
12. Currency denomination, originally Turkish.
13. Big sack.
14. General Sultan Pasha, a big landowner who betrayed Arabi in the midst of the battle and went over to the other side.
15. Khedive Tawfiq.
16. *Azmat al-muthaqqafin*, (Cairo, 1961), pp.13-28, 49-51.
17. Estate.
18. Friday 26 January 1952.
19. *De la décolonisation à la Révolution Culturelle, 1962-1972*, (Algiers, 1973), pp.43-45, 217-228.

6. Arab Unity

ABD AL-RAHMAN AL-KAWAKIBI
(1849-1902, Syria)

An essayist and political theoretician, Kawakibi was born in Aleppo and fled to Agypt in 1898 to escape the persecution of the Porte. There he became a close friend of Khedive Abbas Kilmi, at a time when a resurgent Egyptian national movement, including notably the National and Umma parties, was beginning to make itself felt. Al-Kawakibi himself was an active member of the editorial team of *Al-Manar*, the journal created by Rashid Rida to promote the thought of M. Abduh.

Kawakibi had two main purposes in his more important writings: firstly, to establish the primacy of the Arabs within Islam, and to displace a decadent Turkey — hence his call for an Arab spiritual Caliphate; secondly, he sought to entrench the separation between temporal political authority and spiritual authority. His aim was both to provide a framework of civilization for an Arab unity centred on Egypt and to protect the sovereignty of the national movement in political affairs.

With this project, Kawakibi stands out clearly as one of the great precursors of the radical tendency within Islamic fundamentalism — what we now think of as political Islam — which has become a central aspect of change in the modern world. It was a cause well served by the crystalline elegance of Kawabiki's writings and by his hieratic eloquence.

Main works: *Tabai al-istibdad* (Characteristics of Despotism); *Umm al-Qura* (The Mother of Villages); *Al-amal al-kamilah* (Complete Works).

The Qualities of the Arabs[1]

The *Umm al-Qura* society's one and only preoccupation is the renaissance of our religion. That is why the society has had to pin all its hopes on the people, dependencies and neighbours of the Arabian peninsula, and strives to inform the Islamic nation of the characteristics of the peninsula, its people and the Arabs in general. However, we believe that it is only by explaining why the society has such a preference for the Arabs that we can avoid political and racial fanaticism. Our approach is as follows:

(1) The light of Islam was born in the peninsula.

(2) The peninsula is the site of the Sacred *Kaabah*.

(3) There we find the Mosque of the Prophet and the sacred ground of his house, his throne and his tomb.

(4) The peninsula is the most appropriate centre for religious policy-making, since it lies halfway between the far eastern reaches of Asia and the far western reaches of Africa.

(5) It is less troubled by racial, religious or sectarian admixture than other countries.

(6) Of all the Muslim provinces, it lies furthest from the hands of foreigners.

(7) The peninsula is most likely to be a land of free men, given its inaccessibility and natural poverty, which protect it from the envy and ambition of others.

(8) The Arabs of the peninsula are blessed with Islamic unity, the religion having first emerged amongst them.

(9) The habit of religion is particularly well entrenched amongst them because it is more compatible with their own social customs than with those of others.

(10) Of all Muslims, they are the most knowledgeable about the principles of Islam, as would be expected since they have been practising the religion longer than anyone else; several *hadiths* testify to the strength of their faith.

(11) The Arabs of the peninsula are the most zealous of all Muslims in the preservation, support and glorification of their religion; zeal for the Prophet's cause is a living force amongst them, in the Hejaz, in Yemen, in Oman, in the Hadramaut, in Iraq and in Africa.

(12) The religion of the Arabs of the peninsula is still governed by the example of rectitude set by their forefathers; it provides no opportunity for either excess or confusion.

(13) Because of their Bedouin character, the Arabs of the peninsula are prouder and have a more intense feeling of themselves as a community than any other Muslims.

(14) The princes of the Arabian Peninsula are descended from noble parents and are married to nobles of good family; their honour is unsullied and their line unmixed.

(15) Of all the Arabs, those of the peninsula are the oldest nation of refined civilization, as is shown by the proliferation and excellence of their literature and wisdom.

(16) The Arabs of the peninsula are more capable of coping with tribulation than any other Muslims, and are best equipped for journeys and residence abroad, as they have never succumbed to the servile habits of debauchery.

(17) The Arabs of the peninsula have preserved their race and their customs better than all other peoples; they may associate with others, but they do not intermarry.

(18) The Arabs of the peninsula are more jealous guardians of their freedom and independence than any other Islamic nation; they are the most vehement in their rejection of oppression.

(19) It is true of the Arabs in general that their language is the safest haven for knowledge of all the tongues spoken by Muslims; the noble Qu'ran ensures its survival.

(20) The language of the Arabs is the common language of all Muslims, numbering more than 300 million.[2]

(21) Arabic is the mother tongue of 100 million Muslims and non-Muslims.

(22) The Arabs were the first nation to adopt the principle of equal rights and to avoid great extremes of social inequality.

(23) The Arabs were the first to introduce consultation in public affairs.

(24) The Arabs are more familiar with the principles of a socialist way of life than any other people.

(25) The Arabs are amongst the most noble of all peoples when it comes to respecting treaties, the most humane in their loyalty to the faith, the most chivalrous in their relations with their neighbours and the most generous in their works of benevolence.

(26) Of all nations, the Arabs are the best suited to be an authority in religious matters and an example to Muslims everywhere; the other nations have followed their lead from the start and will not refuse to follow them now.

SATI AL-HUSRI
(1880-1969, Syria)

Born in Sanaa (Yemen) to a family from Aleppo, Al-Husri was trained in Istanbul as a young official of the Ottoman Empire. He served as Minister of Education in the Faisal government in Damascus, towards the end of the First World War, and eventually accompanied it into exile. Between the wars, he actively promulgated the idea of Arabism notably through intense polemics with the masters of Egyptian literature. In 1940-41, he participated in the Iranian revolution led by Rashid Ali Al-Kilani, who entrusted him with the overall determination of education policy. Although stripped of his Iraqi nationality, Al-Husri was later appointed Director General of Cultural Affairs by the League of Arab States and Dean of the Institute of Arab Studies in Cairo. He was the main theoretician of Arab unity and nationalitarianism, both of which he derived from the unity of the Arab peoples' language and history.

Main works: **Opinions and Propositions Concerning Patriotism and Nationalitarianism** (*Ara wa ahadith fil-wataniyyah wal-qawmiyyah*); **Opinions and Propositions Concerning Arab Nationalitarianism** (*Ara wa ahadith fil-qawmiyyah al-arabiyyah*); **In Defence of Arabism** (*Difa an al-Uroubah*); **Arabism Before Everything** (*Al-Uroubah awwalan*); **Arabism Between Its Supporters and Its Opponents** (*Al-Uroubah bayna douatiha wa muaridiha*).

The text that follows is the simplest and most direct exposition of Arabism I know, by the writer who was its main theoretician.

The Primacy of Arabism[3]

All the countries where the inhabitants speak Arabic are Arab countries, whatever the number of states involved or the various flags flying over government buildings or the complex frontiers which separate the various political entities. All these countries are Arab. The 'lands of the Arabs' are not restricted to the Arabian peninsula alone, as has been claimed; every country where Arabic is the language of the inhabitants forms a part of these lands . . . .

Whoever has links with an Arab country and speaks Arabic, whatever the official name of the state of which he is a citizen, whatever his religion, or doctrine, or descent or family history . . . is an Arab . . . .

Arabism is not restricted to the inhabitants of the Arabian Peninsula, nor is it specific to Muslims. On the contrary, it extends to all those who have links with an Arab country and who speak Arabic, be they Egyptian, Kuwaiti, Moroccan, Muslim, Christian, Sunni, *Jafarite*[4] or Druze, Catholic, Orthodox or Protestant. They are all children of Arabism, provided they have links with an Arab country and speak Arabic.

The existing Arab states were not constituted as so many distinct entities by the will of their inhabitants or because of any natural necessities; rather, the repartition was the outcome of treaties and agreements concluded between the states which dominated the Arab Countries and shared them out among themselves. The same applies to the present frontiers between Arab countries; they were not drawn up according to the interests of these countries and their inhabitants; rather they were the outcome of endless haggling and manoeuvring between imperialist powers determined to look after their own interests.

The present differences and divergences among the Arab states — notably in their administrative, legislative and economic institutions, and in their political orientation — are all a legacy of the period of foreign occupation. They were born out of imperialism and are both recent and purely contingent.

The Arabs are a single *Umma*: Egyptians, Iraqis, Maghrebis are the peoples and branches of a single *Umma*, the Arab *Umma*. The so-called 'Pharaonic tendency' has had little impact and in recent years has lost most of its adherents and all of its epigones. The Pharaonic era has been buried in the sands of time for thousands of years. The Egyptians of today have no understanding of the language of the Pharaohs and have no beliefs in common with them. It is thus quite illogical to want to go back to eras dead and gone, to quiz a mummified corpse.

Naturally the sons of Egypt have a right to be proud of the glories of the Pharaonic civilization which their ancestors built. The sons of other Arab countries are also entitled to be proud of the civilizations which have arisen in this part of the Arab homeland since the dawn of recorded history, just as the Egyptians can be proud of the ancient civilizations which flourished in other parts of the Arab world, such as the Sumerian civilization in Iraq and the Phoenician civilization in Syria.

But the fact remains that the Egyptians cannot turn their backs on Arabism by claiming a link to the Pharaonic civilizations. Each Egyptian must realize that the Pharaonic civilization, like the Sumerian, Assyrian and Phoenician civilizations, is dead and gone and cannot be brought back to life.

Arabism is very different; it is part of the living present, not of the mummified past. It is no exaggeration to say that Arabism is overflowing with energy, having just awakened from its long slumber. It is not the final flourish of a prodigious past but the starting point of a radiant future which will witness the creation of the 'United Arab State' and the advance of the renascent Arab *Umma* to the greatest heights of science and civilization.

MAKRAM EBEID
(1889-1961, Egypt)

After studying law at Cairo and Oxford, Ebeid joined the Wafd as soon as it was formed and was sent into exile in the Seychelles with Zaghloul and Nahas. A brilliant orator, a master tactician and an eminent representative of the Coptic intelligentsia, he became secretary-general of the Wafd and negotiated the Anglo-Egyptian treaty of 1936. His dissensions with the entourage of the then president of the party, Mustafa al-Nahas, eventually led him to leave the Wafd; he then founded the Wafdist *Kutlah* party (1943) and campaigned with the rightist parties against the Wafd. Along with Sabri Abu Alam, he was probably the most outstanding representative of liberal political thought in Egypt between the wars.

Main works: **The Works of Makram** (*Al-Makramiyyat*); **The Black Book** (*Al-Kitab al-aswad*).

We have chosen the text that follows because it illustrates the Wafd's itinerary, from the ideal of the Egyptian homeland to the cause of the Arab world. The Wafdist version of Arabism is national, cultural and political; religious factors are seen to have played little part in it. The reader will note that this passionate and specific defence of the Arab ideal is the work of an eminent Coptic politician and thinker.

The Egyptians Are Arabs[5]

We are brothers in the struggle to save our homelands and win our freedom. Catastrophes reinforce the bonds uniting their victims, and we are talking of nations united by a shared language, a common tradition and the same fundamental sociological characteristics.

The history of Arabism is made up of continuous links, forming a closely knit chain. The ties of language and culture are more pronounced in the Arab countries than in any other area of the world. Religious tolerance was born, prospered and still exists between the members of different religions in the fraternal neighbouring countries. Who then can doubt that my phrase 'the Egyptians are Arabs' encompasses affinities and ties that have never been broken by geographical boundaries or political ambition, despite all the efforts that have been made to divide the Arab countries, kill their inhabitants' Arab spirit and disunite and persecute those who work towards Arab unity. That unity undoubtedly constitutes one of the major foundations of the modern renaissance of the Arab East, which so needs unity and solidarity in the face of the European wave which has submerged it.

The Arabs need to believe in their Arabism and in all its constructive features which, in the past, helped them to build a flourishing civilization and subjugate the European countries for so long.

We are Arabs. We must always remind ourselves, in the present era, that we are Arabs, united by suffering and hopes, welded to one another by catastrophe and pain, forged on the same anvil of injustice and defeat; we have all become alike in every aspect of life.

We are Arabs in this open struggle, which is developing in all of Arabism's territories, to win complete freedom and revive the glory of Arab civilization, to improve our public affairs, to guide our youth towards high ideals, to educate our people soundly so as to shake them out of the inertia of the past years, encourage them to look after their own interests, awaken them from their slumbers and light up the path before them. They will then see contemporary life in its true colours and will be able to distinguish between that which serves their cause and that which is harmful to it; they will choose that which will enable them to build a new life based on the glories of the past, with all that that means in terms of spiritual strength and celestial faith, yet solidly attached to the best of what the era has to offer in the way of scientific progress and industrial production.

Yes, we are Arabs, both in this way and in terms of the history of the Arab civilization in Egypt and the closeness of our ancestral stock to that of the Semitic tribes who emigrated to our country from the Arabian Peninsula long ago. That is why we have to strengthen our solidarity, work co-operatively towards a shared glory and build up that Arab unity which rests on common hopes and sufferings, and on our history, our language and our specific national characteristics.

Arab unity is an effective reality, but it requires an organization whose task it will be to constitute a front against imperialism, preserve national specificity, ensure prosperity, develop economic resources, encourage local production, intensify exchange and mutual interests, and co-ordinate relations . . . . Our destiny will lead us to rally round a common ideal and purpose, to unite in a single bloc, joining our countries together in a single national league or in a great homeland made up of several territories, each with its own personality but all with the same general national characteristics, all solidly linked to the great homeland.

ABD AL-RAHMAN AZZAM
(1891, Egypt)

After completing his medical studies in Britain, Azzam played an active part in the Egyptian National Party, served in the Libyan war (1911-12), and travelled extensively in Europe and the Arab world during and after the 1914-18 war. A disciple of Muhammad Farid, and a close friend of the General Aziz al-Masri, his faith in the unity of the Arab peoples was based on history and the needs of the liberation struggle rather than on religion; hence his constant call for tolerance and humanist values.

As Secretary-General of the League of Arab States right from its inception in 1945, he contributed decisively to shaping its spirit and structures until he left in 1952. He now lives in Saudi Arabia.

Main works: **The Hero of Heroes** (*Batal al-abtal*); **The Immortal Message** (*Al-Rissalah al-khalidah*); **The Arab League and World Unity** (*Al-Gamiah al-arabiyyah wal-wihdah al-alamiyyah*).

The following extracts from his speech at the Ewart Memorial Hall of the American University of Cairo on 4 January 1946 outline the philosophy of liberal Arabism, stressing the anti-racist and populist character of Arab civilization.

The Arab League and World Unity[6]

We Arabs have inherited a noble tradition from the 7th Century renaissance, and we call on men today to espouse its values, not as a religion, since men are free in their choice of beliefs, but rather in terms of the ideals, principles and rules adopted by our ancestors, which can help bring about international unity, perpetual peace and the brotherhood of man . . . . I will, if I may, explain some of the principles on which we will base the message the Arabs will carry, as they enter a new renaissance under the auspices of the League of Arab States; a message which has its source in their history and their character.

The first of these principles is the Arabs' refusal to recognize racial or national differences as a justification for one people's domination over another . . . . Men are all equal, and none is superior to others. An Arab is not superior to a non-Arab unless it is as an individual with exceptional personal qualities. Nor should the white man be adjudged superior to the black or yellow man. Indeed, our Arab nation encompasses both Whites and Blacks within the limits of this vast homeland which cherishes all its sons.

The second principle bears on man's natural rights. We say that man is the son of Adam . . .; each man is on the same footing as all the others as far as rights and duties are concerned . . . .

The third principle is, essentially, that we do not recognize class differences. The rich and the poor, the weak and the mighty are all equal within our social system. We thus reject the recent development of class war, a new phenomenon to which we must find an effective solution.

However, if we retain our present lifestyle, through which the Western capitalist nations have perverted us, then our message will lose all meaning and become a message of oppression, enabling one class to exploit another. We must therefore rally to our true ideals and to the qualities of our noble heritage, which ensure that the poor are guaranteed the support of both the community and the state, that they receive their share of education and of life's opportunities, and that they can gain access to the highest positions in the state through hard work and their own merit . . . .

Before we were invaded by the materialist Western civilizaion, during the period of our social decadence, people were in the habit of looking after each other as relatives, neighbours, people from the same district or even as fellow countrymen. They took it for granted that they were all brothers, that life in this world was transitory and that they would never enjoy the blessings of the life eternal if they gave themselves over to pleasure and abandoned the poor to their misery . . . . If we are presented with a choice between two evils — extremist capitalism or the escape into Communism — we have to say that our message endorses neither the one nor the other. Whilst the former ensures the happiness of one class, the second comes along to chop off its head, but in time will engender the opposite of what it sought. We refuse to accept either Anglo-American capitalism or Russian Communism. God has made us a mediator nation and has chosen us to bear witness. I feel that he wants to send us out again as his messengers, in a world which shall, God willing, be reformed with our help.

This is no fatuous claim but the words of a believer. I believe that everything which is now happening in the world is only the preparation for a new message, and I have faith in God, who put us here on this earth and made us the inheritors of the Pharaohs, the Babylonians, the Phoenicians, the Chaldaeans, the Carthaginians, the Aramaeans and later the Arabs, who bequeathed us the great religions preached by Moses, Jesus and Muhammad and who has sent us these long tribulations in order to purify us. I have faith in the message of this new nation, the nation of the future. . . .

I cannot conceal my apprehension concerning the danger to civilization posed by the policies of the great powers. I feel it is my duty to be extremely frank and to beg you, O Arabs, to fulfil your humanitarian mission. You are indeed a nation torn between East and West; if you come to understand your mission, if you refuse to be the plaything of these tyrants or to submit to influences from both North and South, if you launch an appeal for peace and plead for all men to live as brothers sharing a faith in humanity, that all races and individuals may become equals, and if you struggle for all this not just for one year, but for ten or twenty, then you will be truly worthy of your mission, you will save civilization and put the affairs of the civilized world on some basis other than materialism and power politics. You are the heirs of religions and civilizations that go back to the dawn of history. Let endurance and tolerance be your main qualities as they were amongst your forefathers.

If you ask me what this new Arab League is, I will tell you that it is the core around which I see these great hopes being realized . . . . It is a pact which everybody should approve of, since we co-operate under its auspices on the basis of the principle of equal rights between all states. Our League recognizes no differences between big and little states. Egypt, the most populous and territorially largest of the member states, as well as the richest in resources and culture, is in my eyes absolutely equal to the smallest of the fraternal states, be it Lebanon, or Transjordan or whatever . . . . We hope that the United Nations will one day come to understand that there is no big and small in matters of co-operation. We co-operate to maintain peace amongst ourselves and our common happiness; we co-operate to improve our economies, our cultural and social conditions, and to build, over time, a united social edifice.

The central problem both for today and for tomorrow is the freedom and independence of the Arab peoples. The Arabs will no longer tolerate imperialist domination, and since the foundation of the Arab League they have struggled unrelentingly to achieve their freedom . . . . In the eyes of the Arabs, nothing justifies the existence of the League more than its outspoken position on Arab affairs. The League demands the evacuation of all foreign troops from all Arab territories, starting with Egypt. Furthermore, the League has expressed itself frankly on world affairs, defending justice and liberty everywhere, be it in Indonesia or in a defeated Germany.

You will doubtless recall that the Arab League has clashed with the Jews during the last six months, in a violent conflict with this weak and scattered people who deserve our sympathy more than any other, since the Jews are our persecuted cousins. Thoughout our history, we have been their friends and protectors. But the calamity of Zionism grips them fast, the Zionism that was fuelled first by British arms and then by American money, so that the Jews would be able to build a foreign imperialist state on Arab land. The Zionists are a curse to the Jews themselves as well as to us Arabs. We continue to offer the Jews the hand of friendship and refuse to engage in any criminal persecutions.

But what can be done about a people who have appeared like an eruption of evil amongst us, full of imperialist pretensions and delusions of domination? We call on the Jews of the whole world to repent and to remember that they have brethren in the East who have no wish to add to the sum of their woes. We beg them to come back to their senses and to lead the misguided back onto the right path . . . . I believe that with the grace of God and guided by the lesson of recent events, we will eventually win, but when we do so, we will not scatter the Jews as the Europeans once did, for that is not our way, nor was it that of our forefathers. When they see our perseverance and how sacred we hold the freedom of the individual and the group, they will understand that we are their brothers, that they can live amongst us just as our Christian brothers have done, and that they can rise to the highest offices in the common homeland of the Arabs.

. . . We Arabs seek no conflict of hatred between races, sects or classes. Whoever has lived in our countries, has grown up in the framework of our culture and has been proud of our honour is one of us. We believe that war will be outlawed, that the world will not dare embark upon another war which would mean the ruin of civilization. We, therefore, refuse to prepare for war, just as we refuse to associate ourselves with imperialism, exploitation, domination or conquest. We want to see fraternity amongst men and we believe that the world is one planet, populated by men whose destiny it is to be happy and to help each other, the rich aiding the poor and the mighty giving succour to the weak. We participate in the United Nations Oganization in order to participate in the creation of a new, united, cohesive and co-operative world. Our call is sincere before God, and our message is one of love and brotherhood. I will close with the immortal words of Omar to Amr, the conqueror of Egypt, when he had vanquished two empires: 'How is it that you have reduced men to slavery when their mothers brought them into the world free?'

MAHMOUD MASADI
(1911, Tunisia)

Mahmoud Masadi is the key figure in Tunisia's modernist cultural renaissance. An *agrégé* in Arabic, he became the editor of *Al-Mabahith* (1944-47), and then, in 1958, Secretary of State for National Education, in which capacity he completely reformed Tunisian education. As

a nationalist militant active in the Destour since 1933 and Deputy General Secretary of the UGTT, he was deported in 1952-3. He now serves as Minister of State advising the Prime Minister.

He sought to create a prudent synthesis between historic Arab, and especially Tunisian, culture, and the modern currents of European literature.

Main works: **The Dam** (*Al-Sadd*); **The Genesis of Forgetfulness** (*Mawlud al-nisyan*).

The Third Congress of Arab Writers (Cairo, 9-16 December 1957) had taken 'literature and Arab nationalitarianism' as its general working theme, thereby underlining the rapid rise of the wave of Arab unity after Suez. M. Masadi, the President of the Tunisian delegation, pleaded passionately for political liberalism. The following extracts are from his very controversial report to the congress.

The Idea of Arab Nationalitarianism[7]

(1) In proposing 'Arab literature and nationalitarianism' as our theme, we are juxtaposing two concepts. But whereas the former needs no definition and is familiar to all of us, the latter concept, Arab nationaltarianism, is not so self-evident; . . . it is by no means a simple concept, given the multiplicity of its characteristics and the diversity of its various constitutive elements.

A first group of these elements has already been excellently analysed by Dr Taha Hussain and other colleagues. Amongst such elements are the unity of our language, which is Arabic; the unity of our literature, which is Arab; the unity of our culture and civilization, which are broadly Arab and Islamic, although they have been influenced by non-Arab and non-Islamic cultures and civilizations and have profitably incorporated contributions — both recently and in the past — from men who were neither Arab nor Muslim. Such then are the characteristic constituents of the first great group of elements which make up Arab nationalitarianism. The elements in question are partly spiritual and partly historical and inherited; some are rooted in the past, others are features of the modern world.

It is in this sense that the Sudanese delegation proposes the following formulation of Arab nationalitarianism: 'A spiritual league formed by the collectivity of men for whom the Arabic language carries an inheritance which is their shared rallying point.' However, alongside this first group of inherited elements, both static and dynamic, there are other elements constitutive of Arab nationalitarianism which are more tied to a specific time and place, less separable from the tumult of events and circumstances. These elements are unlike the spiritual values which result from the experience of nations over the ages. Rather, they are material things which emerge as part of an evolving reality in each era and each country. I refer to the economic and political interests and the social needs peculiar to this or that Arab state, which are the products of a specific geographical, economic, political and social context. There can be no doubt that interests and necessities of this sort are determined by 'the way things are' as Ibn Khaldun puts it; they change as their context changes. For those of us who prefer an efficacious realism to myths, sentimental confusion, and the realms of the imagination, it is obvious that man cannot dominate and control these factors as he chooses, even in the service of the nationalitarian goals he has chosen.

The fact remains, however, that Arab nationalitarianism cannot be based only on a community of civilization or on the assumption of shared material interests; it requires a third constitutive factor, which draws on the other two and yet is distinct, a psychic factor without which the very existence of Arab nationalitarianism as a viable force is open to doubt. That factor is the shared will to live together as a community. There can be unity of language, unity or close kinship in literature and culture, as is the case amongst the Anglo-Saxon countries, or there can be political and economic interests in common, as there are between many countries of the world, without the outcome being a specific, unique nationalitarianism.

The most distinctive feature of Arab nationalitarianism, and the most enduring, is the perpetual renewal of this common will for a shared, united or integrated social existence, encompassing every cultural, sociological and political dimension of the united entity in some cases, or a few specific aspects at other times. Although its content may vary, our nationalitarianism is deep-rooted in our people's hearts and will remain a vital instinct and energy, linking individuals and communities. This will to unity may manifest itself as a defensive response, stimulating combative energy whenever the joint entity is under attack; all our forces will then be concentrated on the area under threat, be it our language, our religion, our economic interest or our political independence. It was this unity which stood fast against cosmopolitanism, protected the Arab *ethnos* from decadence and contempt, fought against Byzantium in the days of the Beni Hamdan[8] and al-Mutanabbi and resisted the Crusader armies, defending Islam and its territory. But perhaps it has only achieved its fullest development in the modern era, when faced with the imperialist wave which submerged all the countries of the Arab and Muslim world. It was then that Arab nationalitarianism really emerged as the defender and regenerator of Islam, with Muhammad Abduh and the religious reformers. The outcome was a religious culture, the work of the scientists and writers of the modern orient who have laboured for a century and a half to revive, renew and promote Arab literature and thought, in the course of this blessed modern renaissance which we are still living through today. The same impulse also led to the economically liberating policies of the various national movements which struggled against imperialism until, one by one, the Arab homelands were liberated, culminating in the heroic and glorious struggle of the Algerian people.

MICHEL AFLAQ
(1910, Syria)

**Having completed studies in history at the Sorbonne (1932) Aflaq took
up a teaching post and, in 1940, created the Party of Arab Resurgence
(Baath)[9] which set itself the task of forming a united Arab homeland free
from imperialism. At the time of Suez, the party fused with Akram
Hourani's socialist party and adopted various socialistic formulations.
Since then, Michel Aflaq has emerged as one of the main theoreticians
of Arab nationalitarianism, a bitter enemy of Arab Communism and,
for a while, a potential rival to Gamal Abdel Nasser for the leadership of
the movement for Arab unity.**

    Main works: **For the Resurgence (***Fi sabil al-baath***); The Battle of the
Single Destiny (***Marakat al-masir al-wahid***).**

Arab Unity Above Socialism[10]

The Arab question must be seen as a whole and treated as such. I believe
that there are those who concentrate on unity alone and thus promote the
disaggregation of the Arab cause. The Baath party considers our national
cause to be a single cause, and believes that its success depends on a far-
reaching Arab upheaval, an upheaval in thought, in economic and social
conditions, in people's very souls and not just in politics . . . . When we say
that the correct solution to our national problem is a Baathist upheaval, we
simply mean the following: the Arabs have been living a period of
decadence for several centuries, and not just since their colonization by the
West. The conditions which have developed in our countries over the last
several hundred years have very deeply perturbed and disfigured the structure of the nation and have caused a disjunction between the idea of an Arab
nation and the reality, so that our nation is no longer able to react in a
healthy way to the demands of life.

    The upheaval required is precisely the attempt to reinstitute a healthy
and direct interaction between the nation and the realities of life. On the
basis of this simple definition, it is clear that politics, in the traditional sense,
cannot diagnose the ailment and prescribe a cure, just as it cannot change
anything fundamental in our lives. What is it then that we require? . . .

    Our economic problems . . . are serious and are always at the forefront
of our thoughts and endeavours; however, we look upon them not as the main
problem but as the reef we run into whenever we try to approach the main
problem. The real issue is how we are to give our nation back its soul, to
ensure that the Arab and the nation as a whole recover a positive, active,
determined and correct attitude to life, consisting for the individual Arab in
a mastery of his destiny and for the nation in a good grasp of its purpose and
aims, and an understanding of how to achieve those aims. Corruption,
especially in economic affairs, acts as a barrier to the nation's self-

awareness and appreciation of the value of its mission. In practice, our theory of upheaval translates into a struggle in the broadest sense, to re-educate the nation and teach it to meet difficulties head on, that it may rediscover its now dormant strengths and benumbed determination.

As we have pointed out, the struggle must be understood in the broadest sense of the term. We are talking of a struggle both against external forces (be it Zionism or imperialist domination) and against corruption at home, be it political or social injustice, exploitation, intellectual poverty, fanaticism, intolerance, narrow-mindedness or lack of compassion. When we call on our citizens to struggle against this state of affairs, we are not just aiming to change the specific situation; we are trying to restore to our people an awareness of their real worth and of the true purpose of their lives.

. . . Starting from our unitary conception of the Arab cause, we do not believe that it is possible to separate Arab unity from socialism. Arab unity is a higher value than socialism and is more advanced, but the demand for Arab unity will remain an abstract and theological notion, and in some cases a harmful delusion, if it is not put in its real context. That context is the sentiments of the people; the Arab people are, after all, the only force capable of making Arab unity a reality.

Consequently, our identification of unity and socialism gives the ideal of unity its substance. One might say that socialism is the body and unity the soul. On top of the countless forces in conscious and unrelenting opposition to Arab unity (the imperialist and Zionist forces being amongst the most dangerous) and the domestic forces that sacrifice the most vital national interests and aspirations to their private interests, one must also take into account all the dogmatism, ignorance and backward customs which prevail in our society, impeding any new measures requiring abnegation and effort; nor should one forget all the various forms of fanaticism — communalist, regional or ideological — which divide and undermine our national structure . . . . It is indispensable for us to face and overcome these factors, and to do so we must draw on sources of energy which can match such obstacles. The only such source is the people. But even if the people are well disposed towards unity, as is natural, it is of little avail if they remain powerless and in chains. However, if we prepare the people for struggle, for a free and honourable life, if we get them used to this struggle, then unity will become a practical question and a practical demand. That is why our party is not just a socialist party, and why socialism is not its primary attribute; it is an Arab party, a party of the Arab renaissance, which implies upheaval . . . .

The idea of resurgence (Baath) seeks to rise above both the logic of fanatical nationalism and the logic of internationalism. The former takes the national interest as its be-all and end-all . . . . The latter takes world revolution as its real aim and the specific interests of each nation as means to attain that end. The logic of the Baath links nationalitarianism and humanism, making them almost synonymous. It does not treat humanity as something more elevated than the nation, which would imply that nationalitarianism was only a temporary stage. The very logic of world revolution implies neglect of the essential needs of each nation *qua* nation, since everything is subordinated to the needs of the world revolution; whilst such a logic may sometimes concern itself with the specific needs of each nation, it does so at a superficial and artificial level, and only in terms of a fundamental political approach aimed at building the kind of worldwide public opinion which would give such a revolution its impetus and orientation. The upshot is not only that certain basic needs within each nation are not satisfied but also that the logic is self-contradictory in that it cannot achieve what it proclaims as the goal of revolutionary logic. The correct approach to world society in fact consists in satisfying the specific requirements and solving the problems of each nation in the light of the relevant specific circumstances peculiar to that nation, in all their complexity; the ability of each nation to draw on its own distinct experience will enable it to enrich other nations.

We cannot stress too strongly that the resurgence movement is a national movement, in that it stems from within the nation itself, which gives it much greater freedom of action, since its ideas and plans are inspired by the interests of the Arab people themselves. It derives both its material and moral strength from this position. Its material strength stems from the fact that the movement cannot but respond to the needs of the nations and the prevailing conditions of the country; this unalterable fact enables it to speak and act with more courage and frankness than any other movement, without ever having to contradict itself or suddenly change its line . . . .

From this material strength there flows a moral strength; the movement is fortified by the support of the great mass of the people, which enables it to accentuate its revolutionary character and to be more straightforward in its revolutionary action . . . . Outside of their organized partisan minorities, the other movements are not in any position to draw on a (political) consciousness capable of interpreting all their half-truths, lies and lack of frankness as to real goals.

MUNAH AL-SULH
(1926, Lebanon)

A historian and political philosopher, al-Sulh was born into one of the great families whose role in the national history of contemporary Lebanon is an integral part of the Arab long march. A journalist, publicist and academic, al-Sulh was the leading light of the Arab Cultural Centre in Beirut, a focal point of the Arab world's contemporary cultural renewal. In 1973 he was appointed cultural adviser to the president of the republic. During the calamitous events which have befallen Lebanon from 1975 onwards, he has emerged as one of the most influential mediators.

Main work: *Al-Islam waharakat al-taharrir al-arabi* (Islam and the Arab Liberation Movement).

The highly influential and recent work from which our extract is drawn lies firmly in the great convergent tradition of radical political Islam and populist socialism embraced by Sultan-Galiev after 1917. The reader will note once again the central concept of cultural anti-imperialism, an idea which is steadily gaining in strength.

Islamicity and Arabism[11]

When the Arab masses refer to their being Muslims in the context of a political situation or of a civilization, they usually mean to underline that they refuse to be vassals of the West and that they feel themselves part of an historical and geographical whole, with their own values, roots and inheritance. In a word, these masses share the same principles as the vanguards of Arabism and the Arab liberation movement. The only difference is the clarity with which they perceive reality and their ability to express it; their commitment and attachment to the national and human reality is no less.

Sometimes, by proclaiming their Muslim faith, the popular masses seek to signal their positive commitment to this dimension, thereby telling the intellectuals and the Westernized pseudo-vanguards: 'I belong to one world and you belong to another: we are different.' The popular masses, by clinging to their Islamicity, proclaim that they are in tune with the personality of the nation, not that they lag behind it.

It may even be that through their Muslim faith the popular masses experience a level of harmony with Arab aims and a willingness to serve those aims greater than the most sincere of nationalist intellectuals, so true is it that the content of the popular masses' attachment to Islam is, at heart, identical to the content of the Arab liberation movement . . . .

Although the popular masses rarely allow themselves to put their religious commitment above their commitment to the nation, the progressive Arab intellectual is always reluctant to recognize this fear in terms of a commitment to revolutionary purity and the rigour of his ideals; but the truth, if he would only admit it, is that he dreads to give the Arab liberation movement the density and efficacity which would turn it into [a force] going far beyond the dedication, self-sacrifice and determination that he can muster. He says, 'The popular masses are not yet Arab, they are still Islamic,' because he himself has still not become as Arab as the masses and because his sense of being Arab lacks the intensity with which the masses feel themselves to be Muslims . . . .

Historical necessity itself, along with development of the Arab unity movement has ensured that the birth of this movement took place in a much more healthy way than was the case for many other nationalities. Right from the start, history freed the Arab nationalitarian movement from any of

the ambiguities which result from non-nationalitarian religious commitment, since the Arab nationalitarian movement was given its original
impetus through armed struggle with another Islamic state, Turkey. The
question of the relationship between religion and nationalitarianism was
already largely decided in the first days of the Arab nationalitarian movement. Despite this, certain intellectual and progressive Arab circles have
refused to accept that the differentiation was established not to protect
nationalitarian thought from the incursions of reaction, but rather to keep
Islam as an issue out of the revolution. These circles insist that the differentiation between being Arab and being Muslim has not been clearly
established, with the implication that there is a contradiction between the
two terms. These circles are determined to pursue the differentiation between being Arab and Islam because, consciously or unconsciously, they
dread the call for interaction between these two different realities and the
consequences of a revolutionary upsurge of both Arabicity and Islam, and
of the Arab liberation movement, on the basis of such interaction. It is as if
these circles sought to allocate roles, casting Islam as reactionary and the
enemies of that reaction as progressive . . . . The popular masses throughout
the Arab world insist on their Islamicity as a form of allegiance to the fundamental aspects of the national question.

The reactionary imperialist conspiracy consists in precisely this: to convince the vanguards that the Islamicity of the popular masses is
qualitatively different from the Arabism of the vanguard, and to give the
popular masses to believe that the Arabism of the vanguard is of a different
nature from their own Islamicity. It then becomes easy for imperialism to
adopt what attitude it chooses, positive or negative, to that sector of
Arabism represented by intellectuals distanced from their cultural heritage
and the popular masses, or to that sector represented by an Islamicity distanced from the axis of nationalitarian aspirations. These options are in fact
perfectly suited to the interests of the cosmopolitanism which is the underlying content of the philosophy of imperialist cultural penetration in our
region . . . .

A huge portion of imperialism's efforts goes into building up a certain
vision of Islam, both in the eyes of the Arab citizen and in those of the world
at large. Imperialism bases its endeavour on an approach to Islam as a fundamental and efficient force in life and on an understanding that the
possibilities for imperialist ingress into Arab life depend largely on the type
of vision the Muslim and non-Muslim Arabs of the Islamic world have of
Islam. Imperialism's underlying aims do not stop at building up a vision of
Islam in the minds of Muslim Arabs alone; the way Islam is seen by all
Arabs is the target. Imperialism fully understands that the relationship bet-
ween Islam and Arab nationalitarianism is different from the relationship of
Catholicism to French nationalitarianism, or of Protestantism to the United
States, or of Orthodoxy to Greece. It also understands that the relationship
between Islam and Arab nationalitarianism is different from that between
Islam and the nationalitarianism of Iran, or even of Turkey. The Arab

nation was formed and entered into history by its own efforts, and Islam was born and reached its apogee in giving birth to the Arab nation. It is thus impossible to establish a deceptive and completely artificial separation between the life of Islam and the life of the Arab nation, in the past, in the present or in the future. The heritage, values and concepts of Islam constitute the major part of the national culture of any Arab — be he Muslim or non-Muslim.

How does cultural imperialism wish us to see Islam? The two visions proposed to us are apparently separate and contradictory, although fundamentally they serve the same ends. The first vision casts Islam either as the cause of the backwardness of the Arabs, and perhaps even of international life in general, or as a religion just like any other religion, with a role in Arab life identical to the role of other religions in other countries . . . . Imperialism has succeeded in its efforts to convince certain revolutionary intellectuals that a revolution in Arab life would have to begin with a revolution against the rites and prescriptions of Islam . . . so that, according to this imperialist logic, the first step the revolutionary must take before engaging in revolutionary activity is to proclaim his atheism or at least his rejection of Islam . . . . The second dangerous vision is the one imperialism has sought to implant through the orientalist schools, some of which proclaim the sacred character of the institutions of the past, especially in the fossilized forms they took during the era of decadence. These institutions are depicted as shining examples of perfection, as the *nec plus ultra* of life and as the only path compatible with the capacities, conditions and mentality of the Arabs. The idea is then that if the Arabs are to succeed, they owe it to themselves to revive these institutions, in their old form, confirming to the letter everything about them that is fossilized, rather than rediscovering their spirit, their ideas and the principles on which they rested . . . .

Imperialism thus kills two birds with one stone: the intellectual who believes that there is no road to progress other than over the ruins of Islam, and the intellectual who holds that the only course is a return to institutions of the past, presented as the only institutions which can be truly Islamic. The first type is found predominantly amongst thinkers, 'revolutionaries' and the reformist parties; the second type abounds in the universities, amongst academics and the sons of wealthy families who live a life of luxury as extravagant as anything the West has known. Neither type has in any way been able to convince the masses or to reach out to the man in the street . . . .

If we look at the problem from the point of view of the Arab liberation movement, we notice that, on the contrary, now that Islam has been liberated from the relative oppression it suffered under imperialism and reaction, it has become a natural and powerful support to the Arab liberation movement, as its essence requires. Islam has become the property of the masses. We will only be able to propel our nation into the age of movement with the wholehearted support of the popular masses in so far as we understand their Islamicity, and turn our backs on a frozen transcendent intellectualism contaminated by the interests and ideological poison of certain intellectuals. No one who considers Islam today in any country whatsoever can fail to realize that it is an oppressed value and hence a revolutionary force. That is precisely what makes Islam the historical twin brother of the Arab liberation movement . . . . Arabism is never weak when Islam is strong, only when reaction, regionalism, provincialism and cosmopolitanism prevail . . . .

We have to make up our minds: is the Islamicity of the popular masses a burden for the Arab nationalitarian movement, or is it an additional dimension of this movement? That is the question we would ask of the leftist converts to ideological alienation and of the right, united by self-interest, each in their own way determined to keep Islam out of the revolution.

Notes

1. *Umm al-Qura* (Cairo, 1931), pp.193-197. *Umm al Qura* (Mecca) was first published in *Al-Manar* (Cairo, 1901-1902).
2. In 1901-1902. Presently estimated at about 600 million people.
3. *Al-Uroubah awwalan!* 4th edition (Beirut, 1961), pp.11-13,.113-114.
4. Shiites.
5. *Al-Makramiyyat*, presented by Ahmad Qassem Goudah (Cairo), pp.147-150.
6. *Al-Gamiah al-Arabiyyah* . . . (Cairo, 1946).
7. *'Himayat al-adib wal-qawmiyyah al-Arabiyyah', Al-Adab*, Vol.VI, No.1, 1958, pp.26-28.
8. Ruling dynasty in 10th Century Syria.
9. The Arabic word 'baath' does not mean 'renaissance' (Nahda) but rather 'resurgence'.
10. *Marakat al-masir al-wahid*, 2nd edition (Beirut, 1959), pp.34-39, 51-53.
11. *Al-Islam wa harakat al-taharrir al-arabi* (Beirut, 1973), pp.50-68.

7. The Problematic of Socialism

MUHAMMAD RASHID RIDA
(1865-1935, Syria)

A disciple and epigone of Muhammad Abduh, Rida was the real architect of fundamentalist Islam's evolution towards philosophical coherence and political activism. His fine classical Islamic training and good grasp of modern culture, his deep revulsion for the corrupt practices of certain Sufis, his interest in the ideas of Ghazili and his concern to revivify a decadent Islamic Orient all combined to make him, from 1894 onwards, the favoured disciple of Muhammad Abduh, whom he was later to interpret in his own way.

He came to Egypt as a refugee in 1897, and in 1898 founded *Al-Manar*, which was to be the ideological crucible of political Islam right up to 1935, notably by its formative influence on the future leaders of the Muslim Brotherhood.

Rida's central concern was the need for unity between the faith, the nation, the state and political activity; without such unity, he believed there could only be weakness. In his call for the restoration of a double Caliphate — by the Turks, of necessity, and later, more genuinely, by the Arabs who alone could carry through the *ijtihad* (interpretation) — he proposed a political philosophy and a programme of action geared to the spiritual renaissance of modern Islam. He naturally took part in a great many of the religious and political activities within the Islamic and Arab context.

Main works: The Caliphate (*Al-Khilafah*); Al-Manar and Al-Azhar (*Al-Manar wal-Azhar*); The Story of the Eminent Master, Sheikh M.A. (*Tarikh al-ustadh al-imam al-shaikh Muhammad Abduh*); Al-Sunnah wal-shiah; The Muhammadan Inspiration (*Al-wahy al-muhammadi*); Interpretation of the Holy Koran (*Tafsir al-Qu'ran al-hakim*).

Given that the political dimension is understood as the fundamental one for the renaissance of Islam, it follows that it is from this point of view that Muslims must interpret the movements and revolutions which shake the world. Hence this analysis of Bolshevism, drawn up in August 1919, which enables us to understand the resonance of Communism

in certain long oppressed and humiliated traditional sections of the population.

Socialism, Bolshevism and Religion[1]

European communiques and press articles fulminate against the Bolshevism which has spread throughout Russia and the neighbouring territories of Asia and Europe. It is presented as an outburst of anarchy, murder, sedition, slander and pillage, an expression of the collapse of law and order. All the advanced states are terrified that Bolshevism will insinuate itself into their countries and sweep away their institutions, their laws, their religion and their moral values.

It is precisely this fear which leads to doubts and questions regarding the sincerity of this barrage of criticism. If these terrible activists were really so opposed to religion, so antithetical to rationality, so hostile to culture and science, there would be far less concern that they could destroy religion, culture and social institutions! God's law, which is the basis of all society's laws, is there to maintain that which is good. The public has grown used to hearing politicians denigrating the good, praising what is evil and multiplying untruths. People thus have high hopes of Bolshevism, even if they are unfamiliar with its nature; they want to understand its meaning and to be kept informed of its institutions.

The British and their allies are fighting Bolshevism with all the means at their disposal: words, deeds, money, even religion. Britian has entrusted part of this offensive to Sheikh Bakhit, Mufti of Egypt, who has issued a *fatwa*, formulated as the answer to a question, in which he proclaims that Bolshevism is forbidden by Islam and by all religion because it supposedly recognizes no rights to wealth, reputation or blood. The *fatwa* even suggests that Bolshevism is essentially akin to Persian Mazdaism and Zoroastrianism. Many writers, from Al-Azhar and elsewhere, have riposted from religious or historical points of view. The Egyptian newspapers have joined the fray. But the Egyptian government has photographed the manuscript of the *fatwa* and has printed many copies, none of which were distributed in Egypt. They were, it seems, intended for certain Muslim countries of Asia where Bolshevism has gained a hold.

We have often been asked about Bolshevism. What is it? Is it harmful, an undiluted evil as the politicians and the *fatwa* suggest? Or is it generally good, or good for some and bad for others?

Here is our answer. After much research, we have formed the impression that Bolshevism is the very essence of socialism. It proposes to abrogate the ambitious power of the capitalists and their firm supporters, the governments, who promulgate materialist laws designed to destroy the rights of the factory hands, peasants and other workers in their own countries and to help them colonize weaker foreign countries. The literal meaning of Bolshevism is 'the majority'. In other words, the true government of any people will rest with the majority, that is to say the workers, as soon as the power of the financiers and their supporters, the mighty, has been overthrown. This is precisely what happened in Russia after the fall of the tyrannical and unjust dynasty of the Tsars. (Not that this injustice and tyranny prevented the governments of the so-called democracies in France and Britain from seeking an alliance with the Tsars in order to appropriate Ottoman and Persian territories.) The remnants of the Tsarist forces rose up against the Bolsheviks and fought to regain power. Everywhere in the world those in authority will do everything in their power to combat insurgency, whether they have right on their side or not. If the furious invective against Bolshevik harshness has any foundation, then surely this is part of the explanation. No government can pretend it would have acted differently. The Bolsheviks' lack of experience of government was another factor. Disorder, revolt and misery were everwhere. The Bolsheviks had no opportunity to temper their severity and harshness.

The following should be quite clear: Nobody should think that the actions and institutions of the Bolsheviks are in keeping with Islamic principles of government or that Muslims faithful to their religion could follow them. But that is not true only of the Bolsheviks. All the laws established in Europe and even in the East, in Egypt and the Ottoman Empire for instance, are in some way contrary to Muslim law. Muslims hope for the triumph of socialism, a triumph which will abolish the slavery of peoples — of all workers — even if they reject that which runs contrary to Muslim law in socialism as in other doctrines. Until the socialists embrace Islam they cannot invoke the laws of Islam in the name of their cause.

Reproduced below are some extracts from an article which highlights the intentions of the people. It is taken from the journal *Souriya al-Muttahida* (United Syria), published in Mexico:

> Read what I have to say with great care, O rich merchant. Socialism stalks the entire planet. *'Vox populi, vox Dei',* as the Latin proverb has it. In other words, when the majority pursues a necessary goal, it cannot be prevented from attaining it, for the majority embodies the truth and truth is an irresistible force.
>
> With every day that passes, it becomes clearer that might is right, and that the majority is mightiness itself. This was apparent during the war provoked by Germany. The peoples of the world decided that Germany's war against France, Belgium and Serbia was a crime against humanity. The majority turned against her, despite her military strength, her diabolical submarines, hellish aeroplanes and enormous cannons. The majority attacked Germany from all sides. As we have said, such a majority is the embodiment of truth.

Public opinion, the will of the majority; that is socialism. Bolshevik is the Russian word for 'majority'. It implies a demand that world peace be built on solid and just foundations and that decent living conditions be provided for the workers in every part of the world.

The reader should not be astonished when we say that 99% of the world's inhabitants are socialists or Bolsheviks. They represent the people whose voice, according to the proverb, is the voice of God. It is the people who bring down governments and overthrow kings and thrones. And it is the people whose rifles protect the rich man's possessions, his wives and children, his land, his herds and his factories. It is the people who die that the rich man's wealth may grow.

Activity! Work! That is the advice fathers give their children. Throughout their childhood, children hear the same thing repeated to them by their masters. The rulers too exhort the people to work: work brings happiness; without it there is only ruin. The working people represent 99% of humanity. The happiness or the ruination of a country depends on them. It is they who are sent to war to maintain [national] security, help the oppressed and judge the oppressor. Surely their rights should be held sacred and respected?

Two states break off friendly relations. The reason? One of them covets a fertile piece of land or a lucrative mineral deposit belonging to some rich individual. The other state then sends all its people to die on the battlefield in order that the rich owner may retain his property. The first state sends all its people to die so as to appropriate the property and sell it to some financier from its own country. The worker abandons his plough, his pick, his saw or his hammer. He leaves his house, his wife and his children exposed to hunger, nudity and contempt. He dons his rifle and goes to brave death amidst the thunder of the cannons, the clash of sabres, the fountains of blood, to defend the rich man's property, land, minerals and factories. Meanwhile the rich man lolls on soft cushions, enjoying his women and his wine.

The people do all this in the name of the homeland; a homeland of which not an inch belongs to them. They come back trembling from the human carnage, exhausted, sick, pale, to find their wives and children gripped by hunger, cold and destitution. And then the government tells them 'get to work!'. Once again, the poor worker's day is spent at his plough or wielding his pick. But he still does not get a decent wage; at most, he can buy a little food, of poor quality, and a few rags.

Generations and centuries have witnessed the grief and suffering of the people. If they ever sought to break the iron yoke of the rich, the latter's accomplice in crime and prevarication, the government, would attack them. The people were thus forced to submit to injustice; equity and goodness were driven out by fear.

But today the people are not as they were yesterday. They now control the armed forces, the supplies, the railways and the communications network. 100 million Russians, in areas which are amongst the most fertile and richest in minerals, coal and oil, support the workers' demands and have formed the world's first popular government. The peoples of central Europe have demonstrated their support for popular government. The workers of France, Italy, Switzerland, and the rest of Europe, America and Asia are also clamouring for the downfall of their respective governments and the creation of popular (Bolshevik) governments. They do not fear their governments because they know that the soldier with his rifle or the sailor on his gunboat is one of them. They know that it is they who drive the trains and make the cannons and the shells. Everything is in the hands of the people. It is on them that the universal revolution and the instauration of a reign of peace and justice depend.

But none of this will happen unless popular governments sensitive to the peoples' needs are set up. Such popular governments can only be established once the fortunes of the wealthy have been distributed [to the people]. The wealthy thus have to be fought if the just demands of the people are to be met. Only coercion and force will bring them down. The rich will suffer throughout the world, but the blame for that will not lie with the people; it is the rich themselves, with their hunger for absolute domination, who will have brought their fate upon themselves.

AL-TAHER AL-HADDAD
(1899-1935, Tunisia)

A key figure in the Tunisian and Arab national renaissance, Al-Haddad was a trade unionist, a politician, an ardent feminist and a lyrical and mystical poet; his thought and work have been and remain a living source of inspiration to the present generation.

After completing secondary school at Zaytounah, he became an active militant in the Destour, from the time of its formation in 1920. In 1924, responding to the call launched by Dr Muhammad Ali, he threw himself into the struggle for the creation of a General Union of Tunisian Workers (UGTT), which he saw as an essential ingredient of social justice and as a way of radicalizing the national movement. Because of his struggle against the assimilation campaign (the law of 20 December 1923) he was exiled in 1925.

On his return, he published a book on the philosophy and history of the still emergent Tunisian workers' movement, and a work on the emancipation of women based on the religiously inspired themes of Qassem Amin, interpreted from the point of view of political democracy. As was to be expected, this latter work aroused the fury of traditionalist religious circles.

***Main works*: Tunisian Workers and the Growth of the Workers' Movement (*Al-Ummal al-tounisiyyoun wa zuhour al-harakah al-niqabiyyah*); Tunisian Women in Society and Under Religious Law (*Imraatouna fil-sharia wal-mujtama*).**

The extract below shows the author's concern to affirm both his faith in socialism, following the 1917 revolution which he salutes in his

Preface, and the gradual character of social evolution, which he takes as an historical necessity specific to Tunisia. The worker's movement, led by Farhat Hashad, and the Tunisian national movement have made these two themes their own.

Tunisia and Socialism[2]

At the head of the movements which marched victoriously towards a better future were men of science who had dedicated themselves to the service of humanity: they studied the history of mankind, natural law, social life and the social system best capable of ensuring humanity's happiness. After centuries of such study, the work of the European prophet of socialism, Karl Marx, was published; it is now considered as the summum of humanity's dreams, expressing principles founded on the support of all sincere and upright workers.

Eventually, these forces took the form of powerful parties organized to struggle against capital, rejecting its right to exist and striving to uproot its ever more tenacious hold. Many European countries underwent violent upheavals, notably as a result of the establishment in Russia of a government which embodied the dreams of socialism. In the other European countries, two forces — capital and labour — continue to clash, in a conflict whose violence varies from country to country; for instance the workers' parties in France constitute a major element in the struggle against capitalism, despite their internal divisions. In Italy, on the other hand, fascism has succeeded in stifling the workers' movements and the defenders of capitalism attribute Italy's improved financial situation to Mr Mussolini's government. Applying its fascist principles, the latter has been able to maximize the exploitation of the workers, by lowering workers' wages, increasing the working day from eight to nine hours and extending this practice to cover agricultural as well as industrial labour, thereby increasing production and reducing consumption.

Measures aiming to increase production, reduce wages and impose more and more general taxes which do not bear on capital and which fall mostly on the workers have become contemporary capitalism's main concern, especially in those countries where confidence in financial stability is low. There are those who would like to see a fascist regime installed in France, but they cannot proceed thanks to the strength and vigilance of the workers' parties.

The old world, awakened by the thunder of bombs, has been considerably influenced by such movements, but this influence is gaining ground only slowly and must advance at its own pace, given the forces that are ranged against it. The main preoccupation of the old world is to rid itself of the Europeans who range over its territory, exploiting it purely on the principle that might is right. The old world must thus equip itself with everything the West uses in the way of science and other weapons. The day the Western governments recognize that the old world has attained some real measure of power, they will strive, if internal dissensions do not prevent them, to ensure that the order of this world is a capitalist one; and that will not be the end of the story . . . .

As we have already indicated, Tunisian society has little cohesion. A general awakening following the Great War and certain limited experiences have prompted the beginnings of an awareness of suffering and the need to do something about it through social solidarity. This feeling is still at an early stage and people are not yet ready to accept the idea of revolution as a means of social change, even if the strength of the idea is growing . . . .

In practice, the question is more serious: the necessary premises for the kind of social revolution which can be prepared by propagating the revolutionary spirit are still absent in the Kingdom of Tunisia, where European forms of social evolution, the development of resources, the organization of assets and the extension of activities have not yet developed. With the exception of the Israelites, the average Tunisian trader continues to sell from his tiny stall . . . ; our biggest industrialists, in terms of wealth and the scope of their activities, employ barely more than ten people; the same applies, more or less, to the most enterprising Tunisian *fellah* on his farm. We are still a long way from the mines, factories and warehouses into which hundreds or thousands of workers swarm to earn their daily bread.

The world revolution preached in Europe is based on the class struggle and clearly has little relevance to a country like Tunisia, especially given the state the country finds itself in at present as a result of overall world politics; class struggle in our country lacks the necessary basis and, if it serves anybody, it certainly does not help the principal protagonists.

The Kingdom of Tunisia cannot afford a revolution, even one directed against the ruling regime. The nightmare we are living through and the poverty which has befallen us might give cause to believe that the country is on the verge of an explosion. In practice, however, the elements necessary for success are lacking. What Tunisia really needs is to develop social forces armed with the knowledge required for the country to take possession of its own resources — permanent, peaceful and fundamental forces which can provide the basis for a free and happy life. Only then will the nation be ready to elicit from within the will, the ideas and the capacity to govern itself, without which it will never attain any of the goals it has set itself.

Any nation which does not draw on its own resources to achieve its ends will never realize its hopes. No nation can attain a worthwhile level of development by relying on any foreign state, party or association. Life, liberty, strength and sovereignty are only to be found in the depths of one's own soul, one's own thought. As long as its soul and mind remain inert and benighted, no amount of suffering and woe can make the nation into anything other than a blind and deaf tool in the hands of others, who would quite naturally use it to suit their own ends.

The idea of co-operation is in itself fine and good. But it can only be truly realized when the two partners are of equal strength . . . . A country in

Tunisia's present state cannot accept co-operation; its need for all its forces and for its own integrity is too great. It can accept aid from whoever offers it, but only providing there are no strings attached — [the nation's] freedom of thought and action is sacred and the right to take its own decisions must never be sacrificed . . . .

Present-day Tunisia's paramount need is for social reform. Every class must participate in this endeavour, despite the differences in their living conditions. The kind of differentiation which exists in the European countries, and which has led several communities there to set themselves goals which seem so distant to us, does not as yet exist amongst the Tunisian people. We must proceed in keeping with our own nature if we are to achieve our ends . . . .

History, ancient and modern, shows that by respecting an established order of social class, nationalism bears within itself the seed of terrible conflicts in the future; the class struggle between workers and nationalists in Europe is an example of what can happen when the general meaning of the term 'national' is distorted to refer only to the most privileged and wealthy class, namely the capitalists. The fact remains, however, that man can always draw profit from past experience, to the extent that the framework in which he operates allows him to do so. Is it realistic, in a country like Tunisia, for the classes to clash straight away to avoid conflicts between them in the future? Given the situation of the country and the sword of Damocles that hangs over our heads, the answer is simply that the question does not deserve serious consideration . . . .

The growth in Tunisia of a social movement based on general co-operation between classes which are not so distant from one another, a movement which would set out to inculcate a sense of values and promote public education, would be of immense value to the country as a whole and would pave the way for acceptance of the socialist ideal instead of accentuating differences [between classes] and increasing the antagonism between them.

The General Union of Tunisian Workers was formed on the basis of such principles and to serve these ends.

SALAMAH MUSA
(1887-1958, Egypt)

Musa was one of the founding fathers of Egyptian socialism, along with Tahtawi, Shamayyil and Antoun. He visited Britain in 1908 and soon became a disciple of G.B. Shaw and H.G. Wells. His book on socialism (1912) was the first Arab work of the kind. He defended the scientific approach and evolutionist theory, campaigned for political democracy and socialism, and produced an extensive body of critical, literary,

philological and religious writings. In 1920 he founded the Socialist Party and in 1930 launched *Al-Magallah al-Gadidah*, a journal which was to remain central to Egyptian radical thought up to the Second World War.

Musa was repeatedly persecuted by right-wing governments and was excluded from public life during the last years of his life, as the Islamic ideology grew stronger. The opus he left is a fine blend of Oriental spirituality, Renaissance humanism and a socialism in which he retained the essential analyses of Marx and the Fabians.

Main works: **Socialism** (*Al-Ishtirakiyyah*); **Arabic and Contemporary Rhetoric** (*Al-Lughah al-arabiyyah wal balagah al-asriyyah*); **Today and Tomorrow** (*Al-Yawm wal-ghad*); **The Book of Revolutions** (*Kitab al-thawrat*); **The Education of Salamah Musa** (*Tarbiyat Salamah Musa*); **Forbidden Writings** (*Maqalat mamnouah*).

The second edition of his autobiography provided Salamah Musa with an opportunity to draw up a spiritual testament in the year of his death. It is a vivid expression of his faith in rationality and science and his commitment to the struggle for freedom and socialism. The bitterness which colours the work as a whole prefigures the 'crisis of the intellectuals' but this text remains, nonetheless, a real hymn to culture.

Credo of a Socialist[3]

What do you believe?

I believe in Christianity, Islam and Judaism. I love the Messiah and admire Muhammad. Moses enlightens me, I meditate on Paul and am attracted by Buddha. I feel that they are all my spiritual parents, that I live in harmony with them and draw from them an inspiration to truth, honour, mercy and nobleness of spirit.

I also believe in love of nature and the majesty of the Universe. I do not overlook the religious meaning of the theory of evolution and remain attentive to the procession of all living things, of which man is the crowning glory. Indeed I find this religious meaning in the beauty of womankind, the sacred character of maternity and the honour of humanity. I believe in Tolstoi, Gandhi, Voltaire and Bacon.

The only image hanging over my bed, where I can see it as I rise in the morning and as I prepare to sleep is a picture of Tolstoi, the humane man.

In a word, the core of my credo is humanity, with all its philosophers, prophets and writers, with all its courage, intelligence, mercy, magnanimity, beauty and honour.

But my credo is not some naive compound of placidity and resignation. I have turned away from such attitudes and do not regret it. Certitudes may be more peaceful, but as Bertrand Russell has it, doubt is nobler. I am fortunate in that culture has enabled me to attain to a total vision of life and the

Universe. I believe that a man can only develop a heightened religious consciousness through culture and by acquiring a comprehensive vision of the Universe, keeping his reason and his heart in harmony with the universal movement of life and humanity's hopes. This leads him to elaborate a personal standpoint and may cause him considerable anxiety. Religion is, after all, a personal standpoint which cannot be generalized, which is why it owes it to itself to remain permanently anxious.

There are dozens of fundamental books which have shaped my life and my personality. However these books have been like the scaffolding used in building; the moment the house is complete, the grid of iron and wood surrounding it is taken down. That is why I dismantled Nietzsche, and dozens of others, when I no longer needed them as the scaffolding from which I built my personality.

When I meditate on my personality and objectives, I feel that I am playing the same role, in 20th Century Egypt, as the men of the Renaissance did from 1400 to 1800. That is why I feel a spiritual kinship and a sacred sense of mission with Leonardo, Voltaire, Diderot and their fellows. That is why I have preached reason instead of faith, and independence of spirit instead of respect for tradition.

Of all the men of the Renaissance, the one I feel the closest affinity with is Leonardo da Vinci. Like him, I believe that a mature spirit should not restrict itself to either literature or science or philosophy, but should on the contrary unite them in order to draw out their quintessence, which is a philosophy of life.

If you wish for more details, dear reader, you should know (1) that I believe in truths, hence my attachment to science which is the body of truths; (2) that if a conclusion is inescapable and the fruit of scientific consideration, I accept it. That is why I believe in the socialist future of the world, and of Egypt, and work towards realization; indeed the contemporary economy presages its advent; (3) that I believe there is no stability in the world, the universe and society, since evolution is the essence of matter, of living things and of societies — which is to say that it is the basis of all existence. Social rigidity thus amounts to pernicious opposition by the wicked to the laws of life and the universe.

In terms of intellectual culture, I have attained the most a man of my age can pretend to. The seeds of future ideas are still germinating in my mind and I have many projects in hand. My overall purpose is to transform Egypt from a weak Oriental country, locked in its agricultural and other traditions, into a modern European country reliant on science, industry and the independence of its own personality, and with an economic structure oriented towards socialism.

As I see it, socialism constitutes the practical application of the humanist doctrine. We have already implemented the first stage of socialism, in that we have replaced the monarchy with a republic. We have struggled against feudalism and have built factories. Many of my fundamental hopes have been realized.

In the last analysis, socialism means that the people are paramount;

more, that they are everything. Hence my struggle in the press to create a popular Arabic writing style and to ensure that literature, science and culture as a whole should be within the reach of the people and not the privilege of a particular class.

I have been reproached for having written about *meloukhia*, *bamiah*[4] and beans. Those who criticized me did so because of their distance from the people and their attachment to overblown literary doctrines according to which one should never lower oneself to mentioning such vulgar dishes, concentrating instead on 'entertaining the spirit'. I hold the contrary view that the writer's vocation is a humanitarian mission with the service of society and the promotion of mankind as its aim. The poor amongst our people, those whom foreign imperialism and local despotism have impoverished and starved, have no need of our descriptions of the beauty of a flower or the fragrance of jasmin. Humanity, not beauty, is the purpose of literature. And humanity demands of the humanist writer that he concern himself above all else with the subsistence of the people. Flowers and jasmin can wait . . . .

As for my lifelong work in the press and in literature, it can be considered either as a failure or as a success. From the financial point of view, it has undeniably been an almost complete failure. I took up journalism in 1914, when I published a journal called *Al-Mustaqbal*, and have stayed in the same profession until today, with interruptions of a few years here, a few months there. I have worked for many newspapers and journals, I published *Al-Magallah al-Gadidah* for 14 years and have written over 40 books. And yet, despite all this, I have had to sell everything I inherited simply in order to live. The Ministry of Public Education spent not one *millieme*[5] on one of my books, nor did it ever subscribe to *AL-MAGALLAH AL-GADIDAH*. Amongst my contemporaries, there are journalists who have, over the years, earned some 30 or 40,000 pounds. The Ministry of Public Education would sometimes spend up to a thousand pounds on copies of their books. Similarly, there are several monthly or weekly journals to which the Ministry of Public Education paid subscriptions of at least 20 or 30,000 pounds. Egyptian broadcasting went so far as to treat me as if I were not Egyptian. Others have given 400 or 500 conferences over the last ten years, while I have given only five. Many writers have won prizes for which I never even qualified. That is their success, and my failure.

My success is of a quite different nature. It is to have transformed the youth of Egypt and the Arab East, and to have inculcated in them courage, independence, faith in science and contemporary thought. I helped them to change, to live a new life and acquire some idea of the future, its promise and its dangers. I succeeded in developing, for their benefit, a writing style which was capable of expressing what they needed to understand. Similarly, I did not hesitate to stress the need to adopt Latin script the moment I became convinced that our Arabic script was acting as a brake on our scientific progress and on our culture.

I have never locked myself into the ivory tower of literature. How can a man live in a tower when 99% of his fellows live in mud huts?

My success with the young is fully proportional to my financial failure with the governments of the past. I always refused to tie myself to the forces of reaction in their various guises, the same forces who distributed money and land so profusely to their supporters whilst isolating their opponents and causing them harm My arrest, in 1946,[6] on a charge of making propadanda for the republic instead of for the monarchy and for socialism instead of for feudalism, was one of the factors of my success as I understand it; it was also a factor of the failure I am condemned for by our great writers who published endless declamations, articles and poems praising the despot Faruq, to the point that one of them even described him as an example of morality to be emulated by all Egyptian youth.

As I enter my 70th year, I feel that the end is in sight, although it may still be perhaps 20 or 30 years away. When it comes, I will accept it with complete calm. But in the meantime, I hope to keep my intellectual appetite and continue to investigate life, pursuing knowledge and understanding as I have done thoughout my life.

Finally, I would like to die like Al-Jahiz 'with a book resting on my breast'.

AZIZ AL-HAJI
(1926, Iraq)

Born into a middle class Iraqi Kurdish family, Al-Haji eventually graduated from the Ecole Normale Superieure and became a secondary school teacher in Al-Qut. He joined the Iraqi Communist Party in 1945, was arrested in 1948, under Nuri Said, to be released only ten years later in 1958.

He then threw himself into political and theoretical work, becoming Iraq's main Marxist political theoretician; the bulk of his work remains scattered over various periodicals. Forced to leave Iraq in 1960, Al-Haji moved abroad, becoming a member of the High Commission for the Defence of the Iraqi People and one of the leaders of the Iraqi Communist Party. Following the June 1967 war, he returned to the fray and emerged as one of the key figures of Iraq's Marxist-Leninist Party. Armed struggle in the south of the country led to a bloody repression in which Khaled Zaki met an heroic death. Shortly afterwards, Aziz al-Haji withdrew from the political arena and became Iraq's permanent UNESCO representative.

Main works: **Arab Nationalitarianism and Democracy** (*Al-Qawmiyyah al-arabiyyah wal-dimuqratiyyah*); **Our Revolution** (*Thawratuna*); **On Non-Capitalist Development in Iraq** (*Hawl al-tatawwur ghayr al-rasmali fil-Iraq*).

The text below illustrates two important characteristics of Marxism

in the Arab world: on the one hand the stress on the fundamental link between democracy and socialism; on the other, the insistence that democratic reform is a necessary precondition for the introduction of socialism, which the right cannot adopt as its goal.

Arab Nationalitarianism, Democracy and Socialism[7]

The fundamental content of Arab nationalitarianism, as represented by its advanced wing, is its progressive and democratic content. The conscious Arab popular masses draw no distinction between the aims of national liberation and the raising of the standard of living, industrialization, agrarian reform, the enjoyment of democratic political rights and a new departure in international relations based on faith in the ability of all peoples to make their own decisions. Indeed national liberation from imperialism and the determination to do away with every trace of imperialism in all the Arab lands and to eliminate artificial divisions effectively implies the liberation of the broad masses of the Arab people from the worst exploitation humanity has ever known — that exercised by the blood-sucking foreign monopolies which accumulate fabulous profits by imposing frustration, hunger and backwardness on millions of human beings.

That is why the Arab national movement has gained such impetus and has become stronger through the organic linkage of national liberation to political and economic democracy.

However, since the 1930s, we have witnessed the emergence within the liberation movements and in certain Arab countries of tendencies whose slogans and objectives suggest a rejection of democracy. The underlying reasons are to be found in the impact made by imperialist policies geared to exploit and divide the Arab nation. The rise of Nazism and fascist tendencies, and their temporary victory, also played an important role in the pollution of the national movement with non-democratic or even anti-democratic slogans and concepts. Many politically commited Arab men and women, Arab patriots sensitive to the increase of imperialist pressure, felt that the best way to eliminate imperialism and unite the Arabs might be to adopt the Prussian model, taking the unification of Germany as personified by Bismarck as their model and inspiration . . . .

If we are to give a lucid answer to democracy's detractors and enemies, we must first define it . . . . In terms of the present stage of the Arab revolutionary struggle, democratic goals can be defined as follows:

On the economic and social level:[8] (1) The elimination of feudalism and the implementation of fundamental agrarian reform, to the benefit of the great mass of *fellahin*, especially the poorer ones; that is the social axis of the revolution; (2) Industrialization of the country and encouragement of national, public and private capital in industry and commerce; (3) Satisfaction of the everyday demands of the workers; (4) Guarantees given to meet the demands of artisans, employees, smaller artisans and intellectuals;

(5) Generalization of education and culture; (6) Equal rights for men and women; (7) Abolition of reactionary laws.

The question of how to achieve socialism is not on the immediate agenda. Socialism implies the elimination of private national capital, the gradual nationalization of all private enterprise and the transformation of agriculture and craftwork on socialist lines. Such a programme is not in keeping with the needs of contemporary Arab societies.

Propaganda which calls for socialism as an immediate objective cannot be scientific. Furthermore it carries a double danger: firstly it distorts the real meaning of socialism and misleads the masses; secondly it can alienate national capitalists from the national revolution in which they have an important role to play, be it in terms of the revolution itself or in terms of the reconstruction of each liberated Arab country, all of which will still need private capital for a long time to come . . . .

The reality is that socialism is a distant goal. The Chinese experience has shown that it is possible to achieve that goal in stages, by convincing the bulk of the national bourgeoisie itself rather than by force and coercion . . . . It is strange to see such calls for socialism launched in a liberated Arab country which has until now shown itself incapable of implementing a radical agrarian reform and where a layer of rich *fellahin* prosper whilst destitution forces a growing number of poorer *fellahin* to sell their land.[9]

Furthermore, the transition to socialism demands a certain level of mass organization and a certain kind of popular consciousness, neither of which exists at the moment. This does not mean that there is any artificial barrier between the two stages but simply that the first is the natural preface to the second, socialist, stage.

AHMAD BEN BELLA
(1919, Algeria)

Born to a peasant family, Ben Bella completed traditional Islamic studies, became a non-commissioned officer in the French army and served in the Italian campaign. As an influential member of the MTLD, he soon came to understand the inanity of activity within the framework of the French occupation. His stay in Egypt (1952-1954) provided him with an opportunity to broaden his political vision so as to encompass the entire Arab world. On his return to Algeria, he created the 'Revolutionary Union and Action Committee', the acting instrument of the FLN which launched the Algerian national revolution on 1 November 1954.

Kidnapped in the Tunis aeroplane incident (1956), he was released after the Evian agreements, formed the so-called Tlemcen group and became President of the Democratic and Popular Republic of Algeria

(September 1962) then Secretary-General of the FLNs' Political Bureau. On 19 June 1965 he was overthrown by a coup d'etat and placed under house arrest. He was released in 1981, and has since moved steadily closer to the positions of political Islam.

Under his leadership, independent Algeria opted for self-managed socialism, the first major initiative in the 'poor people's revolution' in the Arab world. Eight years after the nationalization of the Suez canal, the themes of his speech on 29 September 1964, on the occasion of the inauguration of the third Saharan pipeline at Laghouat, provide the elements of a progressive national doctrine as to the utilization of the oil and natural resources of the dependent countries once dominated by imperialism. The main passages are reproduced below.

Neo-colonialism and Socialism[10]

The principles which guide our plan of action to exploit our hydrocarbons could equally be used as the basis on which to define the new relations which must be instituted between the underdeveloped countries and the industrialized countries. It is by drawing on these principles that we will be able to put an end to the system of exploitation inherited from colonialism, which drains the natural resources of the former to the benefit of the latter. However, if the underdeveloped countries are to gain recognition of their economic rights and obtain from the countries that exploit their wealth a real contribution towards their industrialization, they must unite to impose respect for their intentions. In the first place, they must finally refuse to play the game whereby the capitalist companies pit them one against another thereby neutralizing them and preventing them from defending themselves effectively. The existence of the Organization of Petroleum Exporting Countries is a happy fact, which promises greatly for the future. Algeria is ready to join in any action which helps to eliminate the exploitation of peoples, and will implement any measures which contribute to increasing the exploited countries' share of the revenues generated through the valorization of their resources.

At present, this share is determined in terms of 'profits'. But the concept of profit bandied about in capitalist theories is inherently ambiguous. If we are talking about the normal return on investment and for services rendered, then there is no problem, providing the state receives its due in the form of taxes paid on any commercial or industrial profits. But if the concept of profit encompasses the wealth inherent in the very fact of possessing a natural resource, then it is clearly misleading, in that it amounts to transferring abroad a part of the national patrimony, subsumed under profits from capital; this is precisely what we mean by exploitation.

To be efficacious and coherent, the actions of the producer-countries will have to be geared to win back all the revenues due to them as owners of these natural resources, which are a gift of nature and not a creation of the capitalists.

Considerable sums would then flow into the coffers of the rightful owners, the so-called underdeveloped countries. These would, as a result, be in a position to escape the bottleneck caused by lack of investment capital and take some major steps towards progress. In particular, they would no longer have to subordinate the implementation of their development plans to the approval of finance organizations serving the interests of the dominant economies.

... But we intend to share the benefits thus derived from our natural resources with the peoples to whom we are tied by a common history and destiny. In the case of gas, we intend to supply our brothers in Tunisia and Morocco and, if possible, other neighbouring African countries, as soon as the technical and economic facilities for transport are available.

Furthermore, the moment we have recovered from the economic effects of the war, we intend to allocate, according to formulae to be worked out opportunely a part of the income derived from our oil and gas exports to help our Maghribi, Arab and African brothers realize their own development projects.

It is worth citing the example of Kuwait, which has granted major loans to other Arab countries at very favourable rates of interest. The efforts of our Kuwaiti brothers have thus made possible achievements which could never have been realized had the relevant projects been burdened with the conditions and charges habitually imposed by financial institutions. We hope that the Kuwaiti example will be taken up and that the solidarity of peoples linked by shared interests and a common destiny will increase.

A bare two years after independence, Algeria is already resolutely on course towards its economic development.

The building of this pipeline, which we are gathered here today to celebrate, marks a critical phase in our development. It symbolizes our determination to further political liberation by economic liberation, in order to fulfil the hopes of our *shuhada*[11] who gave their lives for our national independence. It also exemplifies the desire of the Political Bureau and the Government to respond to the deeply felt aspirations of our working masses, whose support remains the principal driving force of our actions.

This inauguation ceremony is a way of paying homage to the Algerian people at work, and of saying clearly what we see as good and what we see as wrong about our relations with the foreign companies operating in our country. We have clearly indicated the basis on which we wish to engage in a lasting collaboration with these companies and the countries they represent.

We sincerely believe that co-operation is not only possible but also desirable. We hold that all those who honestly wish to take part in our development can count on a secure future in Algeria. In particular, the genius of France, which has set its imprint on this country in so many ways, can still discover a wealth of opportunities to realize its great potential here.

Finally, socialist Algeria calls on all peoples who are struggling for their economic liberation to unite and combine their efforts, failing which all our attempts to storm the citadels of imperialism will be in vain.

Our message is one of solidarity with all fraternal countries, whom we hope one day will play a role in the development of our own resources.

Economic liberation, development, solidarity and peace — those are the themes I have constantly reiterated in the name of Algeria, throughout the magnificent Odyssey which has taken us from Algiers to Laghouat, via Arzew and Oran. Rising above the arduous problems this century has set us, these themes express the hope of our people, who have paid so dearly to join the concert of nations — the hope for a better tomorrow for all mankind.

AHMAD BEN SALEH
(1926, Tunisia)

Later to become a Tunisian statesman and the leader of the left within the regime, Ahmed Ben Saleh had a traditional Islamic education in Tunis, attended the University of Paris and took up a teaching post at the Lycee de Sousse (1948-1951). He became General Secretary of the General Union of Tunisian Workers (1954-56), then, successively, Secretary of State for Public Health and Social Affairs (1960-1964), for Planning and the National Economy, and for National Education (1964-1970). He was Deputy General Secretary of the Destour Socialist Party from 1964 to 1970.

The launch and intensification of the co-operation campaign in the countryside gained him many enemies on the right. Taking advantage of his relative estrangement from President Bourguiba, Ben Saleh's opponents engineered his downfall and had him condemned to 10 years in prison in 1970.

With all his contradictions, Ahmad Ben Saleh's hesitant but stubborn search for socialism makes him stand out as the most notable figure of the new political generation in Tunis, for whom socialism goes hand-in-hand with the intensification of Tunisia's Arab allegiance.

Of all his published writings, this speech given on 9 December 1968 to open a seminar on the management of public enterprises best situates the man and his work.

The Rationality of Development

There are certain elements which must be taken into account in a developing country which has only recently achieved independence and is determined to create a national economy capable of opening onto the outside world precisely because it is national. These can be summed up as follows.

Firstly, when the country concerned is poor in resources, as is certainly true in our case, the essential thing is to ensure that any endeavour is genuinely integrated into an overall effort, as part of a specific sector and as one element with the efforts of the nation as a whole to promote its general development. The idea that the way firms are managed must be responsive to national goals as defined in our Development Plan is quite fundamental.

Secondly, there is the fact that the concept of profit must be retained whatever the nature of the enterprise. This is even more essential when the company is a public or co-operative one, because it is in such enterprises that profits are most needed. In this way capital can be accumulated, the enterprise become self-financing and new companies providing new jobs be started up, thereby promoting the sector as a whole and contributing to the general progress of the country's economy . . . .

Even social life can be based on competition rather than confrontation. Politics too can be a matter of competition and not confrontation. The real point is to strive gradually to convince the present generation that class struggles, and struggles between socialists and capitalists, between people and between nations are *not* inevitable.

In short our apparently purely technical efforts to manage companies are inseparable from a global conception of life which will lead people, nations and economic agents towards coexistence, respect for one another and peace. This global vision of things is what we in Tunisia are proud to call Bourguibism and Destourian Socialism . . . .

To take the matter further, the way enterprises are managed can be evoked. Our approach has concentrated on *goal-oriented management* . . . . In the various European countries it is almost taken for granted that major public companies should receive massive annual subsidies, but in a country like Tunisia, whenever the state grants a loan to a firm or helps to capitalize it . . . people start railing against socialism, depicted narrowly as public companies living off the state. The reality is quite different.

The truth is that the economists from the rich countries, many of whom come to Tunisia as expert advisers, have not grasped that an enterprise is the manifestation of a given society, with given sociological and economic conditions. It is only when this has been fully understood that economic co-operation, the key concern of all the international bodies today, will really be formulated in terms of respect for each country's options and aims; a respect for the wishes of all societies which are really trying to develop and become modern countries . . . .

We will not always be mere consumers of products and ideas. Our ambition, our pretension perhaps, is to help change the way people think . . . . We certainly have no wish to be treated always as people in need, urgent need, of an ever increasing number of experts. This has to be said, if only to inspire cadres of the young nations with self-respect; a self-respect which is vital if — with the help of intelligent sincere experts, under the auspices of the United Nations and certain other countries who understand the differences between societies and the political conditions specific to each — we are ever to contribute to the development of humanity and perhaps eventually send out our own experts to help others, and not merely in the Third World . . . .

It is worth looking at the matter from a less superficial viewpoint. We have seen reports which have been drawn up after one week in the field. We have seen senior experts present reports on the overall economic or financial position of specific countries or public companies. We have had to put up with endless sinister caterwaulings concerning the quality of public companies and their management. But we have held firm, and I can tell our African friends gathered here today that we have to hold firm; but we also have to be merciless with incompetent management . . . .

There is still a long, hard way to go, and the path we have chosen is one of the hardest. It is the path of effort, organization and rational management; it is also the path of careful consideration, avoiding hasty imitation and the incorporation of our policies — especially our economic policies — into an overall framework which is unsuitable because it takes no account of the crucial time element. This element of time, the time which separates us (from the developed world) must always be borne in mind if we are to succeed in taking off intellectually by boosting the management abilities of all the developing countries, and especially of our own country, which is the only one I am really qualified to speak about.

The Egyptian Communist Party
(Egypt)

Founded in 1920, the Communist Party was reborn in 1939, after an eclipse of a few years. It re-emerged as a new movement, a profoundly national movement of cadres operating at a very advanced theoretical level. Gradually, and especially from 1946 onwards, it assumed the role of political think tank for the entire national movement. Its great strength in the towns, amongst the workers and intellectuals, was offset by the chronic dividedness which ravaged it from 1939 to 1958 and by its notable weakness amongst the *fellahin*. Increasingly heavy waves of repression came to a climax in 1952-1956 and more particularly again in 1959-1964. The aim of this repression was more to break individuals and the spirit of the movement, to eliminate the leadership, than to dismantle the underlying networks. A whole generation of Marxist Egyptian youth endured through this dark night and elaborated the analyses and theories which are now a major influence throughout Egypt and in many parts of the Arab world. In this sense, Egyptian Marxism can be seen as a school of thought and action.

In April 1965, a year after the gates of the camps had been opened to all but a few revolutionary Marxists who remained committed to the re-creation on the Party, the Central Conference of the Egyptian Communist Party, by majority vote, decided to dissolve the organization so as to facilitate the concentration of all socialist forces in Egypt within a single socialist party. The extracts below outline some of the arguments put forward when this highly unusual decision was being taken. It should be borne in mind, however, that it was a decision which was vigorously criticized at the time by a substantial section of the movement and continued to be so by the new generation of Marxists which grew up in the middle of the national crisis after June 1967. The fact remains that the following text catches fairly precisely the overall tone of Arab national communism, which has been fundamentally marked by the evolution of progressive thought and action in Egypt.

Egyptian Communism and its Mission; a Balance Sheet[12]

Given that socialism is, in the end, the fruit of the conscious and creative work put in by the working people, the central task of the present situation is the advancement of socialist democracy, by enabling the people to apply it effectively. It is through this practice of socialist democracy that the most complex problems facing the revolution can be resolved, and that the transfer of power to the working people's alliance can be effected. The revolutionary leadership, namely the Free Officers, have already begun to act in order to shift the centre of gravity within the national alliance away from capitalism and towards the working classes, the *fellahin*, the intellectuals and the revolutionarities. We refer to the 'National Action Charter', the fundamental document of the Egyptian state.

The itinerary of the leaders of the 23 July revolution shows that they have adopted a course chosen by the people. It follows that the Egyptian Communists are no longer alone in calling for socialism and social progress, since there are now other forces, which are constantly developing, whose seriousness and commitment to the cause of social progress is undeniable. In considering the problem of the organization and political unity of all the socialist forces in the country, the Egyptian Communist Party must thus take into account these revolutionaries who have endorsed the people's aspirations for the construction of socialism and who have carried out socialist measures. We must also bear in mind all the socialists and unorganized Marxists who, along with the Communists, have raised the banner of social progress. It is in the light of all this that the Central Committee of the Egyptian Communist Party has decided to wind up the Party's independent organizational structure. In the specific conditions of our country such a step is unavoidable if we are to establish the basis for unity amongst all socialists, joined in a single revolutionary organization, a single socialist party.

This historic decision by the Egyptian Communist Party is the result of conscious efforts made by members of the Party to study and understand their specific reality and to fray an Egyptian path to socialism. Our position is rooted in conscious fidelity to the Marxist-Leninist method of understanding the spirit of the time and the central aspect which characterizes it . . . .

Faced with the attempts to revise the (1936) Anglo-Egyptian treaty, the Marxist organizations of Egypt have called for its abolition. Faced with roundabout and underhand attempts to co-operate with the forces of imperialism, the Egyptian Communists have called for the rejection of common defence agreements and the removal of all foreign military bases. Faced with organic and time-honoured links with the imperialist West, the Egyptian Communists have called for political, cultural and economic liberation from imperialism and have demanded the nationalization of both foreign and local monopolies. Faced with the traditional parties' slavish subjection to the Palace, the Egyptian Communists have called for a republic. Faced with total neglect of the problems of the *fellahin,* the Egyptian Communists have called for the elimination of feudalism, agrarian reform and a ceiling on land ownership. Faced with economic dependence on the imperialist West, the Egyptian Communists have called for nationalization of all foreign monopolies. Faced with the reactionary ideas and institutions which degrade and enslave women, debarring one half of our people from any conscious participation in the development of the country, the Egyptian Communists have called for equal rights for women. Faced with the oppression of the people, restriction of its political and trade union rights, and repression and division of the working class, the Egyptian Communists have called for complete political freedom, the right to form trade unions and to organize a united trade union movement, increased wages and shorter working hours, improved services and social benefits, free schooling and the creation of a General Union of Egyptian Workers, as outlined by the Preparatory Committee of the 1945 Trade Union Congress. Faced with the plots of the leadership of the reactionary parties and their attempts to link up first with the British and then with the Americans, the Egyptian Communists have demonstrated their commitment to peace by calling for the creation of a national army independent of all imperialist forces, supportive of the people's cause and alert to the dangers of adventurism and war. Faced with the isolation the imperialists sought to impose on our country through the feudal authority of the monarchy, the Egyptian Communists have called for joint struggle with all peoples opposed to imperialism and for friendship and co-operation with the socialist countries. Faced with attempts by reactionaries to strip Egypt's denunciation of the 1936 treaty of its meaning, the Egyptian Communists called for armed struggle and joined up with the partisans who were fighting on the banks of the canal.

During the years in which the national struggle for liberation intensified, the Egyptian Communists called for unity amongst all national forces. During the period between the Suez war and July 1961, the Egyptian Communists, many of whom had been sent to the camps, called for nationalization of all foreign and local monopolies and constantly stressed the importance of democracy as a way of overcoming social backwardness. The Egyptian Communists have insisted that a common destiny unites all peoples in the ardent struggle against world imperialism; they have always been concerned to link the national content of the Arab nationalitarian cause, as a movement opposed to imperialism, with its class content as a progressive movement of the mass of working people, a movement which aims to overcome social backwardness . . . .

Today the Egyptian Communists are firmly committed to the unity of all socialist forces and to the creation of a revolutionary vanguard party which will bring together all those who are dedicated to the socialist cause. Throughout, the Egyptian Communists have advocated socialism and have made it clear that our people do not struggle just to liberate themselves from the oppression of foreign despotism but also for a better life, in keeping with human dignity . . . .

It follows that the main characteristics of the vanguard party, the United Socialist Party, are as follows:
(1) the Party will draw its inspiration from the sociological and scientific ideology (Chapter 6 of the 'Charter'); (a) there is only one scientific socialism; (b) the application of socialist principles is determined by the patriotic and national reality of our country, by its specific historical characteristics and traditions; (c) the way it applies its principles in our country will be determined by respect for revolutionary Islamic and religious values . . . .

The fact that the Egyptian Communist Party is winding up its independent organization does not mean that its militants are going to withdraw from political activity or retreat into passivity. This decision by the Egyptian Communists is no temporary tactical manoeuvre to gain time, but on the contrary, a step towards the strategic goal — the victory of socialism. It is based on a desire to give priority to considerations of unity between all socialist forces, so that a new party committed to social revolution can arise in the country. The Egyptian Communists are not dissolving their independent party organization simply so that certain individuals can gain high office. We are not going to put all our sacrifices, our fallen heroes and the years of deprivation we spent in the camps onto the negotiating table. The sacrifices we made were made too generously for us even to consider turning them into bargaining counters in some compromise; we offered them humbly, as gifts to our noble people, to their history and their revolutionary tradition, and as a contribution towards a better tomorrow. We say to all our socialist comrades 'The Egyptian Communists, with their long experience of hardship, raise no obstacles to unity. Now it is up to you . . . .'

FUAD MURSI
(1925, Egypt)

Fuad Mursi studied law and political economy at the Universities of Cairo and Paris, where he took his PhD in 1949. He was appointed Professor of Political Economy at the Alexandria University Law Faculty (1950-1959), played a major role in the Communist movement and was one of the leaders of the Egyptian Communist Party from its unification to its self-dissolution (1958-1965). After the great repression, he was appointed President of the Administrative Council of the 'Al-Nasr' national car manufacturing company (1966-68) and a member of the National Council. He served as Minister of Supply from 1970 to 1972 and then as Economic Adviser to the Government of Kuwait. His theoretical and political work in Egypt has continued to develop in recent years.

**   *Main works*: Financial Relations between Egypt and Great Britain since 1939; The Political Economy of Money (*Iqtisadiyyat al-nuqoud*); Currencies and Banks (*Al-nuqoud wal-bunouk*); International Economic Relations (*Al-Alaqat al-iqtisadiyyah al-dawliyyah*); Money and Banks in the Arab Countries (*Al-nuqoud wal-bunouk fil-bilad al-arabiyyah*).**

**   In 1966, Mursi published an important series of theoretical studies, notably in the journal *Al-Taliah*, edited by Lutfi al-Kholi. He dealt at length with the future of Marxism in the context of the fusion of all socialist forces within a single party, the Arab Socialist Union. The pages that follow are from the first of these studies, in which Mursi claims recognition for an embattled but legal Egyptian Marxism as the**

**main current of socialist thought in Egypt, and attacks the manoeu-
vrings of a ruling state capitalist class which has always opposed
revolutionary Marxism. The article was published shortly before the
dramatic events of June 1967.**

Specific Socialism and Scientific Socialism[13]

Scientific socialism constantly runs into attempts to revise it. Some of these
attempts are made by the enemies in order to undermine it, others are the
doing of its own supporters, who seek to incorporate into it alien ideas . . . .
The most skilful attempts to misdirect our socialism are based on the argument that since the forces of production in Egypt have not reached the level
required for the construction of socialism, we are not yet ready for a
socialist system.

In 1957, Wahib Mesihah expressed this view in a little book entitled
Economic Development in the Shadow of Capitalism. He criticizes the
call for socialism issued by the country's leaders and claimed that: 'We will
believe in socialism when we have a powerful productive apparatus capable
of flooding the country with goods, for we will then be faced with too low a
level of consumption, restricting the outlets for our products.'

The implication is that the leaders of the revolution should not have
attempted the passage to socialism in 1961; that they should have ignored
the acute class struggle, the damage the big capitalists were doing to our
economic development, the pressing need for change in the national
economy and the steady fall in the standard of living of the working people,
simply because 'production had not yet reached its peak'.

It was the Egyptian capitalists, the people Mesihah was speaking for,
who estimated that the plan adopted to double the national income in ten
years was beyond the real capacity of the economy and that, even if it were
successfully implemented, it would be at the expense of the profits they
intended to keep for themselves. That is why they were so violently opposed
to the 1959 law setting a ceiling on income and waged such a determined
campaign against the country's economic development, hiding behind the
slogan 'Don't sacrifice this generation for the sake of those to come'. Once
the transition to socialism had been instituted, they immediately refor-
mulated this capitalist slogan as a socialist slogan, so as to reduce the
energy with which the leaders of the revolution pursued the transformation
of society. When Yahia al-Gamal speaks of Arab socialism, he hurriedly
adds that he 'refuses to consider the individual as a being whose existence is
devoid of meaning, and cannot accept that the individual and individual
liberties should be totally sacrificed under the pretext that the individual
and individual liberties are not fundamental values, that only social values
can be fundamental . . . .'

Such responses are to be expected. What is more surprising is that these
capitalist arguments often find a ready response from socialists. Indeed, it is

sometimes suggested that since our productive forces are still under-developed and our relations of production remain immature, our socialism must have been imposed upon us from above and cannot have sprung from the working classes themselves.

The theory in question is exposed very lucidly in certain writings of Mus-tapha Tiba, a central tenet of whose work is the idea that our epoch is 'characterized by the increased importance of consciousness, by man's definitive liberation from the laws of social determinism, and his increasing ability to plan his own future and decide his own fate untramelled by the workings of social laws'. Man has in fact supposedly become able to shape these laws in a way which furthers not only his own interests but also those of humanity as a whole.

This is an admirable and attractive vision, but it is, unfortunately, Uto-pian and quite unscientific. It rests on two ideas which run counter to a scientific interpretation of history: firstly, the idea that our epoch is charac-terized by the growing importance of man's consciousness and his increas-ing liberation from the laws of social determinism; secondly, the notion that in our era man has become capable of freeing himself from social laws.

In other words, the author is saying that nowadays social evolution is shaped by the development of subjective awareness rather than by objective laws. Such a thesis does not hold water even in the most advanced socialist countries, where giant strides towards socialism have been taken and man's extraordinary powers have been amply demonstrated by the conquest of nature and of space.

It should be recalled that:

(1) Freedom does not mean the abolition of objective necessity: it consists on the contrary in the discovery and understanding of the laws which regu-late necessity, which will always be with us.

(2) Man can liberate himself from the laws which regulate society only to the extent that he has come to know them through a process of discovery. Freedom thus does not consist in abolishing the laws which regulate society or distancing oneself from them. It consists, on the contrary, in coming to grips with them.

(3) It is not scientific to invite man to 'cease being the slave of social laws'. What we seek is to eliminate the workings of certain laws and bring others into play. We wish to free ourselves from capitalist social laws but to submit to the social laws of socialism.

The various attempts to have scientific socialism rejected often involve the idea of replacing it with a socialism endowed with specific national characteristics — an intermediate and peculiarly Arab socialism.

Hussain Fawzi al-Naggar argues that 'Arab socialism is a new kind of socialist thought; it rejects historical materialism and is based on a new interpretation of history'.

Salah Mekheimar writes: 'When we look at the Charter and try to draw out the elements of our scientific theory of [social] evolution and of our attitudes towards absolute determinism and social relativism, we are immediately forced to choose between determinism and relativism, between a linear and multilinear causality which are in fact constantly interacting and influencing each other.'

Rifat al-Mahgoub writes: 'The implementation of Arab socialism implies recognition of two premises which are not accepted here: recognition of the fact that socialist thought leads to a single theory, or, given the multiplicity of socialist theories, recognition of the fact that socialism as applied in Egypt is the application of a specific pre-existing socialist theory.'

Toeimah al-Garf writes: 'We fundamentally reject Marxism, because it is an essentially materialist theory.'

Abd al-Moghni Said argues that 'the road to an intensely desired unity cannot be the unification of doctrinal terminology geared to impose a rigid way of thinking on all socialists.'

All these authors are expressing their wish to differentiate themselves from Marxism or even their hostility to Communism. And when Rifat al-Maghoub writes: 'the course we have chosen is the opposite of Communism, which consists in dispossesing the wealthy, whereas we are only concerned to provide wealth for those who have nothing'; it is immediately apparent that his hostility to Communism has led him, without his realizing, to mutilate and distort our experience. Surely we have already proceeded with the expropriation of many of the wealthy, as well as providing land for many of those who had nothing. In any case, how could the destitute be provided with assets if not by dispossession of the rich?

To call for one specific kind of socialism is thus, in practice, to refuse to recognize the fact that there is only one socialism, which takes different forms . . . .

The fact that there is only one socialism in no way means that socialist experiences are of only one kind or are all alike. Each socialist experience takes place under objectively different conditions. Each people, in carrying out its socialist revolution, adds something new to history and contributes to the development of the theory. There never has been and never will be a revolution which does not change as it goes along and which proceeds strictly according to a pre-determined plan. Socialism may be indivisible, but its implementation is subject to the national conditions of the countries concerned, in our case the Arab countries with their particular historical characteristics, their revolutionary traditions and their respect for the revolutionary and religious values of Islam. Nothing prevents someone being both a socialist militant and one of the faithful.

Let us take just one example. The dictatorship of the proletariat is well known to be one of the fundamental principles of Marxism. Nonetheless, Marxists today are revising this principle, not in order to abolish it but so as to develop it and work out what is the most suitable form it can take in the modern world. Most Marxist thinkers of today have reached the important conclusion that there can be a variety of transitional stages on the way to socialism, and diverse forms of people's power. Indeed, history shows that the socialist revolution can develop either from a democratic revolution or from a struggle against fascism or from a national liberation movement.

At present, an absolutely new socialist experience is underway. After a victorious national struggle for national liberation, several countries which have recently won their independence have embarked on the transition from national revolution to socialism, by nationalizing such bastions of foreign capital as the banks, the insurance companies, foreign trade, transport and industry. They have not established the dictatorship of the proletariat but have opted instead for various forms of popular power.

I believe the objective bases for this new historical venture are as follows:

Firstly, this new possibility rests on broad social alliances, incorporating classes other than the working class; classes which, in today's world, are capable of assimilating the ideas of scientific socialism. Power thus rests upon a wider base made up of several classes.

Secondly, this new historical opportunity is based on the fact that the revolutionary class alliance exercises coercion at a lower level and against a narrower range of other social classes. Democracy is thus open to a broader range of social groups.

Thirdly, the possibility is based on a public sector which takes a socialist or semi-socialist form according to the nature of the regime. But this sector constitutes the most advanced model of economic development. It plays a leading role in economic growth and begins by organizing the petty production sector, which is the majority sector, striving to establish an increase in the productivity of labour higher than the increase in the real income of the workers. This is essential if the society is not to eat up its capital and destroy the sources of future accumulation and increased production . . . .

There remains one last question which cannot be avoided: why has our country witnessed such frequent and varied attempts to modify scientific socialism? The underlying causes of these deviationist tendencies are to be found in the relative backwardness of our forces of production, the high incidence of low-income petty production in our towns and countryside, and in the fact that our society is made up mainly of peasants. Socialism thus appears to many people as an ingathering of the poor, whose material and spiritual resources are so limited that no one can be allowed to own more than anyone else; a regime of austerity is supposedly thus made inevitable by the very low level of consumption. Such a social landscape is fertile ground for anarchist and Utopian socialist ideas. It spawns a mistrust of all authority, even that exercised by the people, and is responsible for the impossibility of forming an organization with a proper structure and foundation, and for the tendency of organizations to degenerate into talking shops. It leads to the demand for absolute equality, even though equality means equal opportunities for all, not equal shares, and to the propagation of ideas favourable to the extension of small scale land ownership and the continuation of petty production, which is by its very nature underdeveloped . . . .

These approaches underestimate our economy's tendency to move spontaneously towards capitalism. The Kamish events and those that followed have surely shown how strong the tendency for the peasantry to fall into opposing rich and poor groups has become, and how easy it is for capitalist forms of agriculture to evolve.

Under such conditions, the intellectuals appear as the most important representatives of petty capitalism in the towns and countryside. Although many of them have sincerely embraced the principles of scientific socialism, there is no shortage of casuists who adopt reformist positions for fear of abandoning capitalism. They make no effort to transcend the limits of the national revolution or the peasant movement and they camouflage their reformism and the exhaustion of their revolutionary drive with resounding but empty phrases. Such apathy is contagious and even contaminates the ranks of the workers themselves . . . .

But what gives the ideology of petty capitalism such unaccustomed vigour are the conditions peculiar to our own country, notably:

(1) The inadequate development of class and political consciousness amongst the masses, and especially amongst the working class, so that socialism sometimes appears not as a clearly understood historical necessity but as a noble transition inspired by considerations of equity.

(2) The propagation of socialist ideas is, we repeat, due to the conversion to socialism of the nationalist leaders when already in power. The defence of socialism is thus seen as something which comes from above, imposed by leaders and administrators.

(3) The diversity of forces committed to scientific socialism, and the multiplicity of their ideological background, political traditions and social origins.

One last word. There are no sacred rites or established formulae for converting men to socialism. It is not necessary for people to adopt Marxism or to endorse proletarian class struggle for them to be socialists. It is possible for the most fervent capitalist to become a socialist if he drops his capitalist fictions and comes round, even slowly, to a socialist viewpoint. For somebody to become truly socialist, he must fulfil only one pre-condition: that he link his life to the life of the people, trustingly and honestly. That is a good enough start; the rest will follow, naturally and simply, as time goes by.

KAMAL JUMBLATT
(1917-1977, Lebanon)

A Lebanese statesman and writer, Jumblatt was born into one of the great Druze families. After studying literature and philosophy at the Sorbonne, he went in for law at the Saint Joseph University in Beirut. He worked as a barrister, was elected to parliament in 1943 and founded the Progressive Socialist Party in 1949. In the course of his career he held several ministerial portfolios — national economy, agriculture,

education and public works — and led the struggle of the Lebanese political forces committed to the Arab national movement and opposed to the isolationist policies of Camille Chamoun.

Jumblatt's political doctrine cast socialism as the best means of promoting the most complete expression of individuality. A deep and mystical faith was an integral element of his approach. A talented writer and a popular orator, Jumblatt rapidly emerged as the moderator of the Lebanese national movement and for several years presided over the forces supportive of the Palestinian resistance. During the civil war which ravaged Lebanon in the late 1970s, when foreign troops moved into both the south of the country and Beirut, he was assassinated by those who saw him as the apostle of a united, reconciled Arab Lebanon.

Main works: *Haqiqat al-thawra al Lubnaniyyah* (The Real Lebanese Revolution); *Fi ma yata adda al-harf* (Beyond Words); *Thawra fi alam al-insan* (Revolution in the World of Man); *Fi ma yata adda al-marksiyyah* (Beyond Marxism).

Why Am I a Socialist? [14]

Because I love justice, fraternity and freedom. Because I feel that if I am fair to others, I am being fair to myself and if I am unfair to others, I am unfair to myself. Because I seek accommodation with everybody and all-encompassing agreement, like a musical phrase which is only complete if all the different constituent sounds are balanced and accommodate each other. Similarly agreement and harmony must reign between people on the one hand and the rights that they have by law and by natural justice on the other. That is what we mean when we speak of justice.

I am a socialist because I believe that work with no capital is not fulfilling and that work — the gateway to all natural forces and to the capacities of the individual, which are themselves one of those natural forces — is essential to capital. Capital remains a potential which cannot be realized unless it is transformed into work. Work cannot be distinguished from capital, from any capital whatsoever, for without capital there can be no work, since work is itself the realization of capital, of unused productive capacity or potential. It is class attitudes, both on the part of the workers and on the part of employers, which have separated capital and labour and established a distinction between them. But a man's thoughts, his body, the money he earns through his work are inseparable from the thoughts, body and wages of others, since they all exist as part of capital's potential.

The goal of the Socialist Progressive Party is not to exacerbate class attitudes, nor to adopt them as a method or an object, but rather to eliminate class affiliation by the way we formulate our Constitution.

The historical struggle between the classes, which has so exhausted the most vigorous forces and their potential and has dissipated so much human effort in differences and constant internecine strife, must be overcome. These efforts, these forces, these potentials must change and work together to understand and master the secrets and nature of the soul, and thus complete the course of evolution and fulfil mankind. That can only happen if we manage to forge individuals and communities who are united in a stable society which is conscious of its own destiny and based on love and reconciliation, that is to say on the power of comprehensive evolution.

I am a socialist because I believe that evil, all evil, both in the Communist system and under what is called individualistic capitalism, stems from the naive separation between capital and labour, a separation which ensures the primacy of one social group over another in both those systems.

I am a socialist because I believe in the need for synthesis, agreement and unity between labour and capital, two elements which cannot be separated naturally or spontaneously.

I am a socialist because I believe that socialism is a faith which must become entrenched in men's hearts before it can be implemented in systems and institutions.

ABDALLAH LAROUI
(1933, Morocco)

A historian and political theoretician, Laroui was born to a great Moroccan family. He studied in Paris, participated actively in the Moroccan national movement, notably alongside Ben Barka when the National Union of Popular Forces was established, then continued his researches during a long stay in Egypt. After a period as visiting professor at the University of California, he took up his present post as Professor of History in the Faculty of Arts of the Muhammad V University in Rabat, and concentrated his efforts on analysing the Arab ideology and the Moroccan and Maghribi national movement.

Main works: **The Contemporary Arab Ideology; A History of the Maghrib; The Crisis of the Arab Intellectuals.**

In the text below, Laroui retraces Marxism's Odyssey through the contemporary Arab world.

Objective Marxism[15]

. . . Could Marxism thus be the logical basis for the Arab ideology, in other words the only possible systemization of all its presuppositions? It may be so; but what Marxism are we talking about? . . .

Economics

As we have shown, it was through economics that Marxism was first introduced into Arab thought. This origin was to have a profound influence on the form Marxism took in the Arab world.

The first question we must face is that of the origin of capitalism, a question which is essential for the Arab ideology and which demands an answer that owes nothing to Weberian or racist analyses. Marxism provides two answers, both referring to effects as well as to causes: the pillage of the Orient by war and unequal exchange, and more fundamentally, the disruption of old agrarian structures by a steadily developing monetary economy . . . . The important thing is to grasp that there is a certain way of reading Marx, which is by no means arbitrary and indeed has some title to our attention. It is a way perfectly suited to the problem we constantly face, since it accounts for the differences between East and West whilst preserving their essential unity by relating their divergent evolution to a combination of fortuitous causes; at the same time it stresses the necessity of the process as a whole: neither the race nor the religion of the less advanced peoples is brought into the explanation . . . .

Next, we must have a theory of capitalist growth . . . . Determinism in any form, that of Comte or de Toqueville for instance, is certainly welcome in the Arab world,[16] but none is as all embracing as that attributed to Marx. Determinism is welcome because it traces back a differentiation which over time has become almost irreducible, to a minimal and, above all, fortuitous divergence. Let us go back to the beginning, and everything falls into place: science, the novel, painting, politics, local administration, even hygiene, manners and taste. All this no longer requires us to imagine a succession of creative acts, a fantastic series of strokes of genuis; it is no longer essential for the peasant to be hardworking and ingenious, the merchant a brilliant businessman, the bourgeois an empire-builder, the navigator adventurous, the emigrant a farsighted dreamer, the publicist brave, the poet a visionary and the philosopher encyclopaedic in his wisdom before we can hope to get going. They all become the fruits of a single seed. We no longer need to compare the two histories sector by sector, only to be brought low at every turn by the wealth of the West. We can concentrate on that one crossroads, where, purely by chance, the West headed off in one direction and found itself on a broad well-paved concourse, while the Arab East took the other path and lost itself in the wilderness. In such a Marxism, the Arab ideology finds the wherewithal to fight back against the visions of a Claudel, who sees God setting stars to guide the navigators towards their destiny, or of a Schumpeter, who endows the capitalist leaders with an ever-alert spirit of innovation, or even of that history of philosophy which casts each system as a challenge to God.

Finally, there is the question of how we are to heal ourselves. Two key decisions sum it all up: nationalization of foreign trade and agrarian reform, the two preconditions for industrialization. This therapeutic strategy is a quintessence of the history of capitalism in its simplest form, as exemplified by France. Previous visions, both clerical and liberal, sank into the most banal eclecticism, be it Qasir Amin's feminism or political education as prescribed by Muhammad Abduh and Taha Hussain, or community and rural development as echoed in Allal al-Fasi's 'Auto-critique' (in which he goes so far as to propose the outline of a model village), or mobilization of youth, or whatever. These fragmentary solutions neither produced convincing results, nor helped us towards a correct appreciation of the weak points of our society. In contrast, a Marxist analysis has no difficulty in providing us with an Archimedes' fulcrum: other reforms fit in neatly around our basic economic decisions, forming a complete system. Mobilization of the countryside makes sense in the context of agrarian reform, just as adult literacy complements the drive for industrialization. . . .

But what readers are looking for is a practical guide, not an impeccable theoretical analysis. Even Rostow forces his reders to go back to the sources which he himself has drawn on so extensively, albeit without acknowledgement.

It is worth remembering that many of our national planners were trained at Cambridge or Berkeley. In forming autochthonous liberal thought, Western technocracy gives it a common language with the Marxist intelligentsia, which naturally immediately proves its superiority by a more complete systemization. A few years on, and the West is appalled by the rapid progress of a Marxist influence which it has itself, quite unconsciously, helped to develop.

Sociology . . . .

The notion of class is, at first, grasped in terms of the traditional framework, and easily takes on the ethical content of a struggle for purity and honesty. The traditional activism of Islam gives politics that harsh tone which ultimately stems from the historical extraneity of the groups mentioned earlier. Reformism, once religious and now political, is always moralistic and violently opposed to the corrupt classes. No doctrinal pacifism can justifiably preach patience or tolerance: only force overcomes criticism.[17]

In its first days, a national state can deny that the existence of class is relevant to the present or future, but it cannot apply the same logic to the past. The petty bourgeoisie has struggled too long against feudalism and the liberal bourgeoisie to forgive and forget. Indeed, old resentments will sometimes be artificially revived to justify the regime's more controversial measures, just as the liberal state would sometimes use demagogy to fan old hatreds against the local bourgeoisie, in an effort to hide its own class character.

Thus, even when class no longer figures in the political arsenal, it is used as a way of elucidating our cultural history. It then loses its ethical halo and becomes one element in the general movement of the whole society towards positivism. Since the eclecticism and subjectivism of the classical critiques are no longer helpful, the idea of class is used as a first step towards an objective appraisal, allowing us to introduce a little order in a fairly tangled history. The concept thus has few serious detractors. For instance the book *On Egyptian Culture*,[18] which remains the only substantial essay in which the idea of class is used to appraise contemporary literary work in Egypt, has still not been refuted in any methodical way, despite its obvious weaknesses and the fact that it is more programmatic than analytical in its approach. What was so welcome was its systematic and objective methodology, breaking with forty years of literary exhibitionism. Only foreigners have been sarcastic about its naive dogmatism, which by explaining everything in terms of a single cause ends up by explaining nothing. For the Arabs, on the contrary, it struck an original chord.

This use of the concept of class in cultural criticism is, however, too unilateral, indeed it is ideological, but it is nonetheless not wholly inadequate as some would claim. As we have already seen, class analyses — including this one — were justified not directly in terms of the structure of Arab society, but indirectly, in terms of the structure of Western society, since the Arabs still constantly refer to a Western model in all their thoughts and deeds. Our writers may subjectively reject class differentiation or pretend not to see it poking out of the surface of reality — which is possibly justifiable, up to a point — but they nonetheless employ concepts which can be shown to incorporate a vision of the West which undoubtedly does have a class signification. Such significations are thus present in all Arab thought, albeit mediated in various ways. Naturally, the pedagogic requirements of political struggle and action and of the Marxism we are describing are incompatible with such mediations, which are thus necessarily dispensed with.

Class analysis, as a scientific endeavour, is thus perfectly justified by the historical reality and is in no way devalued by the simple polemical form it takes in the action of a liberal national state in its early stages.

Finally, *on the ideological level*, the Marxism which can meet the logical demands of Arab thought is not one Western philosophical system amongst others; it serves as a systematization of systems . . . .

Marxism offers a simplified and unitary vision of Western history: classical philosophy culminates and is fulfilled in Hegel, as the latter is in Marx. Modern times can be summed up in three dates: 1688, 1789 and 1848, and in one concept: the bourgeois revolution. Economic history from the Crusades and the enclosures up to the period of British commercial hegemony in the 19th Century is encapsulated by the development of the capitalist system. All these events, and other partial or subsidiary manifestations can then be reduced to a single cause. No Arab relives the thought of Descartes or Spinoza in the way that certain Westerners can relive it. Instinctively, the Descartes the Arab grasps is the correctly labelled Descartes who fits neatly into the Hegelian-Marxist system. When one of us inadvertently finds himself wading through a modern philosophy without a guide, we lose the ability to think critically and have to fall back on merely literary forms of expression.

This need for a system, imposed by the primacy of action, becomes particularly apparent in the crisis of contemporary Arab philosophy. In our countries, either thinking is conceptual, in which case a commentary on Marx is eventually taken as a starting point, or the concept is ignored — as happens in the majority of cases — and falls into eclecticism.[19] In fact Marxism's role is in many ways reminiscent of the position of Aristotleianism in classical Arab thought.

Marxism as the summation of the West; that is what contemporary Arab thought has unceasingly been looking for during the last three quarters of a century. The moment technophilia dominates the national state, the choice is between Marxism and impotent eclecticism. The West can indulge in Bergsonism or phenomenology, but the Arab East can read with advantage only that which has been integrated into the Hegelian register.[20] When an Arab is a Bergsonian, he stops thinking about his own life, he thinks like a frontiersman, entirely turned towards the West.

In the past, the Arabs had their own way of reading Aristotle, a way which suited them and was in many respects unlike the Greek reading. Today, their situation calls for a particular reading of Marx, and although it has not yet been systematized and is still more of a possibility than a reality, such a reading can already be demarcated from other readings current in the West or adopted individually by Arab intellectuals.

How are we to qualify and judge this Marxism we have sketched so roughly? It is an objective Marxism, if by that term is meant that it appears as a necessary consequence of ideologies already current in Arab society. It is reduced to a positivist level, as we have shown; as a way of approaching economics, sociology and the history of ideologies, it presents no essential methodological difference from the positivism of Comte or Spencer. The Arab understanding prefers it to those others simply because it offers a more coherent system which is more critical of the bourgeois West.

Because of these two characteristics, this Marxism is in part effective and in part still hypothetical: effective because it emerges here and there in the practices of the state and in individual positions; hypothetical because it often appears under a borrowed name, as Cartesianism, Philosophy of the Enlightenment or Darwinism. These guiding ideologies are merely the fragments of systems and their unity and justification is to be found only in Marxism reduced to its positivist level. That is why we say that the latter is still partly hypothetical; it is the invisible hearth in which are brought together all the ideologies in the light of which Arab society seeks to restructure itself. But hypothetical does not imply arbitrary.

To sum up, let us say that this Marxism inspires the majority of those who are building the national state, even if it is not officially endorsed.

According to some Westerners, the political defeats suffered by the Arab Communist parties are due to the mechanical application of over-crude concepts, the fruits of a negative and now thankfully revolved era of European Marxism.[21] But then these innovators cannot explain how a small number of Marxists, often in prison, can have such influence on the policies of their state, or how such insignificant groups can, in certain cases, exercise real cultural hegemony.

Once again, we are running into the duality described earlier . . . . The political failures of the Marxist parties certainly do not stem from any incomplete analysis of reality, but from the fact that society has not yet assimilated the experience of liberalism and technophilia — a fact which is determined by history itself rather than by any human intervention.

Thus the Arab consciousness, faced with the need for action, gives the same answer to both positivism and Marxism, an answer which seems paradoxical at first sight: yes to the system, no to the method.

ABD AL-FATTAH ISMAIL
(1939, South Yemen)

The general public knows little about the People's Republic of Yemen, which grew out of the old British Protectorate of Aden. Yet it is an important centre of political evolution in the Arab world, sitting as it does at the junction of Africa and the Indian Ocean.

Starting out as a worker in the BP refinery in Aden, Abd al-Fattah Ismail soon won himself a reputation as an efficient political and trade union organizer and repeatedly suffered the consequences.

When the first republic was established, he was appointed Minister of National Orientation and Union (with North Yemen) Affairs. He then led the struggle of the National Liberation Front against Qahtan al-Shabi's FLOSY, culminating in the creation of a socialist republic. He is now Secretary-General of the NLF and one of the five members of the ruling Executive Committee. The report below, published in 1970, examines the difficult equation between underdevelopment and the socialist revolution.

Underdevelopment and Socialist Revolution[22]

The first step is to unite the forces of the NLF around a common programme, so as to exclude any possible conflict and clear up the issues which have led to disagreement amongst the leading members of the Front at a time when they should have maintained their unity in order to carry out their own programme.

Secondly, we must take into account and draw in all the progressive groups outside the NLF, calling on them to work with the NLF party to mobilize all those who want social reform and agree with the ideas, principles and programme of the NLF.

The programme envisages the creation of legal government administrative bodies and active co-operation between the provincial administrations and the administration in the capital. It also recommends that all forces be mobilized to ensure that the administration that is set up is honest and progressive.

Later, it covers the armed forces and how to mobilize them in order to consolidate the revolution by means of a programme which demands greater loyalty on their part towards the administration and the party than towards the army's own programmes, or anybody else's.

Economic problems are also dealt with. The programme makes it plain that the national economy must liberate itself from domination by imperialist private businesses.

Peasant relations of production are discussed and a plan is envisaged to free the agricultural workers from personal domination by means of a land reform, and to free the economy of the towns from imperialist domination.

The NLF proposes to initiate a programme which will enable it to transfer control of the economy from capitalist to government hands.

The government's programme of social reform is geared to encourage the creation of student, worker and trade union federations within the new structure, so that these forces can defend and help the government and the country's progressive movement in their efforts to achieve the goals the party has set itself.

Concerning culture and the choice of education system, a very clear plan has been drawn up to establish a new system free of bourgeois influences and the forms of education which prevailed in the past. We seek to create a new progressive education system which will serve as the basis for the democratic and social thought of new generations.

The Arabian Peninsula and the Arabian Gulf have been subjected to centuries of domination, during which the imperialists appropriated ever-increasing quantities of their resources and wealth. The emergence of a new, progressive and democratic regime in the southern part [of the Peninsula] represents a threat to the imperialists, who fear the possible expansion of the revolution and the growth of a democratic group which would expel them and cut off their flow of profits from the Arabian Peninsula.

The new Saudi-North American machinations aimed against the new South Yemini regime are part of a plan to crush all progressive regimes in the Arabian Peninsula and in all the Arab countries. The emergence of a new and progressive regime in South Yemen, the result of armed struggle against the British, has brought social change to the Arabian Gulf and has encouraged a revival of all the progressive parties and elements in the region. Unity amongst the progressive forces has been established and the same model of struggle against the British has now been adopted throughout the Gulf. One example is the Dhofar Front, which regroups other Gulf forces and fronts struggling for the liberation of the region.

Our foreign policy is a faithful reflection of our domestic policy, and we declare ourselves to be an integral part of the progressive revolution in the entire Arab world, which is in turn an integral part of the tricontinental revolution which will free our peoples from imperialist domination and institute a democratic and socialist system.

On the domestic level, we are struggling against capitalism and imperialism in order to realize a social reform based on the same principles which most progressive regimes in the world have used to that end, and in order to establish a democratic socialist regime in the southern part of Yemen.

All this means that we are enemies of imperialism and capitalism and friends of all the progressive parties and regimes of the three continents. That is why we have opted for a socialist and democratic form of government on the same lines as other socialist governments in the world.

As an integral part of the Arab progressive movement, our aim is to free the Arabian Gulf from the sheiks and kings, to liberate it and help the Palestinians win back their country. We are part of the most progressive movement in the world. Our first goal is to unite South and North Yemen under a single socialist and democratic structure.

We have the same programme and affiliation regarding the rest of the world as all other democratic and socialist parties struggling against capitalism and imperialism. The tricontinental movement is an example of the struggle between progressive and imperialist capitalist regimes. We too are a small example of that struggle.

We are opposed to apartheid and racial segregation in any part of the world and hold that equality between nations must prevail. We are also opposed to nuclear weapons and their proliferation. We believe that the progressive governments' only friends are those of the socialist camp; but the existing division between the latter makes it difficult for them to help progressive regimes and greatly benefits the imperialists. Furthermore, it enables the imperialists to attack the smaller progressive countries with impunity. We sincerely believe that only a united socialist system can break imperialist domination of the world. The Middle East's problems are the result of conflict between progressive regimes, and of imperialist domination over the Arab world.

Zionism is the instrument used by imperialism to attack the Arab world. The Israeli government is imperialism's means of ensuring domination over the resources of the Arabian Peninsula. Palestine is an Arab country which belongs to the Palestinians, and as long as the latter are denied access to their home, there will be no peace. The United Nations resolution is limited to the post-5 June events but makes no mention of what happened before. Without a resolution which tackles the problem at its source by enabling the Palestinians to return home, there can be no peaceful solution and no settlement.

We believe that the liberation of Palestine and of the recently occupied territories will only be achieved by supporting the just war in Palestine and in all occupied Arab lands. The support of all progressive regimes for this struggle is the only way to resolve the problem which has been a major concern of the United Nations ever since the state of Israel was created in

1948. The struggle in Palestine is part of the very same struggle which is being waged in Vietnam, Korea, South Africa and throughout the world.

The only way to achieve peace in the Middle East and to resolve the Palestinian problem is to support the armed struggle of the Palestinian people in the occupied territories.

ABD AL-KHALEQ MAHGOUB
(1924-1971, Sudan)

General Secretary of the Sudanese Communist Party, for which he won wide recognition within the national movement in Sudan, Egypt and throughout the Arab world, Mahgoub received his grounding in Cairo during the critical 1940-46 period. He rapidly emerged as a creative force, a mediator, and a lucid and perspicacious statesman who greatly influenced the policy of a democratic national front based on the autonomous existence of a powerful Marxist party.

The May 1969 revolution marked the consecration of this policy: four ministers represented the Marxist wing within the Numeiri government. In Spring 1970, the counter-revolutionary rebellion of the traditionalist Mahdist sect was curbed, thanks to the decisive joint action of the army and the popular masses. Nonetheless, the government decided to expel A.K. Mahgoub, who found asylum in Cairo and a good friend in President Nasser.

On 24 July 1971 a progressive military *coup d'etat* attempted to overthrow General Numeiri's regime but two days later, the direct intervention of several Arab states enabled the deposed head of state to regain power. A massive witch hunt against the Sudanese Communist Party was then initiated. Arrested on 27 July, hastily dragged before a mock tribunal in the middle of the desert and condemned to death. Abd al-Khaleq Mahgoub, the General Secretary of the party was executed a few hours later at dawn, on the 28 July 1971, along with the General Secretary of the Trade Union Federation, Shafai Ahmad al-Sheikh, and the Minister for Southern Affairs, Joseph Garang.

Mahgoub's writings were mainly published in the party journals, *Al-Maidan* and *Akhbar al-Usbu*. The following two texts illustrate the life and death of the man who created and led the largest Communist party in the Arab world. The first text defines the party's general line in 1969. The second, a report to the February 1970 Consultative Conference of Party Cadres, establishes the Communists' position towards the army and the putschist temptation.

For a New Democracy in Sudan[23]

The revolutionary movement of 25 May 1969 confirms that despite the counter-revolutionary activity and constant pressure exercized by neo-colonialism against the national liberation movement, the balance of forces in the world during the 1960s has not shifted in imperialism's favour. It is possible for any particular country to break through imperialist encirclement and the barrier of counter-revolution. Although the counter-revolution succeeded in our country in 1965, the popular movement skilfully operated a tactical withdrawal, whilst retaining most of its key functions in the mass organizations. This tactic enabled it to regroup, to defend democratic liberties, and to condemn both economic backwardness and attempts to push the country towards capitalism.

The popular movement waged an unrelenting struggle from October 1965 onwards, right up to 25 May this year, when a group of patriots and progressive officers, expressing the aspirations of the people, overthrew the reactionary and counter-revolutionary regime and handed power over to the National Democratic Front. The advent of the new government has given the revolutionary movement a new impetus, allowing it to close ranks and propose new solutions to the problems the country has suffered from for centuries — solutions oriented towards non-capitalist development. From within the revolutionary movement, there crystallized a precise programme of development and modification of the state apparatus, a new approach to the national question in southern Sudan and a strategy for radical change in the education system.

There are parallels between the events of 1964 and 1969, but there is also an important difference. In October 1964, the unarmed popular masses succeeded, thanks to the sheer scale of their movement, in overthrowing the military dictatorship of the reactionary forces. But there was then no alliance with the armed forces of the country, who could have protected and defended the people's authority. What has happened now is the opposite: the popular movement, despite a certain lack of unity, has managed to exercise considerable influence on the political situation in the country. The power of the reactionary forces has been broken and authority now rests with the progressive military and the national democratic forces.

Thus the popular masses now have an opportunity to broaden the movement and unite it under the aegis of a democratic government. In my opinion, the essential development problem facing our country at the moment is the organization of a National Democratic Front in which the revolutionary elements will play a clearly defined role by intensifying the country's political life and increasing mass support the partisans of progress and the new regime. It is important that this front should propose a democratic solution to the problems of the South, with a view to forming a solid union between the national groups in the South and the democratic forces in the North.

I estimate that at the present stage the Communist Party must play a decisive role in the political life of our country. It is at the moment the only organized revolutionary force. The other organized force is constituted by reactionary elements who lack neither the means nor the opportunity to act. It is clear that should the latter succeed in blocking the activities of the Communist Party and its organizations, or in reducing its direct contact with the masses, the balance of power would shift in their favour. Naturally, the reactionaries will seek to bring about such a situation; they fully realize that the Communist Party is now in a position to act effectively amongst the masses.

Another important problem, resolution of which was one of the objects of the October 1964 revolution, concerns the economic and social development of Sudan. In this domain any swings to the right or to the left are to be avoided. The path is clear, and a bitter struggle has already begun.

The old path, based on capitalist development, is no longer justifiable, either in economic or social terms. The old regime proved incapable of solving the serious problems faced by the country after independence had been won. That is why, as was announced in the first declaration of the new regime, the path of non-capitalist development is the only one which will lead our country towards peace and the pinnacles of the 20th Century. We follow this path with a realistic appreciation of our country's situation. We know that we are being held back by the centres of foreign influence in Sudan. In order to set out on the path of non-capitalist development, our country must above all free its economy from foreign influence and then take further relevant measures. We take into account the fact that the economy of our country has been under the influence of the Western economy for a long time, in fact ever since British imperialism established its domination here.

We are not opposed to economic and commercial co-operation with any country in the world, providing it is on a basis of equality and mutual advantage. We also understand that the many resources of our country will only be fully utilized if we opt for non-capitalist development. Our country will progress only if judicious use is made of these resources. We will now also be able to co-operate with the friendly socialist camp which can contribute substantially to the creation and development of the material infrastructure of the Sudanese economy. The material and moral support of the socialist camp is decisive if we are to create the conditions necessary for the stability of the new regime and for the development of the revolution, despite the efforts of neo-colonialism and organized counter-revolution.

The future of the Sudanese revolution, which is now going through the national democratic phase and preparing to enter a new phase, depends on the efforts of the Communist Party and of all the relevant reactionary forces to create a National Democratic Front.

The experience of our revolution shows that the formation of the National Democratic Front presents several particularities linked to the living conditions of our people. The most significant is that the front does not form an integrated and centralized whole, but juxtaposes classes and groups, each of which is differently structured according to the degree of consciousness and organization of each sector of the front in the country's various regions.

The new government formed on 25 May 1969 has declared its intent to extend the October 1964 revolution. It has given the National Democratic Front new opportunities to implement the major changes which are so indispensable to its unity and its ability to accomplish the tasks of the democratic revolution.

The Sudanese Communists Against Putschism[24]

The Communist Party bases on an economic and class analysis its appreciation of those social forces whose interest lies in the achievement of the national democratic revolution. It says, 'The forces which make up this front are the working masses, the agricultural workers, the revolutionary intellectuals and national capitalism; the leadership of these forces rests with the masses of the working class.'

Starting from this analysis, the armed forces can be said to figure in the composition of these [national] forces according to their class status and distribution amongst the various social categories.

There is the petty bourgeoisie (the majority of the officers), and there are the sons of peasants and the working class elements who make up the ranks. The armed forces thus cannot be taken as a new and distinct social category or class to be added to those class forces with an interest in the success of the democratic revolution in our country. In its struggle to ensure the success of the democratic revolution, the Communist Party bases itself on a class policy oriented towards the working class and peasant masses, and seeks to establish a permanent alliance between them. That is the core of the Communist Party's activity. The party's attitudes and activity, therefore, have a class basis, resting as they do upon the masses whose interest lies in the success of the national democratic revolution.

There is a misguided view according to which the national and democratic groups within the armed forces ought to occupy a vanguard position in the Communist Party's activity, simply because these groups are armed and are thus supposedly in a better position than others to settle the problem of power quickly and effectively. As I see it, such a view is both false and non-Marxist.

The democratic revolution is the revolution of agrarian reform, which can only achieve its logical goal by calling on the great mass of workers amongst the peasantry and mobilizing them for struggle in political, economic and intellectual domains.

The socialist revolution is the revolution of the majority of the working people; it is carried through on the strength of their increased class consciousness, their support and their effective participation at the highest levels of revolutionary activity.

The moment the misguided view in question is systematized, it becomes a full-blown putschist theory, which demands that the Communist Party renounce its work amongst the masses and the difficult task of raising their level of consciousness, organizing them and training them in the course of practical and ideological confrontations. Instead, the party should supposedly seek to organize a 'progressive putsch'.

Let us pose the question more broadly and more frankly, in terms of the relation between armed struggle and popular struggle. We Communists reject the theory that a minority should seize power in order to hand it over subsequently to the masses. As I see it, this rejection is a basic ideological premiss of Communism, an integral part of the way Communists conceive of the revolution. Indeed Communism as a science has evolved in the course of a long struggle against precisely such a theory, in the context of the overall struggle against ideals alien to the working class movement . . . .

The mere seizure of power by means of minority action, be it civil or military, without taking into account the role of the masses, without the factors which lead to the maturation of a revolutionary crisis being present, and without considering the role of the working class in the state concerned is indicative of a non-Communist ideology, and in the case of the underdeveloped countries, of a petty bourgeois ideology . . . .

Our way of seeing things is expressed in a report submitted to the Central Committee in March 1969, entitled 'Towards an improvement of leadership work one year after the Congress'. Here it is stated that: 'The putschist tactic, as an alternative to mass action, represents in the last analysis the interests of the bourgeoisie and petty bourgeoisie within the forces of the National Democratic Front'. When I wrote that, I meant to indicate that we must reject any tactic which neglects work amongst the masses, retreats before these difficulties, renounces the Communist conception of the revolution as the ultimate form of mass activity and fails to recognize the principle of the revolutionary crisis in which the overall situation is seen as the precondition and crucial factor of the revolution's success.

The putschist tactic is a non-Communist ideology. Such a tactic may appeal to bourgeois officers seeking to overcome the crisis of authority by pushing the country abruptly along the evolutionary path, or to democratic officers basing their actions on a petty-bourgeois ideology. In my opinion, the coherent ideological attitude of the Communists is not influenced by the particular form in which power is seized through armed struggle, be it an armed uprising of the formations organized by the Communist Party amongst the masses or armed groups operating from within the regular army.

What was once only an historical expectation has now become part of what is realizable through patient struggle to unite the forces of the revolutionary masses. Such a task implies, amongst other things, a contradiction with the national bourgeoisie — with every fraction of the national bourgeoisie. That is why the hesitant attitude which consists in refusing to proceed with our revolutionary work amongst the people is effectively a rightist attitude, and in many cases amounts to rejection of the task facing the Communist Party in the struggle to prise the leadership of the mass movement away from the national bourgeoisie.

Notes

1. *Al-Manar*, August 1919.
2. *Al-Ummal al-tounsiyyoun* ... (Tunis, 1927), Introduction and pp.121-26.
3. *Tarbiyat Salamah Musa*, 2nd edition (Cairo, 1958), pp.272-77.
4. Popular dishes.
5. Equivalent to 1p. sterling.
6. By order of Ismail Sidqi Pasha, his old adversary from 1930-35, as part of the general anti-Communist offensive launched while the Egyptian prime minister was negotiating the Sidqi-Bevin pact.
7. *Al-qawmiyyah al-arabiyyah wal-dimuqratiyyah* (Arab Nationalism and Democracy) (Beirut, c.1958), pp.7-8, 19-25.
8. Only this section is reproduced here, but it covers all the main points.
9. Probably a reference to Egypt.
10. *Alger républicain*, 29 September 1964.
11. Hero fallen on the battlefield, martyr.
12. *Min aql harakah qamahiriyyah wasiah wa munadhdhamah touammin masr al-thawrah! Min agl hizb talii thawri wahid li kull al-quwa al-ishtirakkiyyah!* (Cairo, March-April 1965), pp.1-15.
13. *Al-Taliah*, Vol.II, No.10 (1966), pp.17-29.
14. *Thawra fi alam al-insan* (Beirut, 1967), pp.7-9.
15. *L'Idéologie arabe contemporaine* (Paris: F. Maspero, 1967), pp.139-55.
16. Qasimi's thesis, and its use by von Grünebaum is completely misguided; absolute determinism has always been well accommodated by the religious consciousness.
17. For example the critique of the bourgeoisie in the journals of the Moroccan Trade Unions; the content is often ethical, and framed in terms of decadence, despair, depraved luxury, debauchery, etc. Purely economic criticisms are rare.
18. Mahmoud A. al-Alem and A.A. Anis (Beirut, 1955).
19. Arab essayists exaggerate the importance of our so-called 'philosophers'; their works are all either courses or literary essays.
20. An idea expressed lucidly by Alal al-Fasi in his distinction between the contemporary and the modern; cf. *l'Autocritique* (in Arabic) (Cairo, 1952).
21. G. Martinet, *Un marxisme de notre temps* (Paris, 1962), is a typical example of this type of interpretation.
22. 'Yemen du Sud: sur les sentiers du socialisme', *Tricontinental 1970*, pp.88-96.
23. Extract from *Nouvelle Revue Internationale*, October 1969, pp.106-115.
24. *Al-Hurriyah*, No.577, 26 July 1971, pp.12-13.

8. War and Peace: The Project of Renaissance

AHMAD BAHA AL-DIN
(1926, Egypt)

An Egyptian journalist and publicist, Baha al-Din studied law at Cairo University where he concentrated on political journalism rather than direct political action. As editor of *Rose al-Youssef*, he played an important role in the mobilization of public opinion against the monarchy. His brilliant career in the press was marked by a sound political instinct, a deep sense of culture and an awareness of the place of the Egyptian personality within the broader framework of the Arab world. He served as president of the Order of the Press (1965-68), then as chairman of the powerful *Dar al-Hilal* press and publishing group, for which, amongst other things, he edited *Al-Musawwar*. When Heikal was sacked, he was appointed editor-in-chief of *Al-Ahram* (1974-76), whose great national tradition he maintained. From 1977 onwards, he was based in Kuwait, working as director of *Al-Arabi*, the most important monthly magazine in the Arab world, and continued his activities as a realistic publicist for the beleagured cause of Arab unity and national modernization, notably in *Al-Watan* and *Al-Mustaqbal*. He is now a columnist to *Al-Ahram* (**Cairo**), *Al-Shariq al-Awsat* (**London**), *Al-Mustaqbal* (**Paris**).

Main works: **Faruq, the King** (*Faruq malikan*); **Proposal for a State of Palestine** (*Iqtirah dawlat Filistin*).

The author, who is one of the leading authorities on the Palestine question since 1947, here presents his views on the future of Palestine, in the aftermath of the June 1967 war.

New Life for the Palestinian State[1]

In these times when we are receiving news of the heroic Palestinian resistance in the occupied territories — the first serious step forward, which must be developed more fully — we must draw one lesson in particular from all those we have been forced to face by the catastrophe. The simplest and

198

most important way we can defend ourselves against Israel and keep the Palestinian issue alive — at least until circumstances have changed and we can come out of our defensive trenches — is for Palestine to exist.

The Zionist aggression of 1948 succeeded in cutting away one part of Palestine. And now, instead of preserving what remained of Palestine as a resistant united entity with its own demands, we Arabs have scattered the pieces of it amongst ourselves. The Zionist invasion of 1948 began by gathering Jewish emigrants and refugees from all over the world and turning them into citizens, farmers, workers and soldiers. In contrast, the Arabs have allowed the citizens of Palestine to become refugees and emigrants . . . .

Years passed, during which time the idea of establishing a Palestinian entity and a Palestinian organization slowly ripened and came to fruition. But the organization in question found itself deprived of the most vital asset for expressing the existence of a people and a nation, namely a land of its own! Yet this land existed, albeit in truncated form . . . . The Palestinian struggle was led from Cairo, Beirut and other Arab towns, not from Palestine.

This situation was enough to give the rest of the world the impression that Palestine no longer existed, that there was no longer a people of Palestine who wanted their land back, that the conflict was really between the neighbouring Arab states and a state called Israel . . . .

A state called Palestine must thus from now on serve as our fundamental starting point. Such a state will regroup Jordan, on both banks of the Jordan river, and Gaza; that is to say it will consist of all that remains of Palestine plus what used to be called Transjordan and was, before that, a part of Palestine . . . . The restoration of the name 'Palestine' will have an immense moral and political effect in the world during the next stages of the conflict. When the old original name of the country has been revived, it will be clear that there is a Palestinian state, part of which has been annexed, a state which demands legal redress for that annexation.

It further follows that the restoration of the name 'Palestine' to the land of Palestine must go hand-in-hand with the return of the Palestinian people to the land of Palestine . . . . Those who emigrated . . . to the four corners of the earth, from Canada to Latin America and throughout the Arab world from Algeria to Kuwait, were amongst the best and the brightest of the Palestinian people . . . . The revival of the name 'Palestine' and of the Palestinian state will only be meaningful if it is accompanied by a reversal of the wave of emigration and dispersion, by a massive return and concentration of the Palestinian people, as is natural. Before we speak of a 'return' to the occupied territories of Palestine, we must bring about a return to the parts of Palestine that are still Palestinian. The Arab wall surrounding Israel must cease to be a flimsy collection of refugee tents, full of increasingly destitute people; it must become a mighty rampart of civilization, economically, socially, politically and hence militarily.

It is crucial that life within this new Palestine should be on a par with the

Palestinian people's abilities; that it should be a life which attracts those who have emigrated to return, to fulfil their patriotic duty and promote the Palestinian cause — a life in which opportunities for work, fulfilment and growth will be open to everybody.

This call for a return is no secondary affair. The human factor is fundamental to this national struggle — this acute confrontation between a genuine national destiny and the fate of the invading peoples who seek to establish a new nationality. The human factor will be the decisive force in the end. The core of this human factor is the Palestinians themselves, with the Arabs as a strategic background and source of support. The Palestinian human factor is not just a question of numbers; it also involves the quality of education, of technical abilities and of the economic, political, social and military institutions of the nation.

The issue of the type of regime, whether it be a monarchy or not, is of little matter in this respect. The nation is more important than the style of government. Men may disagree about types of government and the concomitant prevailing conditions, but there is no disagreement about the nation. Nobody would insist that the government of their country be exactly in accord with their own preference before they would accept to live, work and struggle there. Palestinian feeling about returning to their homeland to work and struggle cannot be less intense than that of the Jews, who emigrated from the four corners of the earth to come to a land that they had never seen before, about which they knew little, and whose language they did not speak.

It is essential that the Palestinians who today carry Lebanese, Kuwaiti or Argentinian passports should have the possibility of bearing Palestinian nationality and no other. Let the Palestinians belong to Palestine and Palestine will belong to the Palestinians.

. . . This proposal touches upon a delicate and painful subject, the fate of the Palestinian refugees . . . . Since 1948, a million Palestinians have been living in tents, dependent on the charity of the international rescue organizations. They do not form a coherent civil society; they have no agriculture, no industry, an inadequate education system . . . . They form the majority of those who have been evicted from their lands and their houses . . . .

The question we must face is as follows: is it the fate of this substantial section of the Palestinian people, which has been living in refugee camps for twenty years, to go on doing so indefinitely? I feel that such an unjust and disadvantageous outcome cannot be allowed . . . . Within the overall framework I am proposing, the resurrection of the 'State of Palestine', . . . two goals can be achieved. All these people must move from wherever they are now and settle in that part of the land of Palestine which we still hold. Once in Palestine, these people must become a strong society, with a developing agriculture and industry, an education system and armed strength of their own, so that they can become the 'powerful environment' for the confrontation with Israel rather than remaining caught in the vice of illiteracy, weakness and stagnation . . . . Nothing must be done which would diminish the refugees' demand to return to their homes or which would act as a palliative in any way. It is extremely important that the refugee problem should remain at the forefront of our consciousness, because this problem is the spearhead of the entire Palestinian question. But it is also vital that the refugees should become an efficacious and influential force, a well of Arab and Palestinian potential. These issues of resettlement in the land one lives in, of a life lived in keeping with the possibility of transforming that land into a power base, may not seem to be the primary ones which point towards a rapid and decisive solution. But the attitude involved carries within it initiatives, decisions and actions which will, over time, create a powerful and influential reality.

ALI YATA
(1920, Morocco)

A statesman, Ali Yata was born in Tangiers to a humble Algerian-Moroccan family. He studied in Casablanca then took a correspondence degree at Algiers University. From 1940 to 1945, he worked as a schoolteacher and became an active militant within the Moroccan Communist Party and the National Independence Movement. In 1945 he was elected to the Party's Central Committee and later became General Secretary, in which capacity he decisively re-oriented the approach of his party, the largest Communist Party in the Maghreb, towards revolutionary nationalism. After suffering several bouts of repression, the party took on the name and vocation of the Party of Liberation and Socialism. Ali Yata is presently its General Secretary and also edits the journal, *Al-Mukafih al-Watani.*

From his numerous publications — pamphlets, reports and articles — we have selected his party's report to the Preparatory Commission for the International Conference of Workers' and Communist Parties (Moscow 18-22 March 1969), which a few months later was given as grounds for his condemnation to a long term in prison. His firm and lucid analysis outlines the double problematic of Marxists in the Three Continents and more particularly in the Arab world, faced with the European tradition of orthodox Marxism.

National Liberation and Social Revolution: the example of Palestine

(1) Our first point concerns the national liberation movement.

The unanimous 1960 declaration by Communist and Workers' Parties gave due emphasis to the national liberation movement, which it rightly situated as just below the world socialist system in the scale of progressive forces in the world. The present document abandons that classification and bestows this second place upon the workers' movement in the capitalist countries. As we see it, nothing has happened since 1960 to justify such a change.

True, the socialist countries have played an ever more determinant role in world affairs, and despite certain crises, the overall balance of forces continues to make it impossible for imperialism to institute the reversal it seeks.

True, the capitalist world has been and still is shaken by more and more extensive workers' struggles which have mobilized great masses of people and profoundly affected the economies of the countries concerned. Our sister parties have made progress and even greater efforts, gaining in influence and power.

But the national liberation movements have also developed their struggles. It is worth noting the number of imperialist military interventions and local wars that have been triggered since 1960 in the countries with active national liberation movements in Asia, Africa and Latin America. It should not be forgotten that despite these extremely destructive wars and interventions, the imperialists have not triumphed, for all their efforts both direct and indirect. The fact is that however powerful the means at their disposal, they have proved incapable of overcoming the desire for emancipation of the peoples of the Three Continents or of fundamentally broadening imperialism's political options in the world.

Of course, the peoples engaged in the national liberation movement have an enormous amount of catching-up to do. Often, their social structures are archaic in the extreme, for complex economic and historical reasons, amongst which international imperialism continues to figure prominently. They are waging a difficult struggle in which they must compensate for material and economic inferiority by making exceptional demands on the political consciousness, devotion and spirit of self-sacrifice of the masses. They must start building their new society whilst fighting the imperialist enemy and his various neo-colonial incarnations every foot of the way — in every domain, political, economic, cultural and ideological.

In Africa, for example, these peoples have succeeded in breaking up all the old colonial empires except that of Portugal, which is under constant assault. They have succeeded through long, stubborn and bloody struggles which could only be won after the second victory of socialism over imperialism, the new world balance of power established after 1945. Progressives throughout the world rejoiced over the victories of 1960, which was declared Africa Year in commemoration. Since then, the African peoples have generally been struggling against a new imperialist offensive: neo-colonialism. This struggle calls for new methods, which have not always been forthcoming. Hence a period of relative calm. Hence a wave of reversals imposed by the imperialist onslaught, particularly the various military coups. The disappointment and pessimism of some analysts of these phenomena is nonetheless mistaken and, we believe, the result of an overly superficial approach. For our part, the information we receive concerning the various detachments of the liberation movement in Africa inclines us to conclude that the struggle continues in ever more various forms, that it is growing stronger in certain areas and will develop further in the years to come. It remains as serious a threat to imperialism as it was during our second conference in 1960. The same is true in the other two continents, and especially in Asia.

In our opinion, to recognize the true importance of the national liberation movement for our era in no way detracts from the decisive role of the working class's historic mission.

(2) The second point bears on the situation created in the Middle East by the imperialist-Zionist aggressors.

. . . The crisis in the Middle East is serious in many respects, but we wish to underline one particular aspect of its seriousness. The crisis has already come to a climax three times, in 1948, 1956 and 1967. Each time it was more intense, more bloody and more of a threat to world peace, especially when it is borne in mind that the United States of America, which had until recently at least feigned a certain neutrality concerning Zionist aggression, actively intervened in 1967 by providing the support of the VIth fleet which cruises the Mediterranean. It would be irresponsible to assume that the worst is over. On the contrary, we are convinced that all the territorial annexations, military preparations, imperialist material aid, carefully planned aggressions against Arab states and declarations by Israeli officials indicate that the peak of Israeli aggression is yet to come, and that this war machine, which has proved its capabilities, will be used to the limit by Zionist fanaticism and American imperialism. There are many examples of this kind of escalation, notably Hitler's Germany, a country with which Israel displays many economic, social, military and doctrinal parallels.

The fundamental cause of this crisis must be elucidated. Otherwise, we will be incapable of grasping the true dimensions of the problem and the only solution envisaged will be the search for a balance of power, in other words an arms race which is more likely to have a military than a peaceful outcome.

As we see it, the fundamental cause of the crisis is that the Palestinian people have been denied a homeland and persecuted with a view to their extermination. The problem for imperialism and Zionist colonialism is that this people has not been exterminated. It has survived thanks to its own resistance, the solidarity of the other Arab peoples and the specific international conditions which have prevailed since the end of the Second World War.

Today, the Palestinian people have once again taken up arms. They have learnt to handle automatic weapons. They have decided that they will no longer allow themselves to be mowed down by Israeli soldiers and are determined to win back their homeland, dearly if needs be. No one should overlook, underestimate or denigrate this factor. The Palestinian patriots are waging a noble and sacred struggle. They know that their cause is invulnerable, supported by the Arab peoples and viewed sympathetically by progressive forces throughout the world. They are thus resolved to fight to the last, knowing they have already lost everything and have their country to win.

The international context for their struggle is also favourable, in theory at least. Imperialism has been forced to beat a retreat from huge regions of the world. The socialist countries today constitute a powerful force in world affairs which has staunchly defended the cause of Arab liberation. Imperialism has to make considerable efforts to resist the national liberation movements. The workers' movement in the capitalist countries restricts the reactionary manoeuvres of the ruling bourgeoisies, some of which are beginning to take Arab realities into account, for instance the Gaullist government in France.

We believe that the Palestinian fighters must be assured of the total moral support and effective material assistance of the international workers' and Communist movement. Similarly, we feel that any actions which might cause the Arabs to retreat even further before the Zionist onslaught should be avoided, especially any moves to recognize the state [of Israel], which would amount to a shameful abdication and criminal desertion of our Palestinian brothers.

It follows that the question of the territories annexed in 1967 must be treated firmly but carefully, since the negotiations for their evacuation must not be allowed to mortgage a future which carries enough risks already. Furthermore, these territories constitute only one element of a Middle East problem which encompasses, amongst other things, the national rights of the Arab people of Palestine. It would be contrary to every rule of justice if the Israelis were allowed to profit from their aggression. The occupied territories must be evacuated and indemnities paid to the victims. The Zionist position must never be strengthened by any international initiatives.

By taking into account these views, which are fundamental for the Arab peoples, the progressive camp consisting of the socialist countries, the national liberation movement and the international workers' movement will show that they truly value the anti-imperialist Arab national liberation movement. This is a vital strategic element if we want our forces to remain in the vanguard of the liberation of peoples and of humanity, rather than allowing themselves to be carried along by events, and if we really want them to succeed in carrying out their revolutionary mission.

(3) We come now to our third point.

The proposals before us condemns anti-semitism as a means used by the reactionary bourgeoisie to divide the popular masses and divert them from anti-imperialist or democratic struggles. Our party unreservedly and unhesitatingly supports this view. But we are surprised to note its silence concerning Zionism, given the extent of the damage done by that ideology, which continues to be done, not only in one or the other capitalist or socialist country, but throughout the world and particularly in the Middle East.

We know that one of the major contributions of scientific socialism is to have advanced an historically and politically valid definition of the nation. This definition is a precious asset and a vital weapon for all the people who have struggled or are still struggling to win their inalienable right to national sovereignty. The definition, which rejects chauvinism of every form, and especially racism, restores to patriotism all its purity and worth, and links it to fraternal internationalism, which it clearly distinguishes from cosmopolitanism.

Scientific socialism, fighting in the vanguard of the ideological struggle, was confronted very early on with Zionism in an earlier form, namely Bundism. Marxist theoreticians, and Lenin foremost amongst them, brilliantly refuted Jewish chauvinism and Zionism. Lenin was fully aware that 'Jewish nationalism was in fact just a subterfuge of the imperialist powers who, under the pretence of founding politically independent states in fact create states which are entirely dependent upon them, financially, economically and militarily.' He wrote that in 1920, while preparing for the Second Congress of the Communist International. Right from the start, socialism thus rejected Zionism as a bourgeois nationalist doctrine serving the interests of imperialism, and as a counter-revolutionary, anti-proletarian force promoting religious fanaticism and reactionary subversion.

Zionism is by no means the pure, healthy and legitimate reflex of self-defence that the propagandists claim. Its early manifestations were separatist and divisive reactions against the European workers' movement. It was a reaction by intellectuals who sought to break their national allegiances and who indulged in cosmopolitanism.

Later, during the Second World War, the trial of history showed that true patriots, both Jews and non-Jews, after having fought courageously against Nazism in Europe, set to work rebuilding their weakened nations and struggled to advance democracy, dedicating themselves to the well-being of their people rather than engaging in colonial adventures.

When the Zionists laboriously expound the reasons why the land of Palestine must come to them, they carefully select passages of the Bible which support their claims, but they never mention all the passages which contradict their project. And when their clientele fails to exhibit the necessary degree of religious fanaticism, they invoke racial criteria, without bothering to consider that the most direct descendants of the biblical Hebrews are probably the Palestinians, some of whom remained Jewish whilst others converted either to Christianity or to Islam.

It is worth noting that, if mere veneration of the biblical patriarchs of itself confers some title of ownership over the land of Palestine, then the Jews, Muslims and Christians have equal claims upon it. And history had not arranged things so badly, since, before the Zionist adventure, the three religious communities co-existed peacefully in Palestine and would have continued to do so in the independent Palestine called for by the Arabs; only Zionist ostracism disrupted this harmony.

Be that as it may, we all know that rather than being handed down from on high, Zionism's mission stemmed from much more prosaic sources: first London, then Washington, which also provided the material means with which to carry out their orders. Not only were the Zionists given the territory and the means to evict the previous inhabitants, they also regularly receive enormous subsidies. A report on Israel's foreign resources estimates that the country has received $7 billion in gifts from abroad, mainly from the United States. This figure includes the $1,875 million the German Federal Republic paid as war indemnities, to the detriment of the countries of Europe, who were too socialist for Bonn and Washington to recognize as the real victims [of the war]. Colossal sums have been invested in the Israeli arms industry by the U.S. and the Federal Republic, which also provide constant military aid. Of course the Israelis enjoy the backing of all the anti-Arab racists and enemies of people's freedom throughout the world.

The reason for this support is that Israel serves as the guardian of the oil monopolies' investments and interests in the Middle East, one of the keys to which is the Suez canal. Hence the 1956 aggression following nationalization of the canal, then that of 1967, in response directly to certain problems in Iraq, but above all occupying the entire north-west bank of the canal.

Israel is also used to weaken the Arab national liberation and reconstruction movement. The regimes of the United Arab Republic and the Syrian Arab Republic were direct targets; they survived thanks both to the political maturity of the Egyptian and Syrian peoples, who unmasked the reactionaries, and to the decisive support of the Soviet Union and other socialist countries.

Finally, Israel is an ideal strategic tool for the American imperialists; it acts as their military representative in the Middle East and can at any moment openly become an American base serving longer-range objectives in Europe and Asia. One observer rightly pointed out that Dayan is a far more useful pawn for Washington than Ky in Vietnam.

For all these reasons . . ., we feel that it is indispensable that our document should analyse Zionism, expressly condemn its essence, its manifesttations and its goals, and devote to the question the time warranted by its importance.

(4) Our fourth point bears on the question of unity. The projected document rightly denounces the aggressivity of imperialism, which has grown over recent years, albeit without great success.

In our opinion, a critical note must be introduced. There can indeed be no doubt that if the socialist countries, the national liberation movement and the international workers' movement had been truly united, both within each category and as a whole, imperialist aggression would not even have been able to win the few tactical victories that it has. The peoples would have been spared great sufferings, years of struggle would have been shortened, and tremendous potential could have been devoted to political, social and material progress and reconstruction . . . .

We feel very strongly that the divergences and differences between the various workers' and Communist parties do not stem only from the different situations of each party. The workers' and Communist movement no longer represents the entire world revolutionary movement. The emergence and growth of the national liberation movement has changed the context. The difficulties of the international Communist and workers' movement also stem from the fact that it no longer represents the only front of the struggle. This contradiction is perfectly solvable for those who are armed with a tried and tested scientific doctrine, inspired by a great ideal and keen to resolve the contradiction in the first place. To do so, we need to develop loyal and ever more fruitful co-operation between the Communists and the national liberation movement, to co-ordinate the efforts of every detachment and to carry solidarity and fraternity to the highest possible political level.

This rapprochement between Communists and the national liberation movement must not be jeopardized by the other problems we face. It must be pursued unremittingly, both for immediate tactical reasons and in view of more distant goals, for it will eventually become a factor facilitating the solution of the other problems, in that it will mean greater unity amongst the forces of world revolution.

(5) This brings me to my fifth and final point. We have already stated that the unity between the socialist countries, the international workers' movement and the national liberation movement is fundamental. Taking into account the principles defined in 1957 and 1960 concerning the eminently revolutionary character of the national liberation movement, as well as the political reality that in the Third World the revolutionary movement is not necessarily led or represented by a Communist party but by other parties inspired by socialism, we, and other fraternal parties, proposed at the first consultative session that our international conference should be opened up to these forces. Our conviction was and remains that the unity and co-operation of the socialist forces and the national liberation movement cannot be a merely unilateral gesture, but must necessarily stem from confrontation, dialogue and shared experience.

The majority of the fraternal parties decided to keep the International Conference of Workers' and Communist Parties separate and to organize a World Conference of Anti-Imperialist Forces at a later date. We accepted the decision, but we now note that the projected document makes no mention of it. We feel that not only should that decision be mentioned in the present document, it should in fact be emphasized, explained and presented in detail, since it is of such crucial importance. We must now set about investigating the practical steps required to prepare and ensure the success of this major world event.

ALI SABRI
(1920, Egypt)

An Egyptian statesman and leader of the left within the military regime, Ali Sabri was born to one of the great liberal bourgeois families. He completed Arabic and French studies in Cairo then attended the Military Academy and the School of Aviation (1939-46). He made his career in aviation, notably during the Palestine war (1948), and became a member of the Free Officers group, serving as their liaison officer with the Western powers in 1951-52. After Nasser took power, Sabri became head of the president's political cabinet and took an active part in the Anglo-Egyptian negotiations over the evacuation at Bandoeng (1955) and at many other conferences. He also served as Egypt's delegate to the Security Council's sessions on Suez (1956).

Sabri brought this considerable experience and his keen sense of organization to bear when he assumed the responsibilities of President of the Executive Council of the UAR (1963-65). Following the National Congress of Popular Forces, he became General Secretary of the Arab Socialist Union (1965-67), of whose central secretariat he remains a member. He was later Vice-Prime Minister and was appointed Vice-President by President Sadat, who sacked him on 1 May 1971, accusing him of building a parallel power base. He was released in 1981.

Ali Sabri's evolution fully illustrates that of the Egyptian national bourgeoisie. His patriotism and acute sense of the international balance of power led him first to accept and then to become the epigone of socialism within the state and the one-party system. He saw the future of Egypt as resting firstly on the deep-rooted alliance between the armed forces and the working people (he assumed political and military command of the air force following the defeat of 1 June 1967), secondly on the alliance between Egypt and the Soviet Union.

Main work: The Years of the Socialist Transformation (*Sanawat al-tahawul al-ishtiraki*).

The following interview, granted on 6 March 1971 to Hatem Sadeq, (President Nasser's son-in-law and an editor of *Al-Ahram*) sums up his key theses.

Dialectic of the War of Liberation

Since the battle of 1967, Egypt has not achieved the kind of investment we sought and planned for in peacetime. The annual levels of investment after 1967 were barely higher than they had been in previous years, and development requires a constantly increasing volume of investment. We now invest £E300 million a year in new production and service projects; in 1965 the figure was from £E350 to £E370 million. The armed forces' budget has doubled and has increased by about £E250 million a year. In other words, had it not been for the battle at hand, we would have been able to invest bet-ween £E560 and £E570 million a year; the difference between this figure and current investment figures — £E300 million — represents the burden that the battle imposes on our economic development. We must also be aware of the effects of this battle upon social change which itself has a direct bearing on development . . . . We must remember that, as far as Israel and its supporters are concerned, the purpose of the 1967 aggression was not just the acquisition of territory but also the disruption of our plans to ensure the prosperity of our society. The enemy's fundamental aim is to bring influence to bear upon Egyptian society by weakening us economically and socially, hoping thereby to reduce our ability to challenge its illegitimate designs in our region . . . .

History presents us with contradictory examples of states which have faced battles and wars. Some of these states, those which did not profit from the opportunities a war opens up once it is over, tended towards disintegra-tion and dissolution, whilst the states which mobilized and organized their capacities, and planned the use they would make of those capacities in the battle that follows a war, were the ones which attained ever greater glory and strength. The battle at hand has cost our citizens dearly, both morally and materially . . . . To envisage what will follow on from victory thus becomes a national duty . . . . If we do not start planning right now, when victory comes we will see the potential of our society dispersed and perhaps even wasted, thereby causing dangerous problems which will threaten our national development and integrity . . . . Victory is not the final end in itself, since after the victory we will have to ask ourselves 'for what did we accept all the sacrifices we have made?' To win back Arab land? Yes. To protect the rights of the Palestinian people? Of course, but that is not the whole story. The real aim is to build the kind of society we aspire to, after we have defeated the retrograde forces in the present battle. That is a goal to match the scale of the sacrifices we have had to accept.

There are states that develop and prosper after wars and others that collapse. Some states fall apart morally when the fighting is over, others emerge with an intensified sense of values. In the latter category, one generally finds those states which went to war to defend their territory and the truth . . . .

As prescribed in the National Action Charter and established by our beloved late [President], the Arab Socialist Union is the backbone of everything that happens within our society . . . . We can now draw up a balance sheet of the positive and negative aspects of our experience since 1965. I feel that the negative aspects are due to three main factors:

(1) The Arab Socialist Union exists in the context of a state characterized by the strength and centralization of its administration. Thousands of years ago, Egypt had the first united and centralized government in the world. The Egyptian Government is a strong government; the task of the political organization is to call the administration to account, which the latter will naturally resist with all its considerable might.

(2) Certain leaders are not convinced of the need for a Socialist Union; these leaders even reject its basic philosophy.

(3) By its nature, the Socialist Union is riven by certain contradictions; it is in fact an alliance of the forces of the working people rather than a party . . . . The difference is that the alliance which finds expression through the Socialist Union is between forces sharing a strategic interest but whose tactical or transient interests differ and may even conflict.

Nonetheless, there are many positive aspects to this political organization. To take just one example, drawn, it is true, from the great loss we have suffered, consider the calm, resolute and constructive continuity maintained by the Socialist Union after the death of our leader, Gamal Abdel Nasser . . . . The responsibilities which fell upon the Socialist Union after his death were far greater than before. The Socialist Union, as a mass organization, must work at a high rate to compensate for even part of that loss . . . . Gamal Abdel Nasser was endowed with qualities which we shall not see again in a single person for many years; in his thought, he was far ahead of both institutions and individuals.

. . . Thus if we are to realize fully the potential effectivity of the Socialist Union in the battle at hand and the one to come, we must entrust it with even more duties and responsibilities; I emphasize: duties and responsibilities, not powers . . . . I fully appreciate that both within and without the Socialist Union, the debate has not been sufficiently extended. The extension of this debate presents no danger, even in wartime; every Egyptian wholeheartedly accepts the inevitability of our struggle. As I see it, debate is important not just in order to cope with the present historical circumstances, but also for the long-term future of this country. I cannot imagine our society other than in the context of a powerful and efficacious political organization. The power of our political organization will depend not on orders or 'mobilization' but on the level of debate and the degree of unity and conviction of our people . . . .

Soviet-Egyptian relations have a history of which the High Dam is perhaps the best example. They have a present, embodied in the support the Soviet Union provides us with, for the battle we are fighting. They have a future, already distinguishable in steel-making projects, and the recently signed agreement on scientific and technological co-operation. These relations thus have manifestations in many aspects of life, and like life, they are continuous.

. . . Since 1952, and to this day, the position of the United States of America has been to make war on the UAR so as to prevent it reaching a level of power which would enable it to exercise some influence within the region and beyond — an influence which would threaten the foreign monopolies. The United States hope to weaken Egypt, to force it to remain confined within its frontiers; their approach is fundamentally misguided. The international influence a people has is based on a long history and on its own specific character. Did Britain ever succeed in breaking Egypt's cultural and intellectual influence, even when we were under occupation? How then could such efforts succeed today, now that Egypt is associated with national, social and political principles which have attracted people from as far away as Latin America, who call themselves Nasserists? . . . Our enemies forget that Muhammad Ali had only his military strength to rely on; when that was destroyed, Egypt's role diminished and her enemies were able to impose their will on her. But Egypt's strength in the 20th Century rests primarily on its ideas and principles. Ideas cannot be broken by force; that is the error in American thinking . . . .

We must be prepared for the fact that in the next military confrontation, the enemy may launch a general aerial offensive which will be much more far-reaching than ever before. Similarly, the next confrontation will call for far greater sacrifices than those of the period before the present cease-fire. This is where the organizing role of the people and of the Socialist Union comes in; civil defence, scientific and intellectual preparation for what may happen in the coming battle, and new ways of coping with the problems we face because of the extension of the war are all crucial elements of that role . . . .

Once the battle is over, the struggle for reconstruction will begin. We must be ready to reorient the popular masses, mobilized for self-sacrifice on the battlefront, towards the new battlefront of reconstruction. The present gigantic efforts to prepare the armed forces will have to be redeployed. When we built our missile sites in forty days, at a cost of more than a million pounds a day, it was not so much a strain on our budget as a challenge to our intellectual abilities, to our systems and to our mode of government. The experience we have accumulated in these domains must eventually be used to resolve the administrative, economic and scientific problems of running our towns in a healthy way. The technical experience we gain in time of war is the quintessence of human thought. Electronics is not a science which can only be used to make war, it can also serve to bring prosperity and aid reconstruction.

In the educational field, we must build a system based on our experiences in wartime: the evolution of education is not simply a matter of the need for this or that part of the curriculum. The war itself has provided us with clear answers, in that modern war needs science in every domain — be it electronics, communications, civil engineering or administration — in order words the very areas we need to develop in everyday life . . . . The implication is that our education system must evolve to cope with these specific lacunae; the needs of modern warfare are those of modern life.

On the political level, it is essential that we reinforce our political organization in the course of the present battle, so that this organization can attain the strength which will be required when we pass on to the next stage. One must make the most of a given situation: the fact is that it is much easier to develop the leadership capabilities of an organization during a war than in peacetime . . . . The war is a bridge between the present and our hopes for the future. Nothing more and nothing less than victory will take us across that bridge.

YASSER ARAFAT
(1929, Palestine)

From 1947 to the so-called Six Day War in June 1967, Zionism's political offensive implanted a Zionist state in the land of Palestine, driving
the Palestinians into refugee camps and bringing turmoil to the entire
Middle East.

The offensive was a great blow for Egypt, akin to what happened in
1840 during the first phase of the Arab renaissance. But the Palestinian
people's national tragedy gave rise to an armed national liberation
movement which was to become the vanguard of the increasingly
radicalized Arab national movements. The foundation of *Al-Fatah* on 1
January 1964 thus marked a turning point in the post-Suez political history of the Arab world. 'From resistance to revolution' sums up the programme of the armed Palestinian resistance, which now consists of
several organizations grouped around Fatah. In 1970, the majority of
these organizations joined to form the Palestine Liberation Organization, with Yasser Arafat, the leader of Fatah, as its president.

The October 1973 war put an end to the conspiracy of silence and the
denial of justice that had prevailed. It was a powerful indication of Arab
determination and allowed the General Assembly of the United Nations
to give a triumphal and quasi-unanimous welcome to the President of
the PLO, the symbol of Palestine, on 13 November 1974.

We have chosen the key points of Yasser Arafat's historic speech to
the world's representatives on that occasion.

The Future of Palestine

The roots of the Palestine question go back to the end of the 19th Century,
in other words to the era of colonialism and the beginnings of the transition
towards imperialism. It was at that time that Zionism drew up plans for the
invasion of Palestine and European immigrants came to conquer Palestine,
as they had come to Africa. It was the era in which Western imperialism
was spreading throughout Africa, Asia and Latin America, to establish
colonies and to exercise the cruellest forms of exploitation, oppression and
pillage, at the expense of the people of those continents. It was then that
Zionism installed itself in our country. The consequences of that imperialist
era are still with us today, embodied in the racism practised in South Africa
and Palestine.

In the same way that the demagogues of colonialism, who sought to present their conquests, pillage and constant attacks against the African
peoples as part of a 'civilizing and modernizing mission', the Zionist leaders
disguised their real aims in order to conquer Palestine. Colonialism as a
system, and the colonialists themselves, its instruments, used religion,
colour and race to justify the exploitation of the Africans and their subjection to a regime of terror and discrimination. The same methods were used

in Palestine to usurp our lands and chase our people from their homeland.

Like colonialism, which used the poor, the disinherited and the exploited to set up colonies and pursue its aggression, world imperialism and the Zionist leaders used the European Jews, who were also oppressed and disinherited. The European Jews have been used as instruments of aggression, as a way of setting up a colony, but they were themselves the victims of racial discrimination.

The Zionist ideology was used against the Palestinian people. But the aim was not just to set up a colony in the usual Western manner, it was also to uproot the Jews from their different countries and to separate them from the other nations. Zionism is an imperialist, colonialist and racist ideology, it is profoundly reactionary and discriminatory, and in its most backward aspects can be compared to anti-Semitism, of which it is in fact another facet. When Jews throughout the world are told not to bear allegiance to the country they live in, and not to live on an equal footing with non-Jewish citizens, that is a kind of anti-Semitism. To state that the only solution to the Jewish problem is for the Jews to abandon the communities and nations in which they have lived for hundreds of years and emigrate forcibly to another people's country is to advocate exactly the same position as the anti-Semites.

That is why there is such a close connection between Rhodes, who encouraged colonialism in Southern Africa, and Theodor Herzl, who drew up the plans to establish colonies in Palestine.

After obtaining a certificate of colonialist good conduct from Rhodes, Herzl went to present it to the British Government, hoping to win support for his Zionist policies. In exchange, the Zionists promised the British an imperialist base in Palestine, so as to safeguard imperialist interests in one of the key strategic areas . . . .

The invasion of Palestine by the Jews began in 1881. Before the first immigrants poured in, Palestine had a population of half a million; most of the inhabitants were Muslim or Christian and there were only 20,000 Jews. Each section of the population enjoyed the freedom of religion which characterizes our civilization.

Palestine was a green land, inhabited mainly by Arabs who had built for themselves a prosperous life and culture.

Between 1882 and 1917, the Zionist movement drew about 50,000 European Jews to our country, using trickery to do so. The fact that it succeeded in obtaining the Balfour Declaration from the British Government is yet another illustration of the alliance between Zionism and imperialism. The British had no right to authorize the Zionist movement to establish a national home. The League of Nations abandoned the Arab people, President Wilson's promises and principles went out of the window, and British imperialism, in the form of the mandate, was imposed upon us directly and cruelly. That mandate, granted by the League of Nations, enabled the Zionist conquerors to consolidate their hold on our land.

In the thirty years following the Balfour Declaration, the Zionist movement, in collaboration with its imperialist ally, succeeded in establishing even more European Jews on our territory, thereby usurping the rights of the Arabs of Palestine.

In 1947 the Jews, who owned some 6% of the Arab land of Palestine numbered 60,000. At the time, the total population was 1,250,000.

The result of this collusion between the mandatory power, the Zionist movement and a few other countries was that the General Assembly of the newly created [UN] Organization approved a recommendation to partition Palestine. Pressure was brought to bear and the atmosphere in which the decision was taken was poisonous; the General Assembly partitioned what it had no right to partition — an indivisible territory. When we rejected this decision, our attitude was similar to that of the true mother who rejected Solomon's judgement that her son should be cut in half — a decision which the other woman claiming the baby was prepared to accept. Furthermore, despite the fact that the resolution granted the colonialists 54% of the land of Palestine, they were still not satisfied and launched a terrorist war against the Arab civilian population. They occupied 81% of the land of Palestine, uprooting a million Arabs in the process. They then occupied 524 Arab towns and villages and destroyed 385 in the course of the attack. Finally, they established their own settlements on the ruins of our farms and took over the cultivation of our fields and our orchards. That is the core of the Palestine problem. It is not a religious or national conflict between two religions or two nationalisms. It is not a conflict over frontiers between two neighbouring countries. Rather, it is the cause of a people who have been driven from their land, dispersed, uprooted and, for the most part, condemned to live out their lives in refugee camps.

. . . Not content with all this, racist Zionism transformed itself into an imperialist stronghold and adopted an imperialist strategy and built up a military arsenal in order to fulfil its role. It sought to attack and subjugate the Arab population and to annex Palestinian and other Arab lands. As a result, two major wars broke out, in 1956 and 1967, jeopardizing world peace and international security.

Following the Zionist aggression in June 1967, the enemy occupied the Egyptian Sinai up to the banks of the Suez Canal, the Syrian Golan Heights and the entire West Bank of the Jordan. The Middle East problem thus took on a new dimension. The situation has since worsened due to the enemy's intransigent policy of illegal occupation of these Arab lands, providing a bridgehead for world imperialism's offensive against the Arab nation. Zionism did not respect the decisions and appeals of the Security Council, nor did it bow to world opinion, which demanded withdrawal from the territories occupied in June 1967. Not one of the international peacemaking initiatives prevented the enemy from pursuing expansionist policies. The only alternative left to the Arab nations, especially Egypt and Syria, was to make every effort to prepare themselves to resist this barbarian armed invasion, to liberate the Arab territories and to re-establish the rights of the Palestinians. And that is what they did, once every attempt at a peaceful solution had proved in vain.

This was the context of the fourth war, in October 1973, which showed the bankruptcy of expansionist policy and of rule by military force. Yet the leaders of Zionism are still far from having drawn the lessons of that experience. They are preparing to launch a fifth war, so that they may once again embark on the course of aggression, terrorism, subjugation and war with the Arabs.

Our people are deeply grieved when we hear the propaganda claiming that the enemy has taken desert and uninhabited lands from us and made them bloom; or that the interests of the population have not been harmed by this colonization. Such lies cannot be allowed to pass unchallenged. The world must know that Palestine was the cradle of the most ancient cultures and civilizations. Its Arab people cultivated all its lands for millenia, during which they set an example of religious freedom and treated all the holy places in their care with respect. As a son of Jerusalem, I have the happiest and most vivid memories of the religious fraternity that prevailed in our Holy City before the catastrophe. Our people only stopped practising this policy when Israel was created and we were dispersed. Nonetheless, we are still determined to pursue our humanitarian role in Palestine and will never accept that our land should become a launching pad for aggression or a racist stronghold dedicated to the destruction of civilization, culture, progress and peace. Our people cannot but follow in the footsteps of their ancestors, resist the invaders and assume the task of defending their native land, the Arab nation, culture and civilization, in an effort to save the cradle of the monotheist religions.

It is worth mentioning the Israeli positions which differ from our own: their support for the OAS in Algeria, for the settlers in Africa, be it in the Congo, Angola, Mozambique, Zimbabwe or South Africa, as well as their support for South Vietnam against the Vietnamese revolution. Israel supports racists and imperialists everwhere, and its obstructionism in the Committee of 24, its refusal to vote in favour of the African countries' independence and its opposition to the demands of many Asian, African, Latin American and other states in successive conferences on raw materials, population, food and offshore rights is ample proof of the character of the enemy who has usurped our land. All these facts justify the honourable struggle we wage against him. Where we defend the future, Israel defends the myths of the past.

The deadly enemy who confronts us has committed many crimes against the Jews themselves, for within the Zionist entity, racism is practised against the Oriental Jews. When we were vehemently condemning the massacre of the Jews by the Nazis, the Zionist leaders seemed more interested in exploiting it in order to promote emigration to Palestine. If this immigration of Jews into Palestine had meant their living alongside us and enjoying the same rights and responsibilities, we would have opened our doors to them, as we did before to the Armenians and Circassians who live amongst us as brothers and citizens with equal rights. But what we can never accept is that our lands should be usurped and we ourselves dispersed and turned into second class citizens.

This is why, right from the start, our revolution has not been motivated by any racial or religious factors. It is not directed against the Jewish individual as such, but against racist Zionism and aggression. In this sense, we are fighting for the Jewish individual as an individual, so that Jew, Christian and Muslim can live on an equal footing, with the same rights and duties, free of racial or religious discrimination.

We draw a distinction between Judaism and Zionism. We are opposed to colonialist Zionism but we respect the Jewish faith, for this religion is part of our patrimony. Today, a century after the birth of the Zionist movement, we warn the Jews of the growing danger this movement presents for Jews, the Arab people, peace and world security. For Zionism encourages Jews to leave their country and to adopt an artificial racist nationality instead of their real nationality. Zionism encourages terrorist activity, even though terror has been shown to be inefficacious. The constant emigration of Jews from Israel, which will increase as the bastions of colonialism and racism fall throughout the world, is a further example of the escapable futility of these activities . . . .

We ask ourselves why the Arab people of Palestine should pay the price of discrimination throughout the world . . . . We ask ourselves why do those who defend the situation — if they exist — not take on the responsibility and throw open their country's doors to these Jewish immigrants. Why do they not help them? Why do they not let them in?

The Zionist terrorism which has been practised against the Palestinian people has been registered in official documents distributed right here, at the United Nations. Thousands of Palestinians have been murdered in towns and villages, tens of thousands have been evicted from their land at bayonet point and under the threat of Israeli bombardment. They have abandoned their homes. So many men and women, children and old people have been forced into the deserts and mountains without food or water. Those who witnessed the catastrophe of 1948 falling on the inhabitants of hundreds of towns and villages, on Jerusalem, Jaffa, Lydda, Ramallah and Galilee will never forget their experiences, even if a deathly silence has succeeded in masking these horrible crimes. The vestiges of 385 Palestinian villages and towns destroyed at that time have been hidden and their names erased from the map. During the past 7 years 19,000 houses have been destroyed — the equivalent of the destruction of a further 200 Palestinian villages. Hundreds of people have been mutilated and made to suffer in Israeli prisons. Those prisons are everywhere, no amount of silence can hide them. Zionist terrorism feeds on hate, a hate which has even been vented upon the olive tree, the symbol of our country, Palestine . . . .

For decades, the Zionists have persecuted the leading political, cultural, and social figures of our country, murdering some and terrorizing others. By expelling these individuals, they have stolen our cultural patrimony and our popular folklore, which they pretend belongs to them. Their terrorism has even extended to the Holy Places of Jerusalem, the city of peace, which we hold so dear. They have sought to annex the city and to change its Arab and Muslim character by evicting the Arab population. The fire at the Al-Aqsa mosque and the disfiguration of many historical and religious monuments might also be mentioned . . . .

The small number of Palestinian Arabs who were not expelled by the Zionists in 1948 are now refugees in their own country. Israeli law treats them as second class citizens, or perhaps one should say third class, since the Oriental Jews are the second class citizens. Their land and property were confiscated and they have been subjected to every form of racial discrimination and terrorism. They have been the victims of bloody massacres, as at Kfar Kassem, and have been forced to evacuate entire villages only to be denied the right to return, as in the case of Ikrit and Kfar-Birim. For twenty-six years our people have lived under martial law . . . .

The Israeli leadership has perpetrated constant acts of terror against those of our people who remained in Sinai or the Golan Heights during the occupation. The bombardment of the school at Bahr al-Bakar and the factory at Abu Zabal were acts of terrorism that we shall never be able to forget. The total destruction of the Syrian town of Quneitra is another eloquent example of the systematic terrorism and crime which prevails in our country . . . . When the time comes to make a tally of the crimes committed by the Zionists in southern Lebanon — including piracy, bombardments, a scorched earth policy, the destruction of hundreds of houses and the kidnapping of Lebanese citizens — not even the most unfeeling will remain unmoved at the enormity of what has been done. The violations of Lebanese sovereignty have been flagrant. One underlying objective is the eventual diversion of the waters of the Litani river . . . .

During the last ten years of our struggle, thousands of Palestinians have become martyrs; others have been wounded, mutilated or imprisoned. They sacrificed themselves to resist the threat of extinction, to win back our right to self-determination and to return to our lands.

The Palestinians who live under Zionist occupation resist arrogance and struggle against oppression, tyranny and terrorism. Those who are in prison, or who live in the great prison the occupied territories have become, are struggling to keep their country Arab. They are struggling for their very existence and to preserve the Arab character of their land. They are resisting oppression, tyranny and oppression in every form. It was in the context of our popular armed struggle that our national institutions and policy crystallized into a national liberation movement, covering all Palestinian groups and organizations. The capacities of our people found concrete expression in the Palestine Liberation Organization . . . .

The Palestine Liberation Organization is the only legitimate representative of the Palestinian people. It expresses the aspirations and desires of our people; it tells you of those aspirations and desires and invites you to assume your historical responsibility towards our just cause.

For many long years, our people have suffered the ravages of war, destruction and dispersion. We have paid with the blood of our sons, and that can never be compensated for. We have suffered occupation, dispersion, eviction and terror more than any other people. Yet we have not become bitter and vindictive; we have not become racist; we have not lost the ability to distinguish friends from enemies. That is why we deplore all the crimes perpetrated against the Jews and the deliberate discrimination exercized against them for their beliefs . . . .

Why should I not dream? Why should I not hope, since revolution is the process of making dreams and hopes come true? Let us act together, that the dream became reality, that I and my people may go home to live alongside this warlike Jewish soldier and this touchy Christian bishop, in the framework of a single democratic country where Christians, Jews and Muslims can live together in a state based on justice, equality and fraternity.

Is this noble ideal not worth fighting for, by everybody who loves freedom? The dream is particularly worth while in that its object is Palestine, the holy land, the land of peace, martyrdom, heroism and history.

The Jews of Europe and the United States once struggled for secular states, in which church and state would be separate; they struggled against religious discrimination. How can they then reject such an honourable model for mankind in our holy land, our land of peace and equality?

I call on you to allow our people to establish its independent national sovereignty on its own land. I came here bearing an olive branch in one hand and a revolutionary's rifle in the other. Do not let the olive branch fall from my hand.

War has swept over Palestine, and yet peace will be born in Palestine.

MUAMMAR AL-QADHAFI
(1941, Libya)

Born in 1941 to a humble family, Qadhafi, after the national revolution of 23 July 1952, became a fervent supporter of President Gamal Abdel Nasser, whose mantle he dreamt of inheriting. Following in his mentor's footsteps, he formed the revolutionary core group which overthrew the Senussi on 15 September 1969, and established a republic and socialism in Libya.

Since then, he has embarked upon a stubborn revolutionary offensive within OPEC, the Arab world and in the tricontinental arena, hoping to establish a practical alternative which could hold back the return to capitalism signalled in Egypt in 1975 with the *Infitah*. Support for the

Palestinian resistance, and particularly for its most hard-line elements, is thought to be at the centre of his concerns.

In 1976, President Qadhafi announced his 'third way', which seeks to distinguish itself both from Marxist socialism and from capitalist pluralism. These ideas were outlined in the *Green Book* which signalled the institution of a new form of political organization, the Jamahariyah, the fundamental principles being those outlined below.

Main works: **Speeches;** *Al-Kitab al-Akhdar* **(1976) (The Green Book).**

The Green Book[2]

... Moreover, since the system of elected parliaments is based on propaganda to win votes, it is a demogogic system in the real sense of the word, and votes can be bought and falsified. Poor people fail to compete in the election campaign and it is always the rich — and only the rich — who come out victorious . . . .

The most tyrannical dictatorships the world has known have existed under the shadow of parliaments . . . .

Originally, the party is formed to represent the people. Then the leading group of the party represents its members and the supreme leader of the party represents the leading group. It becomes clear that the party game is a deceitful farce based on a sham form of democracy which has a selfish content based on manoeuvres, tricks and political games. All these emphasize that the party-system is a dictatorial, yet modern, instrument. The party system is an overt, not a covert, dictatorship. The world has not yet passed beyond it and it is rightly called 'the dictatorship of the modern age.'

The parliament of the winning party is indeed a parliament of the party, as the executive power assigned by this parliament is the power of the party over the people. Party power, which is supposed to be for the good of the whole people, is actually a bitter enemy of a part of the people, namely the opposition party or parties and their supporters. So the opposition is not a popular check on the ruling party, but is itself seeking a chance to replace the ruling party. According to modern democracy, the legal check on the ruling party is the parliament, the majority of whose members are from that ruling party. That is to say, checking is in the hands of the ruling party and rule is in the hands of the checking party. Thus become clear the deceptiveness, falsity and invalidity of the political theories dominant in the world today, from which contemporary traditional democracy emerges . . . .

The party system is the modern tribal and sectarian system. The society governed by one party is exactly like that which is governed by one tribe or one sect. The party, as stated above, represents the outlook of a certain group of people, or the interests of one group of the society, or one belief or one locality. Such a party must be a minority compared to the whole people just as the tribe and the sect are. The minority has common interests or a sectarian belief. From such interests or belief, the common outlook is formed. Only blood-relationship distinguishes a tribe from a party and even at the foundation of a party there may be blood-relationship. There is no difference between party struggles and tribal or sectarian struggles for power. And if tribal and sectarian rule is politically rejected and disavowed, then the party system must similarly be rejected and disavowed. Both of them tread the same path and lead to the same end. The negative and destructive effect on the society of the tribal and sectarian struggles is identical to the negative and destructive effect of the party struggle . . . .

The society torn apart by party struggles is similar to one torn by tribal and sectarian struggles.

The party that is formed in the name of a class automatically becomes a substitute for that class and continues until it becomes a replacement for the class hostile to it.

Any class which becomes heir to a society, inherits, at the same time, its characteristics. That is to say that if the working class crushes all other classes, for instance, it becomes heir of the society, that is, it becomes the material and social base of the society. The heir bears the traits of the one he inherits from, though they may not be evident at once. As time passes, attributes of other eliminated classes emerge in the very ranks of the working class. And the possessors of those characteristics take the attitudes and points of view appropriate to their characteristics. Thus the working class turns out to be a separate society, showing the same contradictions as the old society. The material and moral standards of the members of the society are diverse at first but then there emerge the factions that automatically develop into classes, like those which had been eliminated. Thus the struggle for domination of the society starts again. Each group of people, then each faction and finally each new class, tries to become the instrument of governing.

The material base of the society is not stable because it has a social aspect . . . .

Plebiscites are a fraud against democracy. Those who say 'yes' and those who say 'no' do not, in fact, express their will. They have been silenced through the conception of modern democracy. They have been allowed to utter only one word: either 'yes' or 'no'. This is the most cruel and oppressive dictatorial system. He who says 'no' should give reasons for his answer. He should explain why he did not say 'yes'. And he who says 'yes' should give reasons for approval and why he did not say 'no'. Everyone should make clear what he wants and the reasons for his approval or rejection . . . .

Popular congresses are the only means to achieve popular democracy. Any system of government other than popular congresses is undemocratic. All the prevailing systems of government in the world today are undemocratic, unless they adopt this method. Popular congresses are the end of the journey of the masses' movement in its quest for democracy.

Popular congresses and people's committees are the final fruit of the people's struggle for democracy. Popular congresses and people's committees are not creations of the imagination so much as they are the product of human thought which has absorbed all human experiments to achieve democracy. Direct democracy is the ideal method, which, if realized in practice, is indisputable and noncontroversial. The nations departed from direct democracy because, however small a people might be, it was impossible to gather them all together at one time in order to discuss, study and decide on their policy. Direct democracy remained an Utopian idea far from reality. It has been replaced by various theories of government such as representative assemblies, parties, coalitions, and plebiscites. All led to the isolation of the people from political activity and to the plundering of the sovereignty of the people and the assumption of their authority by the successive and conflicting instruments of governing beginning with the individual, on through the class, the sect, the tribe, the parliament and the party.

The Green Book announces to the people the happy discovery of the way to direct democracy, in a practical form. Since no two intelligent people can dispute the fact that direct democracy is the ideal — but its method has been impossible to apply — and since this Third Universal Theory provides us with a realistic experiment in direct democracy, the problem of democracy in the world is finally solved. All that the masses need do now is to struggle to put an end to all forms of dictatorial rule in the world today, to all forms of what is falsely called democracy — from parliaments to the sect, the tribe, the class and to the one-party, the two-party and the multi-party systems.

Democracy has but one method and one theory. The disparity and dissimilarity of the systems claiming to be democratic is evidence that they are not democratic in fact. The people's authority has only one face and it can be realized only by one method, namely popular congresses and people's committees. *No democracy without popular congresses and committees everywhere*.

First, the people are divided into basic popular congresses. Each basic popular congress chooses its secretariat. The secretariats together form popular congresses, which are other than the basic ones. Then the masses of those basic popular congresses choose administrative people's committees to replace government administration. Thus all public utilities are run by people's committees which will be responsible to the basic popular congresses and these dictate the policy to be followed by the people's committees and supervise its execution. Thus, both the administration and the supervision become popular and the outdated definition of democracy . . . .

. . . The General People's Congress is not a gathering of members or ordinary persons as is the case with parliaments. It is a gathering of the basic popular congresses, the people's committees, the unions, the syndicates and all professional associations.

In this way, the problem of the instrument of governing is, as a matter of fact, solved and dictatorial instruments will disappear. The people are the instrument of governing and the problem of democracy in the world is completely solved.

GAMAL HAMDAN
(1928, Egypt)

A specialist in geopolitics and the philosophy of culture, Hamdan studied geography and history, first at Cairo then at Reading. He was appointed professor of the literature faculty of Cairo University, but soon decided to abandon teaching in order to concentrate on his writings, in which he sought to provide a theoretical and cultural complement to the Arab national movement. The ready and attentive response he has found, despite his self-imposed isolation, amongst his peers and especially in the new generation mark him as one of the intellectual leading lights of Egypt and the emergent Arab world. His ascetic thought, attuned to the sweep of history, opens the way for a synthesis between national specificity and modernity which is geared to the project of Renaissance. He stands as one of the greatest intellectual figures in Egypt and the contemporary Arab world.

    Main works: *Al-alam al-islami al-yawm* **(The Islamic World Today);** *Shakhsiyyat Misr, dirasah fi abqariyyat al-makan* **(The Personality of Egypt, A Study on the Genius of Place);** *6 Oktober fi al-stratijiyyah al-alamiyyah* **(The 6 October in World Strategy).**

The October War[3]

Seen in the context of a long process of struggle, the influence and role of the October war can be said to consist primarily in having banished despair for good and in having opened up twin avenues of hope.

    It is well-known that since June 1967, there was one question which haunted us all, an anxiety we barely dared recognize, let alone face: Had Palestine been lost for ever? Would Israel ever really go away, even in the distant future? Or to put it another way, would Palestine ever be returned to us? Was there no hope of seeing the enemy vanish? But now, there is no longer any doubt. The reasons for hope far outweigh the reasons for despair. It is just a question of time. The lost Eden will one day be re-opened to the Arabs, even if that day only comes in the distant future, after many tribulations. History will not stop tomorrow.

    It may seem that there is a dangerous contradiction between how we began our analysis, namely with the threat of losing out to the Zionist invasion, and how we end it, namely with the message that the enemy will one day no longer be with us. But in fact there is no contradiction. Rather it is to be taken as confirmation that our struggle is a struggle to the 'limits', that is to say a struggle with no middle ground, no halfway solution. The victor will take everything and the loser will lose everything. It has always been our fate as a nation to live on the 'limits'; whenever we win, we are called upon to assume an eminent place in the affairs of the world; when we lose, we are in danger of plummeting. The October war settled things in favour of the first alternative once and for all.

Since our great struggle is, in the last analysis, simply a struggle about civilization, as we have repeatedly argued, then we must now ask ourselves what meaning the October war has for civilization. I hold that by crossing the Suez canal, we crossed the Mediterranean, that our eastward advance into Sinai was, in its essence, an advance to the North, towards Europe. It was an advance of our civilization towards the vanguard of contemporary civilization, a crossing of the barrier which separates us from our 'West', and from the era we live in.

How so? We are all agreed, or at least I hope we are, that world imperialism and colonialism, both old and new, built Israel in the heartland of the Arab nation only to force us to remain forever weak and powerless, walled in by isolation and backwardness both materially and culturally, so that the Arab realm would continue to be without value or import, a vast, empty zone of civilization which threatened nobody, its immense body bloodied and mutilated by Israel, and its, as we now know, fabulously rich resources drained by the constant struggle with Israel. Israel, as a principle and as an entity, is imperialism's insurance policy in the region, an endless haemorrhage which drains the vitality of our civilization, sterilizes its future, blocks its evolution, its development, its progress, and drags it down towards the South. In a word, it is a political barrier which prevents our region crossing over the equator of civilization, that line which stretches from the Caribbean, through the Mediterranean and on to the China Seas and which separates the Third World from the advanced world, the impoverished South from the affluent North, Africa and Asia from Europe and America.

Suddenly, the model has broken down, the ineluctable barrier has cracked. The Arabs are moving forwards and a great new wave of civilization and progress is underway. It is thus no coincidence that this phase of the battle has been marked by radical changes in our historical relationship with Europe. A convergence has been established, leading to a new kind of encounter, on the basis of the mutual respect and regard which will one day impose on both parties recognition of each other's equality and authenticity. As we have seen, no two zones in the world are so close to each other, so entwined both culturally and historically — not to mention their geographic proximity — as Europe and the Arab world.

When we look at the map of the world and at the atlas of history, nowhere do we find such propinquity. The history of the ancient and mediaeval worlds is the history of how these two regions shared the world out between them. Their association was sometimes co-operative, sometimes competitive; throughout history these two regions alone competed for, and sometimes shared, world hegemony on a remarkably equal footing. It was also these two regions which jointly laid the foundations of the universal contemporary civilization, be it directly or indirectly; even in their spiritual aspirations, they are united by monotheism and shared religious references. From the ethnic point of view — despite Europe's racism at a certain stage and with no racism on our part now — it is clear that ever since antiquity the broader Middle East has constituted the only white Caucasian zone outside Europe.

Nowhere today are there two regions so close to one another in terms of politics and geopolitics. It is no exaggeration to say that Europe, which has lost much of its influence in world affairs to other more powerful forces, now represents the weakest link in the chain of great powers. It is the hollow point of the advanced North today. In contrast, the Arab world, although it apparently carries far less weight, is much less powerful and, for all its recent progress, is still much less advanced than Europe, nonetheless constitutes the most evolved and progressive sector of the Third World, the richest in resources and the one with the greatest potential for the future. It now stands at the forefront of the laggards, as the South's high point and as the chief force amongst the non-aligned.

The great rift which separates North from South is at its narrowest between Europe and the Arabs, both in terms of politics and in material terms. A rapprochement between them is thus relatively easy. The October victory has bridged part of the psychological, historical and political gap between the two civilizations. We Arabs are now ready to break out of the circle of backwardness and decadence; science and technology are within our grasp and we are ready to join the powerful in their advance and to seek out our own place in the sun.

Now too, on the other side of the line, Europe is anxious to pursue this historical encounter in which new friendships can be forged, new interests served and a new equilibrium sought; Europe too is searching for a new place in a world the very foundations of which are changing. These are the yeast and the letters of credit of a new understanding and rapprochement which the Arabs must strive to appreciate, to accommodate, and to make the best use of — both politically and as a civilization — in their struggle against an enemy who stands opposed to the spirit of the times in every way. In so doing, the Arabs will need a penetrating historical intuition, free of all complexes and sentimentality.

Furthermore, it was not just that the Arabs crossed the sea towards Europe in October; Africa also crossed the desert towards the Arabs, or at least it is beginning to. The victorious and honourable October war has caused Africa to turn back to its Arab vanguard, which has once again become the centre of gravity, the pole of attraction and the apex of power in our continent. The southern half of Africa rejoins the northern half as the whole continent marches northwards, sweeping aside all the artificial complexes and barriers erected by imperialism.

The duty of the Arabs, in turn, consists in moving forwards rapidly and boldly to assume the vanguard role in the continent, to fill the void created by the expulsion of Israel and to ensure that the latter does not get in again by some back door. The Third World constitutes the fundamental domain within which the Arab world will play its new role as a real power, almost as a great power. The Arabs must have no hesitation about making rapid headway towards this goal — as rapid as possible. It would be even better if they drew up a great international strategy, so that they could plan their world role.

That is the message of the 6 October, which must be put into practice *hic et nunc*.

HOUARI BOUMEDIENNE
(1925-1979, Algeria)

Born to a humble family in Guelma, Boumedienne pursued his Islamic studies at Constantine, at the Tunis Zaytounah and at Cairo's Al-Azhar before embarking on military studies in France. Having become a teacher, he completed his military training in Egypt. By 1955 the FLN's war of liberation was underway and Boumedienne was commander of *Wilayah* no. 5, the region around Oran (1955). He rose to the rank of colonel, then became chief of the General Staff of the Algerian Military Forces (1960), in which capacity he organized the military victory of 1962, notably after the arrest of the five 'historic leaders'. He was Minister of Defence in the first government of the Democratic and Popular Republic of Algeria (1962), then Vice-President of the Council of Ministers (1963). In 1965, he was elected President of the Council of the Revolution, overthrew Ahmad Ben Balla and became President of the Republic.

The course of Algerian policy set by Houari Boumedienne can be characterized as an attempt at a synthesis between a populism with socialist overtones, based on Algeria's oil wealth and its advanced infrastructure, and a determination to fulfil a role as the driving force of Africa and the Third World. The continuing radicalization of revolutionary Algeria's policies made its mark and turned Boumedienne into the figurehead of the Third World and the non-aligned bloc. In Algeria itself, Boumedienne fought hard against the new bourgeoisie, notably from 1973 onwards, and intensified his country's Arab allegiance. He powerfully supported Egypt and Syria during the 1973 October war, providing both military aid and diplomatic backing. His approach was

always based on a penetrating vision of the new world balance of power, notably in economic and strategic terms, which made him one of the great statesmen of the Tricontinental and of the Arab revival.

At a time of mounting peril, following the October war and the energy crisis, he addressed an historic message to Dr Kurt Waldheim, Secretary-General of the UN, on 10 April 1974, warning against the new imperialism and pointing out the avenues leading to peace and co-operation.

Let us Sail with the Tide of History!

International relations are suddenly going through a new period of tension, provoked by certain great powers' lack of understanding over questions of raw material resources and development. In our view, questions of energy, of raw materials, or of world inflation represent merely partial approaches to a problem which can only be resolved by the institution of true international co-operation. But such co-operation will never really be established until the international economic order is no longer dominated by the developed countries . . . .

Some developed countries have gone so far as to refuse humanitarian aid to the most impoverished of Third World countries, whilst others have sought to make their grants of aid conditional on aid from other countries, notably the oil-producers . . . . The reality is that this kind of blackmail, which has no precedent in international relations, can only be explained in terms of the resentment felt by certain circles (who have for centuries been used for appropriating the wealth of the Third World peoples) when faced with the fact that these peoples have embarked on an inexorable course which will do away with the exploitation they have suffered. In other words, the majority of developed countries have drawn no lessons from the debate during the last extraordinary session of the General Assembly, and still persist in seeking to solve contemporary problems outside the framework of the United Nations, with no regard for the principles adopted following the extraordinary session concerning the creation of a new international economic order.

It was thus with some perplexity, along with a certain apprehension for the cause of peace and justice in the world, that we learnt of recent declarations by representatives of the great industrialized countries, notably at the tribune of the UN General Assembly during the present session (1973-74).

The aggressivity of these declarations unpleasantly recalls an age we thought had gone for good, and seems, to say the least, rather inopportune in the context of an organization whose primary vocation remains the maintenance of peace and international security based on co-operation and understanding. They amount to serious threats aimed at all the people of the developing countries producing basic raw materials, and particularly at the oil producers . . . .

And yet, the OPEC states have shown that they are conscious of their responsibilities towards the international community and anxious to preserve the opportunity for real co-operation with the industrialized countries. Oil prices were frozen purely and simply to enable those countries to gain better control over the mechanisms of their economies and to control inflation. But despite the freeze on oil prices, in force for the first nine months of this year, not only has the inflationary upsurge continued in those countries, it has reached unprecedented levels . . . .

One cannot help observing that if the freeze on oil prices has had no effect upon the rate of inflation, it is because the real root of the problem lies elsewhere. In fact, far from being creators of inflation, the oil producing countries, along with the other basic raw material producers, are its first victims. The real danger of inflation must thus be sought in the very foundations of the economic system in the developed countries. This system, which for centuries has enabled the Western countries to build up prospering economies, is based primarily on the permanent exploitation of the poorer by the richer and of the weaker by the stronger. One essential characteristic of such a system is that it can only evolve in the context of a constant increase in prices, which constitutes the main source of the equally constant increase in profits accumulated by capital.

In the past, thanks to the surplus value it has extracted from the labour of the working classes, and to the revenues it has appropriated from the raw materials of Third World peoples, the system in the developed countries has been able to cope with the effects of the endemic problems resulting from this constant race to raise prices and, correspondingly, to maximize profits (this is after all what the euphemistic term 'inflation' really refers to).

Today, however, the working class is sufficiently organized to prevent its rights being infringed, and a growing number of Third World countries, having successfully pursued economic liberation, have now won the sovereign right to fix the prices of their raw materials. The system in the developed countries thus finds it increasingly difficult to restrain the level of inflation whilst nonetheless allowing profits to rise higher and higher at breakneck speed.

Now that the Western countries can no longer employ their traditional mechanisms, namely the exploitation of the working classes and the pillage of the wealth of Third World peoples, they are forced to face their own contradictions. If they are really determined to master inflation and thereby put their economies in order, they must attack directly the real causes of the problem, namely the excessive profits of their companies, the rate of return on capital, amortization policies and ruinous expenditure on projects that in no way contribute to the well-being of their people. But they are reluctant to recognize these factors as the real cause of inflation, for these factors are also the pillars of their economic system.

It is thus easy to understand their determination to recuperate their lost privileges, even if in order to replace the superannuated exploitative formulae of the past, they have to introduce newer and more subtle methods of appropriation, such as the mechanisms established under the cover of the struggle against inflation, notably the insistence that it is by natural right that prices in the industrialized countries rise constantly, unlike in the raw material producing countries where there is supposedly an obligation to keep prices stagnant or falling. The price control, which is set out as the objective of these anti-inflation programmes, is in fact simply a manipulation in which static or falling raw material prices help camouflage increased profits and the high margins operated by economic agents within the system of the developed countries. It is mechanisms of this kind which explain the increasing pauperization of some nations, whilst others grow richer. In other words, it is through the exploitation of Third World peoples that many of the developed countries have attained a standard of living far higher than the one they could have generated from their own resources. So at a time when the world believes that colonial domination is coming to an end, that imperialism is retreating before the steady onslaught of the Third World peoples' emancipation movements, and that all humanity is at last entitled to hope for a life of peace and tranquillity based on the equality of all peoples, here we have a resurgence of imperialism in its most implacable form, threatening to impose its dictates on the Third World raw material producing countries.

Having dubbed the OPEC countries' measures concerning prices a political decision bearing no relation whatsoever to economic realities, the spokesmen of certain Western countries take these measures as a pretext to evoke the threat of reprisals against the oil exporting countries. The distinction that is thus gratuitously introduced between how prices are fixed in the industrialized countries and in the raw material producing countries is not the least of the many paradoxes which are being used to sow confusion in people's minds. We are accused of taking arbitrary political decisions, whilst they are supposedly merely playing by the rules of the game. If a Western enterprise can be said to be responding to purely economic considerations when it determines its prices, often on a world scale, in terms of the nature of the market, production costs, amortization, return on investment and the prices of rival products, then by what logic can the measures taken by the oil producing countries be deemed to be inspired by purely political, and thus subjective and arbitrary, considerations, given that the oil producers invoke precisely the same factors, but in terms of their own interests, to determine the level at which their products will be marketed.

If the decision is an economic one in the first case, then so it is in the second. If it is political when taken by a supplier of raw materials, why cannot the same be said when such a decision emanates from a Western company? Unless, of course, one believes that the accumulation of resources must remain the exclusive privilege of the industrialized world and that the countries of the Third World must compromise or sacrifice their future in order to enable this accumulation to continue and to extend itself endlessly; this latter despite the fact that the backwardness the Third World countries have to overcome necessitates a constant and intense level of investment and the mobilization of considerable resources for many years to come. Whatever one thinks of OPEC's decisions, no reasonable man would take them as a valid motive justifying the threats which are presently being directed against its members.

In fact, there is every reason to fear that the campaign mounted against the OPEC countries is simply an attempt to manufacture some pretext, however flimsy, which would justify aggression by those who are waiting to take their revenge on those who have escaped economic domination.

If, by some mischance, such a process were put underway, it would inescapably lead to the dislocation and collapse of the world economy and threaten the very survival of all humanity. It is difficult to see how anybody can both make such threats and call for economic co-operation. One cannot both seek co-operation and interfere, or attempt to interfere, in the domestic affairs of other states in order to impose upon them solutions contrary to their own interests. The Western powers who make such threats seem to think that management of the world economy, which concerns humanity as a whole, is their exclusive prerogative and therefore stubbornly try to hang on to the monopoly of power they arrogated for themselves in the past. Indeed the so-called co-ordination meetings are little less than councils of war designed to draw up a strategy which will enable the powers involved to reconquer the economic advantages they enjoyed until recently at the Third World's expense, and which they lost following the disruption of the then prevailing balance of forces. Let us not forget that the problem of the distribution of world resources has always been posed in such terms, as a balance of forces, not as a simple matter of economic competition.

That is why, as we see it, the United Nations alone can provide a framework and guidelines for the resolution of the economic problems facing humanity today. If we are to maximize the chances of success in the attempt to resolve once and for all the problem of the development of the great majority of mankind, and if we want to prevent this problem eventually becoming the spark that sets off an uncontrollable conflagration, the community of the United Nations must do a great deal more to implement the specific measures laid down in the programme of action agreed by the last extraordinary session of the General Assembly. These measures bore mainly on:

(1) The recuperation by the Third World countries of their natural resources, so that they might obtain fair and remunerative prices for the products and provide themselves with autonomous sources of finance for their development.

(2) The valorization of these natural resources by promotion of industrialization in depth.

(3) The mobilization of complementary financial resources in the form of aid from the rich developed countries.

(4) Adjustment of the debts contracted earlier by the developing countries to the industrialized countries or international financial institutions.

(5) Finally, the effective and immediate implementation of the special programme aiming to attenuate the difficulties of the developing countries most
seriously affected by the economic crisis, taking into account the specific
problems of the least advanced countries and of landlocked countries.

In this respect, it is worth noting that the OPEC countries are already
operating within a framework of human solidarity and shared destiny with
the other Third World countries, and will continue to do so. In this year
alone, the gifts and credits they have granted to other developing countries,
on a bilateral or multilateral basis, represented a far higher percentage of
their Gross National Product than the industrialized countries have
ever provided.

Finally, Algeria reasserts its deep conviction that the only path to salvation involves true international co-operation, which implies a radical
transformation of the established economic structures, a definitive rejection
of the spirit of domination and exploitation, and an acceptance that the old
order is gone for good. Only a transformation of the established structures in
keeping with the tide of history and progress can ensure a harmonious settlement of the great economic problems of today and preserve peace and justice in the world.

GAMAL ABDEL NASSER

**The so-called 'Six Day' war in June 1967 was launched to bring down
the Egyptian state and its leader. On 9 and 19 June, the Egyptian people
demonstrated from one end of the country to the other to keep Abdel
Nasser in power. He proceeded to reorganize the army, the domestic
front and the Arab front. The war of attrition launched in January 1970
wore down the Zionist state's forces and morale but Egypt suffered
heavy losses due to the enemy's strategic aerial and electronic
superiority. A further truce was called, allowing Egypt to reinforce
its capabilities.**

**On 23 July 1970, Gamal Abdel Nasser addressed the 4th National
Congress of the Arab Socialist Union in Cairo. It was to be his last official speech, and can be read as his political testament, in which he
clearly sets out the course for Egypt to follow — a course the spirit of
which he defined in his interview for the *New York Times* in March
1969: 'As you know, we have not been able to realize all our dreams
during the last 17 years because of a variety of problems: the occupation, the 1967 aggression, etc. My dream is above all the development of
the country, electricity in the villages and work for everybody. I have
no personal dream. I have no personal life. There is nothing personal
about me.'**

Political Testament: The Struggle for the Renaissance

On this memorable day, the anniversary of the 23 July revolution, after 18 years of that revolution, we must pause to consider two distinct lines in the UAR if we are to understand the essence, the objectives and the forces which have animated our struggle. The first line is to the south, on the Nile; I refer to the High Dam, construction of which was completed today. The other line is to the north, along the Suez canal. It is the battlefront on which the Egyptian people and the national army are engaged in the noblest and most violent of conflicts. To the south, on the Nile, there rises the High Dam and the giant power station whose twelfth and last turbine began turning today, thereby signalling the completion of one of the biggest electric power stations in the world.

By now, 836,000 feddans of low lying land have been fully irrigated; a further 850,000 feddans have been improved and added to our arable land area. Improvement work proceeds apace. 10,000 million kWh have been added to our national grid. There are now 500 kWh per head, whereas in 1952, the figure was barely 40 kWh.

On the green line, to the north, along the Suez canal, the Egyptian army is fighting. Every day Egyptian youth is giving a fine example of military and national honour.

The Egyptian army, its officers and its commanders, have deployed extraordinary efforts to reconstitute themselves, in circumstances that were amongst the most difficult our national struggle has faced. This army, which the enemy thought finished for decades, has managed to take up the combat again with a rapidity which impartial historians of this period will consider truly miraculous.

The sincere co-operation of the USSR, which was one of the key factors in the construction of the High Dam, has provided the army with the equipment and experts necessary to its reconstitution.

The endless effort deployed by hundreds of thousands of our men and young people who have had the honour of serving in the army in this critical phase has enabled us to achieve a level of combat readiness that neither our friends nor our foes would have envisaged three years ago. The Egyptian Army is today engaged in a battle of special importance, the battle against Israeli air superiority made possible by US assistance following the 1967 aggression. The enemy wanted the Egyptian front to remain open so that his aerial superiority could be used freely. Everyday the enemy carries out raids that last for several hours. Enemy planes fly over our positions and on some days drop up to a thousand tons of explosives, costing nearly a million pounds sterling. The enemy has concentrated his offensive on our anti-aircraft defences, so as to prevent their fulfilling their role on the front.[4]

But the enemy has not succeeded . . . . Between the line across the Nile, at Aswan, and the green line to the north, along the Suez canal, the entire Egyptian nation is resisting, confident, sincere and convinced of attaining its goal. That is the domestic front . . . .

The value of agricultural production increased by 15% between 1967 and 1969. Exports of agricultural products over the same period grew by 40%, despite the war . . . .

These are only some aspects of the agricultural activity of our peasants, who form the great working potential of this country and the fundamental pillar of the popular working forces. These figures are far from the whole story, but I felt they were worth quoting, since our enemy's press media and those of their supporters claim that while we may have resisted militarily, our economy is collapsing.

I want to stress, to you and to the whole Arab nation, that when the Egyptian people decided to resist, in 1967, it also decided to work. Production has increased in every sector, in agriculture and everywhere else. If we turn to industry and to the workers who form the other part of the popular working forces, the picture that emerges against the backdrop of war and danger is just as splendid and honourable.

In 1966-67, the value of industrial production was £E1,077,678,000, and represented no substantial increase over the previous financial year. In 1967-68 it reached £E1,169,419,000, an increase of £E91,801,000, or 8.5%. In 1968-69 the value of industrial production rose to £E1,322,698,000, an increase of £E345,800,000 or 22.8%. In 1969-70, it rose to £E1,424,987,000, an increase of £E344,639,000 or 32%.

These increases are increases in real production, that is, they exclude any price rises. The increases have been quantitative and effective; they have been achieved not only despite danger and war conditions, but also at a time when one of our most important pre-war industrial regions, the canal zone, has been seriously affected. The phenomenon is particularly notable in that our industrial exports have grown by 63% in wartime, from £E82 million in 1966-67 to £E134 million in 1969-70.

The Egyptian people have not stood alone facing war, danger and terror during this admirable and historic period. The entire Arab nation has been beside them, fulfilling its role in the struggle while recognizing its right to assume the greater part of the costs of the battle for the future.

Above all there were the masses, confident in the knowledge that the freedom of the Arab nation was the only objective, and victory for that freedom the only requirement. The Arab masses were aware of every step taken; they rejected all attempts to divert them and remained faithfully committed to their own fundamental freedom. In the first and last resort, this cause, this freedom, this imperative need for victory belongs to them.

The Arab masses have been exposed to psychological warfare in which the enemy has used the most modern methods, great intelligence and much duplicity. But the Arab masses have not succumbed to this psychological warfare. They have attentively followed each stage of the military confrontation and have refused to be tricked by the phoney solicitude of their enemies.

The masses proved capable of distinguishing the windbags and word merchants from those who face death on the battlefield. The masses realized the decisive importance of military action and the full need for political action. They realized that although the objective was clear and unambiguous, the movement pursuing it needed complete freedom of action to cope with a highly mobile enemy, a world preoccupied by the Middle East conflict and an international force comprising both friends and enemies.

The Arab masses did not simply observe all this passively; they did everything they could to help while they awaited results . . . .

The Palestinian resistance made its presence felt and managed to transform the Palestinian people from a refugee people into a warrior people. The Palestinian action made its mark throughout the world, and the *Al-Fatah* organization which launched the action, accepting martyrdom in the service of the liberation of the Palestinian people, has won massive support in the Arab world. The resistance organizations have now managed to agree that a united central committee will in future co-ordinate their actions and objectives.

For my part, I believe that the enemy will seek to sow discord amongst the resistance fighters and amongst all the children of Palestine. But until now, the Palestinian people and the Palestinian resistance have had sufficient maturity to foil all the plots of the imperialists and their agents . . . . Our Arab nation's struggle did not and could not proceed separately from the rest of the world. We have friends abroad, and so does our enemy. If we recall the course of events since 1967 it is easy to pick out those who have been our friends and those who have been Israel's.

When we remember the friends who stood by us in the dark days of 1967, the first, the foremost, the one to whom we owe the deepest gratitude is undoubtedly the Soviet Union, whose leaders, Brezhnev, Kosygin and Podgorny sent me a message telling us not to despair, that the USSR would help us in every way and would supply us with arms to replace those lost in the battles in the Sinai. That was the cornerstone of the reconstruction of our armed forces. The arms from the USSR arrived immediately.

Everybody in the West, in the United States and in Israel insisted that we were finished and that nothing could be expected of our armed forces following the June defeat. Some Israeli leaders declared at the time that they were awaiting phone calls from Cairo or Damascus suing for surrender and asking for the terms of a capitulation.

The Egyptian people, all the peoples of the Arab nation, decided not to accept defeat. But we needed arms for our forces. So when we say that we are deeply grateful to the USSR, it is because we remember that in spite of our enemies' hopes and declarations, the Soviet Union delivered planes, tanks, cannons and arms to us within days of the defeat. In return, we offered the hope that we would resist and, with God's help, triumph . . . , that we would build first a defensive army, then an offensive army which would enable us to liberate the territories usurped from us.

The Soviet Union has also given us political support, both in the United Nations and in the international domain, whereas the United States has helped Israel to remain in the occupied territories . . . .

We must ask ourselves 'What does our enemy want?' It is clear from the Israeli leaders' declarations since 1967 that to this day our enemy still seeks to expand, and thus has no intention of abiding by the Security Council's resolution . . . .

Some Israeli leaders have announced that Israel's frontiers are the Nile and the Euphrates and that the true map of Israel is the one drawn up over 70 years ago by Herzl. That map begins at the Damietta fork and stretches into Iraq, encompassing large areas of Syria, Lebanon, Jordan and Saudi Arabia. That is what our enemy wants.

From 1967 till today, the word withdrawal has not crossed our enemy's lips. When the Israeli leaders answer questions in vague terms rather than speak of withdrawal, they mention the redeployment of Israeli forces . . . . All this shows that Israel seeks to expand at the expense of the Palestinian people and of the Arab peoples as a whole. That is its nature and we must not lose sight of it in this phase of our struggle marked by open battle over the Suez canal front.

Our enemy brings down upon us the hostility of the United States; the American leaders are on Israel's side and supply it with everything it asks for in the way of electronic equipment and military material, so as to prevent us from defending our territory and our children against Israeli raids. Our enemy co-operates with the United States and the United States co-operates totally with Israel . . . .

In fact, a new kind of warfare is being waged for the first time in history: electronic warfare. People say that Israel enjoys technological superiority and that is why it won in 1967. But that is just a way of camouflaging the extent of American collusion at the time. Up until 1967, Israel had obtained from the United States all the electronic warfare equipment needed to paralyze and locate our radar installations and rocket bases, to jam our telecommunications, etc. At the time the newspapers claimed that all this was due to Israeli skill and technology, but it later emerged that all the equipment had been shipped to Israel from the United States.

War today is bitter and complicated, but our armed forces have managed to cope with electronic warfare and to resist, despite all the United States' assistance [to our enemy]. We too need the kind of advanced electronic warfare materials that Israel receives, yet we cannot manufacture it ourselves. It was because of such electronic equipment, delivered secretly to Israel by the United States, that our enemy was able to achieve a rapid victory during the Six Day war . . . .

But despite all this assistance, despite Israel's announcements that it would do everything in its power to break any concentration of Egyptian soldiers and to prevent them from preparing for the crossing of the Suez canal, the training of our troops continues. Egyptian troop concentrations remain in place and the morale of our troops at the front is very high. During my last visit to the front, I spoke to soldiers standing beside the trenches while the enemy was bombarding some of our positions. The officers asked me 'When will we cross into the territory occupied by Israel?'

We have managed to resist and to reconstitute our armed forces. We have mobilized all our potential for the battle, for our great hope of defeating an enemy who understands only the language of force . . . .

Our territories are occupied. Our country is exposed to air raids. We must obtain everything that can help us defend our rights. We are standing up to the Israeli occupation and we know that our fate will be played out on the battlefield. The American press affirms daily that Egypt is preparing to invade Israel by crossing the Suez canal. Our enemies use the term 'invasion' to mislead their own people, who are unaware that Sinai is part of Egypt; they claim that they give Israel arms because it is threatened with invasion. But we are not an aggressive force, we are an energy of liberation, the liberation of our own land. Everybody should understand that: all the parties (to this conflict) and every nation. We simply proclaim and affirm this nation's determination not to cede its territory. No one has the right to force us to do so.

We are working towards the liberation of the occupied territories and we are not prepared to relinquish an inch of them. We proclaim high and loud that this nation will defend its legitimate rights to the very end. Everybody should understand what we mean . . . .

This nation, as I have said, will not give up one inch of its territory; it will not give up its rights, however many weapons and electronics America pours into our enemy's arsenal.

Our nation is not embarking upon either aggression or invasion; we are simply demanding the return of our occupied territories and the restoration of the rights of the Palestinian people — the rights that Israel has usurped. This should be clear to everybody; the consequences are serious.

Notes

1. *Iqtirah dawlat Filistin* (Beirut, 1968), pp.11-23.
2. *Al-Kitab al-Akhdar* (The Green Book) (Tripoli, 1976), Vol.I, pp.6-33.
3. *6 Oktober fi al-stratijiyyah al-alamiyyah* (Cairo, 1974), pp.382-85.
4. The 1970 war of attrition.

9. Two Societies

MUNIR SHAFIQ
(1936, Palestine)

An eminent militant of the Palestinian and Arab national movement, in the great Jerusalem tradition. He became one of the key Communist leaders, undergoing ten years of repression in Jordan, and eventually moved towards a progressive nationalist approach, of which he is now one of the main spokesmen. Currently Director General of the PLO's Planning Centre, he remains a great theoretician and essayist whose penetrating critical thought has had a fundamental influence on the evolution of modern Arab political thinking.

Main works: **Islam and the Battle of Civilization; On the Art of War; On the Strategy of Liberation and the Strategy for a Political Solution; On National Unity and Division; On Palestinian National Unity; Arabism and Islam.**

In the following text, Munir Shafiq shows how deep is the rift within the Arab political class between nationalists and 'good Westernized modernizers'.

This chapter attempts to use an ideological-civilizational term of reference as a basis to the understanding of Islamic societies in general, and those of Arabs in particular. Starting from this point, we find that, created by partition, two societies exist side by side in each country: the historically original society which, generally, has preserved the mode of Islamic society and kept its heritage and traditions, thus retaining the social mode that had existed before colonial control. The second society — the 'modernized' society — formed under Western domination, appropriated to itself a Western type of modernization and, accordingly, this defined fashions of habitation, behaviour, lifestyle, education, thought and concepts, thus creating continuity with the external mode but in a relationship of subservience.

Why an ideological-civilizational standard?

In the light of some Western research methodologies, to adopt the criterion of ideological-civilizational terms of reference to an understanding of Islamic Arabic societies may be considered unscientific. Clearly, however, the societal model of Islamic Arab societies is essentially different from Western models. Thus, to apply such models to an analysis of Islamic Arab societies would, in itself, be unscientific.

Most analyses of the nature of Islamic Arab societies have ignored the duality within these societies, applying only the modernization element, and omitting consideration of the original, traditional element. That the modernized Western-type element was dominant in our countries after the collapse of direct colonial rule, and that there was an attempt forcibly to unite the whole of society under its control may be true, but this does not mean that the older element ceased to exist, or that it necessarily had to legitimate itself by becoming submerged within the modernization trend.

The unique role played by Islam in constructing the mode of Islamic Arab societies provides the rationale for the ideological-civilizational terms of reference, and for distinguishing two societal strands in our countries. Islamic ideology is the crucial cohesive factor, both in the material structures and the social relationships of our societies. When, therefore, this factor is weakened or dispersed the society disintegrates, and its structures, including the economy, can no longer survive.

The viability of utilizing a framework consisting of two societies rests, however, on the degree of accord between this framework and reality.

The Arab and Muslim experience of the wars of the Crusades was bitter, despite victories attained during repeated invasions, and the occupation of some areas from the 12th to the 13th centuries These campaigns, in which hundreds of thousands of people were butchered, and which destroyed, divided and scattered, spreading corruption as they came, failed, however, to destroy the ideological-social-civilization mode of Islamic character. Despite the forceful entry of its weapons and armies, the West was excluded from our society and thus from control of Western societies. This experience demonstrates that while Islam remains strong in the hearts and lives of the people their continuous resistance will render any alien occupation temporary, notwithstanding its strength. This imperviousness was increasingly strengthened by victory against the Crusaders, the defeat of the Tartars and by the fruitless European attempts at penetration from the 16th to 19th centuries. This failure to penetrate the frontiers of the Islamic countries, frustrated Europe's attempt to control the world. The failure was not one of arms only, but also an inability to cope with Islamic Arab societies. This also explain Napoleon's occupation of Egypt; for when he found himself confronted by an impenetrable society he professed himself converted to Islam in order to ensure the durability of his military rule.

Our thesis also explains why colonialist invaders up to the present have concentrated on destruction of the original society, and on imposing in its stead a modernized society lacking the foundations of the original, that is: the foundation of Islam and the human, economical social and Islamic mode of life.

Armed Resistance and Passive Resistance

When the colonialist armies landed on our shores and defeated the regular armies, they were confronted by popular revolutions, largely under Islamic banners. The resistance was courageous, despite the disparity of forces, as witness Egypt and the Sudan, the North African coast, the Arabian Peninsula, Iraq and the rest of the Arab and Islamic countries. The invaders had no respite, and even eventual defeat and massacre failed to achieve surrender. What remained of the original societies turned inwards, seeking to reinforce and preserve their Islamic identity. The original society tenaciously maintained its values, standards and concepts — not owing to stagnation or backwardness, but as a rejection of the invasion of Western civilizations. The controlling Western forces waged war against these societies and described their resistance as a retreat from 'science' and 'progress', suggesting that all our woes, including colonial rule, stemmed from ideological, social and economic backwardness. Thus, our only hope for revival or salvation was to follow in the footsteps of the West.

In the face of military threat, ideological blackmail and temptations and corruptions, there were some who deserted the original society. Various people were involved, but all believed that the only hope for their country lay in the adoption of Western methods and modes. Many elements hostile to colonialism were misled into supporting Western modernization, and thus played a dangerous role in confronting the original society ideologically and civilizationally by placing their patriotic and revolutionary banners and sacrifices in the service of colonialism. The result was to obscure the essence of the confrontation because both the original society's fight for independence and the dependence represented by the modernized society, were thereby eclipsed.

Attack Against the Factors of Independence

Colonialism attempted from the outset to divide the Islamic countries in general, and the Arab countries in particular, because their unity was essential for an independent ideological-civilizational existence. Thus, division caused an inherent weakness and facilitated control and domination. Colonialism, furthermore, could destroy the original societies in the Arab countries only by achieving their distintegration, and so the plan for Arab division was the first step in the plan to destroy the factors of independence.

Colonialism worked to destroy traditional agriculture and existing crafts or professions, and attacked the patterns of ownership, production, distribution, exchange, and communal labour characteristic of the original society. The aim was to remove the basis of independence and substitute a basis of dependence, so that people would dress, build houses, spend their leisure, and raise their children according to Western modes and values. For this reason total war was waged against all aspects of the original society. Psychological war was waged against those who refused to imitate the Westerners: wearing a suit meant 'progress', thinking in a foreign language meant 'knowledge and sophistication'. In short, total absorption of material and ideological exports of the West meant 'progress', 'civilization', and 'modernity'. The arrow of liberation and progress was thus turned against ourselves, and our traditions were represented as 'slavery, backwardness and anachronism', while the colonialists represented 'liberty, progress and civilization'.

The colonialists also set about dismantling the Islamic educational institutions and worked to change the cultural mode of life of the original society. They built modern schools and encouraged study in Europe's universities. Their standards and criteria became dominant, those by which employees, officers, profesionals, intellectuals, teachers, writers and artists had to live by. These conditions suited only graduates from Western schools and universities or those who followed their lead in educational programmes and curricula. Employment within the state, army, companies, banks, or educational institutions became the prize of graduates from Western or modernized schools and universities. The intellectuals of the original society were excluded — a fact which augmented the temptation to enter the modernized society.

The West exploited the situation of minorities and various sectarian contradictions in order to split the original society to which they belonged and to facilitate the erection of the modernized society. One example is that of the Christian Arabs whose historical roots and customs, ethics, and lifestyles made them a part of the original society. The Westerners were surprised on reaching our land to find deeply rooted, commonly held characteristics between all inhabitants of the Muslim area. This did not prevent the achievement of some success later, by the process of modernization that led away from the original society towards subservience to the West. Our thesis applies, therefore, to all members of our community, although care must be taken to see the specificities of each group in terms of the degree of its resistance or surrender to the process of Western modernization.

The war waged against the old society and its values, standards and ethics aimed at its disruption. This was to be achieved by the substitution of values, standards, and customs contrary to all the society's basic foundations. In this manner, the situation of both men and women would be changed, and the society's adoption of new values, standards and customs would render it unable to stand firmly or to advance surely. Society would become like a creature afflicted by disease, unstable in its posture and gait, moving entranced like a prey towards its predator.

This aim has, however, been only partially fulfilled; the original society has continued to resist the invasion, despite receiving many blows and conceding much ground. Furthermore, the modernized society that the West hoped would embody dependence also included elements that resisted colonialism in varying degrees, especially during periods of direct colonial rule and liberation struggle. On many occasions the resistance within the modernized society combined with that of the original society, as witness the popular demonstrations of the 1930s, 1940s and 1950s. Partial victories were achieved in the battle against direct control, and in the creation of independent local governments.

The Modernized Consumer Society

The facts show that the poisons spread by imperialism in order to convert society to modernization have become major obstacles on the path to total liberation from Western control. For the leading patriotic forces that belong to the modernized society have not seen the civilizational dimension of the conflict. That is, they have not grasped the essence of the total war waged by the Western colonialists and imperialists, which is destruction of the original society and construction of a Western modernization society, and so they have not realized that the result has been to maintain subservience, even when the enemies of imperialism are in power.

The Western countries entered the phase of affluence and the consumer society (in the 1950s and 1960s), and the consumer mentality along with consumer goods invaded the world. This in turn meant that the mode of the modernized society became a greater rather than a lesser influence after independence. The role of the state grew and came to stand above all, proceeding to modernize its institutions for which purpose it imported experts, drained resources, increased debts and deficits, and deepened dependence. Policies of migration from agriculture and pursuit of technology and heavy industrialization also played a role in strengthening attraction to the outside (the Marxist programmes are also part of the West's modernization). The achievements during the phase of independence became threatened, while outside control grew, particularly in its cultural and civilizational aspects and way of life. Reality has proved that those elements are an even greater support for colonialists rule than the multinational companies themselves.

The continuation of life according to the modernized mode after the success of the revolution and independence leads towards external dependence, despite good intentions and patriotic sentiment. As long as, for instance, we construct our houses along Western lines, dress according to Western fashions and furnish our homes in Western style; as long as we place our basic needs within the limits of the West's production and goods, run after their experts and technique, and order our education, state, army, and weapons according to their methods, as long as we follow this path we shall never be free from their yoke. We shall present project after project of Western type only to find ourselves alienated from our peoples and unable to escape dependence. To take a simple example from the past, the wearing of Western-type suits instead of our traditional costumes was not only a formal change, one of appearance; rather it meant the end of a large part of our agriculture, industry and professions, and dependence on the outside to the extent that real emancipation was not possible, even if machines were imported in order to achieve independence within their mode. If, however, we had retained and developed our own methods of clothes production, our agriculture, industry, markets and professions would have prospered and developed; we would also have preserved some aspects of our identity and prevented a sizeable number of our young people lapsing into inappropriate attire.

The issue involved here, therefore, concerns the cultural, spiritual, moral and civilizational aspects of the society, as well as those of independence and origin, economic development and prosperity. If the ideological-civilizational foundations of the original society are safe and have not been replaced by the foundations of dependence through creating a consumer society that reproduces that dependence military and economic control is impossible. In this case Western modernization is then sought to fortify the modernized society and infuse new blood, and it thus becomes a necessary condition for the society's existence.

Alienation from the Original Society

The society of Western modernization represents the basis for the development of Western mentality and for secession from Arab Islamic civilization, heritage and history. It is thus a basis for alienation from the original society; we lose our origins within it, and when we think we are advancing we are in fact retreating; we think we are independent whereas we are sinking into dependence, and we work against the masses, although we believe ourselves to be working for their interests. This is because our thoughts, programmes, and plans have lost their popular roots and their historical basis. Alienation from the original society has resulted in the loss of the revolution's base, for the broad masses alone are capable of confronting the enemy in the battle for independence and sovereignty, and of constructing a solid infrastructure that is not deflected by the consumer mode. In other words, such a base resists the mode that ties our countries to the capitals of the colonial-imperialist masters, with their tempting but futile and corrupting attractions.

We are now able to understand what made the civilizational war between the original society and colonialism so bitter from the outset. Each was fully aware of the deeper implications of this war. Each, therefore, opened several other fronts (in addition to the political and military ones), of an ideological or moral nature. Conflict at these levels took place indirectly and its methods often became very complex. Some posed the issue as one of conflict between backwardness and progress, rather than between independence and dependence. Members of the original society presented the problem as a struggle against moral decay, knowing that war against moral decay meant war for independence because decay deprived society of its basic ideological, cultural, moral, vital, productive and existential foundations.

Colonialism attempted to avoid direct presentation of the problem in the desire to obscure the issue. This lured a number of patriotic intellectuals (proponents of modernization) to participate in the battle against 'backwardness'; in reality, these intellectuals were unconsciously assisting in striking at the bases of resistance and independence in their countries. Indeed, they believed themselves to be creating the conditions for resistance and independence by achieving Western 'progress', ridding society of 'backwardness' which was the cause of 'Western domination over the Arab and Islamic countries'. The original society, however, often kept the battle within the limits of ethical and moral issues without invoking the question of independence and subservience, thus avoiding the broader essence of the war, including its political and economic aspects, because a direct confrontation meant massacre. The original society, forming a large majority, could not move without the result being either a victory or a massacre. Bitter experience taught it that patience is crucial, as is unceasing effort, although the conflict took on direct forms now and then, and much blood was shed in the defence of the original society and its independence.

The Two Societies

Following up the thesis of two societies we can now draw additional conclusions:

The Original Society

The original society generally managed to retain a high level of civilizational independence from the West. This meant that preservation of its foundations, especially Islam and its heritage and its non-dependent lifestyles, formed a solid base for the liberation struggle and played an important role in the phase of independence, unity, revolution and development.

It is also necessary to note the negative aspects of this society. The most important of these being:

(a) Struggle against lackey forces that deal or compromise with the enemy from within the original society is more difficult than that against their counterparts in the modernized society. This is because most of such forces have social roots (such as clan leaders), and can fight back on the same ground as the original society, possibly using tribalism, sectarianism or ethnic differences.

(b) The extreme repression suffered by the people prolonged ideological terrorism and injustice, bred a tendency to extreme caution and negativeness, to introversion and even immobility. As a result, its effective forces are powerless to play a positive role in the opening up period, at a time when introversion is no longer excusable and effort is required to provide contemporary solutions for contemporary problems in order to attain victory. Other negative results, to people, of prolonged existence under threats and ideological terrorism, are not mentioned here.

(c) The original society faces a constant challenge under the external control or rule of the modernized society, in terms of elements of Western modernization that manage to penetrate it; only its higher birth rate has helped it retain its numerical superiority. Its subjective resistance enabled it to defend its basic foundations, although it lost some of its battles. Recently, the most dangerous threat to the original society is represented by the huge fortunes made by oil-producing Arab countries, which, in turn, has led to the search for wealth and consumer goods. These items are no longer limited to the modernized society, but are reaching the depths of the original one. It is more difficult to face this penetration than to fight for culture, ideology, ethics, customs and behaviour. We now face the growing demand for consumer goods which are so easy to obtain, and the battle for independence and identity, for our revival and an independent civilization will become more complex.

(d) The original society has for a long time taken a defensive posture, manning the barricades, rather than going on the offensive against the enemy's positions. Its members, therefore, became accustomed to defence and to building fortifications, and need to make a great effort in order to convert to the offensive and to change. A conflict will emerge within the original society when the time comes for a general offensive, and it will become possible to open up to the modernized society in order to absorb it, rather than the reverse. What explains the erection of barriers between the two societies is that in a phase of attack against the original society's ideological and civilizational foundations, opening up to the modernized society meant falling prey to dependence, and to loss of origins and essential formation. Such barriers are negative, however, when the general movement can achieve victory, because one of the conditions for victory is to absorb elements of the modernized society instead of leaving them as tools in the hands of the foreigners.

If the original society has given answers to the problem of resistance that are generally correct, but have not yet answered the post-victory problems, that is not an indication of inability. Indeed, success in the first instance suggests the possibility of success in the second. Failure by the modernized society to solve the problems of resistance is, however, an indication of inability to solve the problems of the second phase, despite all pretensions. This has proved to be the case so far, but the future will be the final judge.

The Modernized Society

(a) The modernized society is a cultural and civilizational dependent of the West in all its modes; it imitates the West in every way. The modernized society is the product of external imposition, not of natural organic development, and so retains the imprints of its birth during its subsequent movement. Creation was an act of separation from the original society and in conflict with it and, despite the weakness of the modernized society and the fragility of its foundations *vis-à-vis* the original society, it imposed its control over the other and founded the unification of both on fracturing the original society and subjecting it to modernization. The contradiction between the two societies is, therefore, essentially deep and carries a tyrannical repressive nature in confronting the original society which, when the conflict deepens is willing to relinquish independence.

(b) Modernized society boycotts and represses the thought of the original society by ignoring or neglecting it, or accusing it of backwardness. The conflict, therefore, is kept within the confines of the modernized society and the opposing thought is completely dismissed until too late.

(c) The modernized society has a divisory nature that alienates it from its country because its ideal is outside. When the majority take the initiative, return of the modernized society to the historical path of its country becomes difficult, and its role in delaying independence and revolution increases. For independence under the leadership of the majority also means ideological-cultural-civilization independence, which is a condition for economic and political independence.

(d) Colonialism, imperialism and foreign domination built schools and universities to produce intellectuals who would provide it with services and help it directly or indirectly in its ideological-civilizational battle — but it succeeded with only a fraction of them. The remainder felt the injustice and insult suffered by the people and the nation, and turned against foreign domination and its agents. These intellectuals fought colonialism, imperialism and foreign domination politically and economically on the basis of political and economic theories derived from European civilizations. Europe has several theories and ideologies that are in conflict, but all are legitimate offspring of European society and the European historical experience and civilization. As a result our intellectuals find themselves alienated from their original society and closer to the foreign mores, which sows the seeds of a basic contradiction with the people and the seeds of dependence. These intellectuals will always face the challenge of independence and emancipation from Westernization, and can succeed only if they turn radically to the inside and shun the outside.

(e) Because it does not represent the people, modernized society does not carry within it a prospect of revolution; a revolution can arise only from within a society, not a revolution of an elite, state, or party. For this reason those intellectuals aspiring to become revolutionaries will find themselves outside the revolutionary process if they do not dare transform themselves and return to the original society in their ideology and civilization.

In a word, to continue existence within the modernized mode, to attempt to retain this mode after independence, means that, objectively, the situation will remain one of dependence on the outside, regardless of good intentions and patriotic feelings.

Division, Unity and the Two Societies

One of the crucial factors that has led to a feeling of impotence on the part of the masses and caused the original society to prolong its negative or indirect resistance, is division. The division of the Islamic countries and particularly the Arab countries into small statelets and entities resulted in their weakness owing to the loss of unity. Division was the most crucial factor enabling colonialism to control our land and build a modernized society with its Westernized state. The modernized society was thus established on the basis of division and interacted with it, forming an organic unity. Together they formed the infrastructure upon which Westernization in thought and mentality rests. They stood in opposition to the original society which, in its basic composition, remained in contradiction with the states erected by division with the modernized society and Westernization. The ideological-civilizational war became dualistic after the modernized society adhered to the division-created states, as the original society entered a war against external colonialist and imperialist forces as well as against local groups which assumed the Western mode.

The modernized society was born in the womb of division. Its state apparatus consolidated division and its economic, cultural and educational institutions were regionalistic. It is no exaggeration, therefore, to say that the modernized society is the child of division. Conversely, we note that the original society was born and bred during broad Arab and Islamic unity over a period of 13 centuries, losing its ability to control and succumbing to the modernized society only after the intervention of foreign bayonets and imposed division. The original society is thus the child of unity, and is oppressed by division.

Comprehension of these two characteristics: the relationship between the modernized society and division, and the original society and unity, allows us to reach important conclusions. The first may be that the original society is the correct basis for action towards renaissance. Furthermore, faithfulness to the aim of real change and development demands eradication of divisionary modernization and identification with the original society. If our conclusions are correct it is clear why the projects for Arab unity and development based on the modernized society and state failed.

Colonialism, imperialism and foreign domination had always aimed at the destruction of the unity of our society and its historical continuity in order to convert it to dependence. The result was the creation of two conflicting societies within one land which entered into bitter conflict that paralyzed their abilities instead of uniting their might against the common enemy. Naturally, unity will not be achieved by wishful thinking, nor by overlooking the basic conflict, nor by refusing to discuss the ideological-civilizational split and what each side represents. Indeed, unity can be realized only through a thorough understanding of each one's reality, capabilities and path. Internal unity and, therefore, general unity and revolution, development and progress in solving the basic problems can be achieved only if we cease to stand within the confines of the modernized society and, refusing eclecticism, take our place under the banners of the original society. That is the condition for eradication of immobility and backwardness, for real progress, for prosperity and overall revival.

Bibliography

I. General Bibliographies

In Arabic

Dagher, Yussef Asad, *Masader al-dirasah al-adabiyyah - 2. Al-Fikr al-arabi al-hadith fi siyar alamhi, al-qism al-awwal; al-rahiloun (1800-1955)* (Sources for literary study - 2. Contemporary Arab thought in the life of its epigones; 1st part: "The Dead" (1800-1955)), Beirut, 1955.

Kahalah, Omar Rida, *Majm al-mouallifin, tarajem mousannifi al-kutoub al-arabiyyah (Dictionary of authors, biographies of Arabic authors)*, 15 vols., Damascus, 1957-1961.

Morouwwah, Adib, *Al-Sahafah al-arabiyyah, nashatuha wa tatawwuruha* (The Arab press, its origins and evolution), Beirut, 1961.

Tarazi, Philippe de, *Tarikh al-sahafah al-arabiyyah* (History of the Arab press), 4 vols., Beirut, 1913-1933.

In European languages

CEMAM, St. Jospeh University, *Arab Culture and Society in Change — A bibliography*, Beirut, 1973.

Clements, Frank, *The Emergence of Arab Nationalism from the 19th Century to 1921 — A bibliography*, Diploma Press, London, 1976.

Grimwood-Jones, Diana; Hopwood, Derek; Pearson, J.D., *Arab Islamic Bibliography*, Harvester Press, London and Humanities Press, Atlantic Highland, N.J., 1977.

Heywood Dunne, J., *Religious and Political Trends in Modern Egypt — A bibliography*, Washington, 1950.

Pearson, J.D., *Index Islamicus, 1906-1955*, Cambridge, 1958.

——————— *Index Islamicus, 1956-1960*, Cambridge, 1962.

——————— *Index Islamicus, Second Supplement, 1961-1965,* Cambridge, 1967.

——————— *Index Islamicus, Third Supplement, 1966-1970*, London, 1973.

Qubain, F.L., *Inside the Arab Mind*, Ithaca, N.Y., 1956.

246

II. Periodicals

(1) Egypt
Apollo; Al-Thaqafah; Al-Gamiah; Al-Magallah al-gadidah; Al-Magallah; Al-Rissalah; Al-Siyassah al-ousbouiyyah; Al-Kateb al-Misri; Al-Kitab; Al-Kateb; Al-Muqabas; Al-Muqataf; Al-Hilal; Nour al-Islam; Magallat al-Azhar; Al-Manar; Al-Fagr al-gadid; Al-Ghad; Magallat ihm al-nafs; Magallat mayma Fuad al-Awwal lil-Lughah, later *Magallat magma al-lughah al-arabiyyah; Magallat magma al-makhtout al-arabiyyah; L'Egypte Contemporaine; Al-Taliah; Al-Magallah al-tarikhiyyah al-misriyyah; Al-Fikr al-muaser; Al-Siyasah al-dawliyyah.*

(2) Iraq
Al-Hurriyah; Majallat al-Muallem al-jadid; Al-Thaqafah al-jadidah; Al-Muthaqqaf; Al-Marifah; Afaq.

(3) Syria
Al-Thaqafah (Damascus); *Al-Hadith* (Aleppo); *Al-Shaba* (Aleppo); *Majallat al-majma al-ihmi al-arabi* (Damascus); *Al-Muqtabas* (Damascus); *Al-Marifah* (Damascus); *Al-Mawaqif al-adabi.*

(4) Lebanon
Al-Abhath (Beirut); *Al-Athar* (Zahlah); *Al-Irfan* (Saydah); *Al-Adib; Al-Adab; Al-Thaqafah al-wataniyyah; Al-Tariq; Al-Mashreq; Dirasat arabiyyah; Al-Hurriyyah; Qadaya arabiyyah; Al-Thaqafah al-arabiyyah* (Beirut); *Al-Fikr al-arabi; Al-Mustaqbal al-Arabi; Journal of Palestine Studies.*

(5) Tunisia
Al-Mabaheth; Al-Fijr; Al-Tajdid.

(6) Morocco
Marakesh (Tetouan); *Afaq* (Rabat).

(7) Sudan
Al-Maydan; Akhbar al-ousbou (Khartoum).

(8) Algeria
Révolution Africaine; Al-Asalah.

(9) Libya
Al-Thaqafah al-arabiyyah.

(10) Kuwait
Al-Arabi; Al-Muslim al-muaser.

(11) Europe and North America
Al-Ihya al-arabi (Paris); *Arab Quarterly Studies* (Evanston, Ill.).

(12) League of Arab States (ALESCO)
Magallat al-buohouth wal-Dirasat al-arabiyyah.

III Monographs

(1) In Arabic

Abboud, Maroun, *Ruwwad al-nahdah al-hadithah* (The Pioneers of the modern renaissance), Beirut, 1952.

Abdel-Malek, Anouar, *Dirasat fil-thaqafah al-wataniyyah* (Studies on the national culture), Beirut, 1967.

—————————— 'Min agl stratijiyyah hadariyyah' (For a civilizational strategy), *Al-Thaqafah al-arabiyyah*, April 1973, pp.116-131.

—————————— 'Al-Nahdah al-hadariyyah', *Qadaya arabiyyah*, I, No.1 (1974), pp.45-54.

—————————— 'Harb Oktober wal-wihdah al-arabiyyah' (The October war and Arab unity), *Al-Marifah*, March 1975.

—————————— 'Tanmiyah am Nahdah hadariyyah?' (Development or renaissance of a civilization?) *Al-Mustaqbal al-arabi*, I, No.3, September 1978, pp.6-11.

Alem, Mahmoud Amin al-; Abd al-Azim Anis, *Fil-thaqafah al-misriyyah* (On Egyptian Culture), Beirut, 1954.

Alem, Mahmoud Amin al-, *Maarek fikriyyah* (Ideological Struggles), Cairo, 1966.

Al-Thaqafah wal-thawra (Culture and Revolution), Beirut, 1971.

Al-Adab, 'Adab al-muqawamah', special issue, 1968, No.4.

Al-Adab, 'Al-Ittijihat al-falsafiyyah fil-adab al-mouaser' (Philosophical tendencies in contemporary literature), special issue, Beirut, 1963, No.3.

Al-Adab, 'Azmat al-tatawwar al-hadari al-arabi' (The Crisis in the evolution of Arab civilization), special issue, 1974, No.5.

Al-Tajdid, 'Fil-thaqafah al-maghrabiyyah' (On Maghribi culture) special issue, I, No.5-6 (1961).

American University, Beirut, *Al-Fikr al-arabi fi miat sanah* (Arab thought in a hundred years), Beirut, 1968.

Amin, Ahmad, *Zuama al-islah fil-asr al-hadith* (The Leaders of reformism in modern times), Cairo, 1948.

Ashtar, Abd al-Karim al-, *Al-Nathr al-mahjari* (The Prose of emigration), 2 vols., Cairo, 1961.

Assad, Naser al-Din al-, *Muhadarat fil-ittijihat al-adabiyyah al-hadithah fi filistin wal-urdon* (Conferences on modern literary trends in Palestine and Jordan), Cairo, 1957.

Awad, Louis, *Al-Muathirat al-agnabiyyah fil-adab al-arabi al-hadith* (Foreign influences on modern Arab literature), 2 vols., Cairo, 1963, 1964.

Awwa, Adel al-; Salibah, Jamil; Gabr, Farid; Garr, Khalil al-; Fakhri, Majed; Madkour, Ibrahim Bayyoumi; Nader, Albert, *Al-Fikr al-falsafi fi miat sanah*, (Philosophical thought in a hundred years), Beirut, 1962.

Azm, Sadeq Jalal al-, *Dirasah naqdiyyah li fikr al-muqawamah al-filistiniyyah* (Critical study of the thought of the Palestinian resistance), Beirut, 1973.

Badawi, Abd el Rahman; Mahmoud, Zaki Nagib; Zakariyyah, Fouad, *Al-Asalah fi-falsafah al-arabiyyah al-muasirah* (Authenticity in contemporary Arab philosophy), *Al-Adab*, XII, No.9 (1964), p.11 ff.

Baheyy, Muhammad al-, *Al-Fikr al-islami al-hadith wa silatuhou bil-istimar al-gharbi* (Modern Islamic thought and its relationship with Western imperialism), Cairo, 1957, 3rd edition, 1964.

—————————— *Al-Fikr al-islami wal-mugtama al-muaser mushkilat al-hukm wal-tawqih* (Contemporary Islamic thought, problems of government and orientation), Cairo, 1956.

Ben Ashour, Shaik Muhammad al-Fadel, *Al-Harakah al-adabiyyah wal-fikriyyah fi Tounis* (The Literary and intellectual movement in Tunis), Cairo, 1956.

Bishri, Tareq al-, *Al-Harakah al-siyassiyah fi Misr, 1945-1962* (The Political movement in Egypt, 1945-1962), Cairo, 1972.

Dagher, Youssef Asad, 'Al-Fikr al-Arabi al-hadith wa mashahir alakihi' (Contemporary Arab thought and its most famous epigones), *Al-Adib*, October 1956, No.72.

Dassouqi, Omar al-, *Fil-adab al-hadith* (On modern literature), 2 vols., Cairo, 1948, 1950.

——————— *Nashat al-nathr al-hadith wa tatawwuratuhou* (The Origin and evolution of modern prose), Cairo, 1962.

Dayf, Shawqi, *Al-Adab al-arabi al-muaser: 1. Fi Misr 1850-1950* (Arab contemporary French literature: 1. In Egypt 1850-1950), Cairo, 1957.

Filistine, Wadi, *Qadaya al-fikr fil-adab al-muaser* (Intellectual problems in contemporary literature), Cairo, 1960.

Ghallab, Abd al-Karim, 'Malameh al-adab al-arabi al-hadith bil-Maghreb' Aspects of modern Arab literature in the Maghrib), *Afaq*, No.1 (1963), pp.13-24.

Gindi, Anwar al-, *Al-Fikr al-Arabi al-muaser fi marakat al-taghrib wal-tabaiyyah al-thaqafiyyah* (Contemporary Arab thought in the battle of westernization and cultural dependence), Cairo, 1961.

Hamdan, Gamal, *Al-Alam al-islami al-yawm* (The Islamic World Today), Cairo, 1968.

——————— *Shakhsiyyat Misr, dirasah fi abqariyyat al-makan* (The Personality of Egypt, a study of the genius of place), Cairo, 1970.

——————— *6 Oktober fil-stratijiyyah al-alamiyyah* (The 6 October in world strategy), Cairo, 1974.

Hamzah, Abd al-Latif, *Adab al-maqalah al-sahafiyyah fi Misr* (The Literature of the press article in Egypt), 7 vols., Cairo, 1950-1959.

Hussain, Muhammad, *Al-Ittiqahat al-wataniyyah fil-adab al muaser* (Patriotic Trends in Contemporary Literature), 2 vols., Cairo, 1954, 1956.

Hussain, Muhammad Kamel, 'Al-Hayat al-fikriyyah fi Misr al-muasirah' (Intellectual life in contemporary Egypt) in *Mutanawwiyat* (Mixtures), Vol.II, Cairo, 1961, pp.43-64.

Hussain, Taha, *Mustaqbal al-thaqafah fi Misr* (The Future of culture in Egypt), Cairo, 1938.

Hussaini, Ishaq Moussa al-, *Azmat al-fikr al-arabi* (The Crisis of Arab thought), Beirut, 1954.

Isa, Sahah, 'Al-Fikr al-siyasi al-misri wa harb tishrin' (Egyptian political thought and the October war), *Dirasat arabiyyah*, XI, No. 1 (1974), pp.3-22.

Kanafani, Ghassan, *Al-Adab al-falistini al-muqawem taht al-ihtilal, 1948-1968*, (Palestinian literature under the occupation, 1948-1968), Beirut, 1969.

Karim, Fawzi, *Min al-gharbah hatta way al-gharbah* (From strangeness to the consciousness of strangeness), Baghdad, 1972.

Kayali, Sami al-, *Al-Adab al-arabi al-muaser fi Souriya* (Contemporary literature in Syria), Cairo, 1959.

——————— *Al-Adab wal-qawmiyyah fi Souriya* (Literature and nationalitarianism in Syria), Cairo, 1969.

Kholi, Amin al-, *Fil-Adab al-misri* (On Egyptian Literature), Cairo,1943.

Khouri, Raif, *Al-Fikr al-arabi al-hadith*, (Modern Arab thought), Beirut, 1943.

Mahmoud, Zaki Naguib, *Taqdid al-fikr al-arabi* (The Renewal of Arab thought), Beirut, 1971.

Mandour, Mahammad, *Qadaya gadidah fi adabina al-hadith* (New problems in our modern literature), Beirut, 1958.

Maqdissi, Anis Khouri al-, *Al-Ittijihat al-adabiyyah fil-alam al-Arabi al-hadith.*

Masiri, Abd al-Wahab al-, *Mawsouat al-mafahim wal mustalahat al-sahyouniyyah* (Encyclopaedia of Zionist concepts and terminology), Cairo, 1975.

Metwalli, Abd al-Hamid, *Azat al-fikr al-siyasi al-islami fil-asr al-hadith* (The Crisis of Islamic Political Thought in the Modern Era), Cairo, 1970.

Murqus, Elias, *Naqd al-fikr al-qawmi* (Critique of nationalitarian thought), Beirut, 1966.

—————————— *Al-Marksiyyah wal-Sharq, 1850-1918* (Marxism and the Orient), Beirut, 1968.

Mousa, Munir, *Al-Fikr al-arabi fil asr al-hadith: Souriya fil qarn al-Thamen ashtar hatta am 1918* (Arab thought in the modern era: Syria from the 18th Century to 1918), Beirut, 1973.

Moustafa, Shaker, ed., *Azmat al-tatawwar al-hadari fil-watan al-arabi* (The crisis of the evolution of civilization in the Arab homeland), Kuwait, 1975.

Naouri, Isa al-, *Adab al-mahjar* (The literature of emigration), Cairo, 1959.

Naqqash, Raja al-, *Fi azmat al-thaqafah al-misriyyah* (On the crisis of Egyptian culture), Beirut, 1958.

Nassar, Nassif, *Nahwa mujtama jadid* (Towards a new society), Beirut, 1970.

Qarmadi, Saleh al-, 'Al-Tarif bi usous al-adab al-tounissi' (Outline of the foundations of Tunisian literature), *Al-Tajdid*, I, Nos.5-6 (1961), pp.5-28.

Sab, Hassan, *Tahdith al-aql al-arabi* (The Modernization of Arab reason), Beirut, 1969.

Safi, Sheikh Othman, *Ala hamish naqd al-fikr al-dini* (On the margins of the critique of religious thought), Beirut, 1970.

Said, Jamil, *Nazarat fil-tayyarat al-adabiyyah fil-Iraq* (Consideration on modern literary trends in Iraq), Cairo, 1954.

Said, Rifat al-, *Al-Sahafah al-yasariyyah fi Misr, 1925-1948* (The Left press in Egypt from 1925 to 1948), Beirut, 1974.

Salibah, Jamil, *Muhadarat fil-ittijihat al-fikriyyah fi balad al-Sham wa atharouha fil-adab al-hadith* (Conferences on intellectual trends in Syria and their influence on modern literature), Cairo, 1958.

Sanoussi, Zein al-Abidin al-, *Al-Adab al-tounissi fil-qarn al-rabi ashar* (Tunisian literature in the 14th Century of the Hegira), Tunis, 1927.

Sarrouf, Fuad, 'Tatawwar al-fikr al-ilmi al-arabi fil-miat am al-akhirah' (The Evolution of Arab scientific thought over the last hundred years), *Al-Abhath*, XV, No.2 (1962), pp.151-212.

Sayegh, Anis, *Al-Fikrah al-arabiyyah fi Misr* (The Arab idea in Egypt), Beirut, 1959.

Sulh, Munah al-, *Al-Islam wa harakat al-taharrir al-arabi* (Islam and the Arab liberation movement), Beirut, 1973.

Shukri, Ghali, *Thawrat al-fikr fi adabina al-hadith* (The Revolution in thinking in in our modern literature), Cairo, 1965.

———————— *Al-Turath wal-thawrah* (Cultural heritage and revolution), Beirut, 1973.

———————— *Al-Nahdah wal-souqout fil-fikr al-Misri al-hadith* (Renaissance and decadence in modern Egyptian thought), Beirut, 1979.

———————— *Al-Thawra al-muadaddah fi Misr* (The Counter-revolution in Egypt), Beirut, 1979; London, 1981.

Tabanah, Badawi Ahmad, *Nahdat al-adab fil-asr al-hadith* (The Renaissance of literature in modern times), Baghdad, 1946.

Taymour, Ahmad, *Alam al-fikr al-Islami fil-asr al-hadith* (The Epigones of Islamic thought in the modern era), Cairo, 1967.

Yaghi, Hasham, *Al-Naqd al-adabi al-hadith fi Loubnan* (Modern literary criticism in Lebanon), 2 vols., Cairo, 1969.

Zakariya, Fouad et al, *Abdel Nasser wal-yasar al-arabi* (Nasser and the Arab Left), Cairo, 1977.

Zuraiq, Constantin, *Fi marakat al-haddrah* (In the battle of civilization), Beirut, 1964, 1973.

(2) In European Languages

Abdel-Malek, Anouar, 'Problématique du socialisme dans le monde arabe', *Nuovi Argumenti* (Roma), (1963-64); *L'Homme et la Societe* No.2, (1966), pp.125-148.

———————— *Robespierre, le jacobinisme et la conscience nationale égyptienne* in *Actes du colloque Robespierre* (Vienna, 1965), Paris 1967, pp.283-303.

———————— *Idéologie et Renaissance Nationale: l'Egypte moderne*, Paris, 1969.

———————— (with A.A. Belal and H. Hanafi, ed.), *Renaissance du Monde Arabe*, Gembloux, Algiers, 1972.

———————— 'The Civilizational Significance of the Arab National Liberation War' in Arussi, Nasser, ed., *The October War*, New York, and *Journal of the Middle East*, Cairo, No.3, 1976, pp.1-23.

Aby-Ghazaleh, Adnan, *Arab Cultural Nationalism in Palestine*, Beirut-Benghazi, 1973.

Abu-Lughod, Ibrahim, *Arab Rediscovery of Europe, A Study in Cultural Encounters*, Princeton, 1963.

———————— ed., *The Transformation of Palestine*, Evanston, 1971.

———————— *Actes du colloque sur la Sociologie musulmane (Bruxelles, 11-14 septembre 1961)*, Brussels, n.d., c.1962.

Adams, C.C., *Islam and Modernisation in Egypt*, London, 1933.

Ahmad, Jamal M., *The Intellectual Origins of Egyptian Nationalism*, London, 1960.

Arberry, A.J., ed., *Religion in the Middle East*, 2 vols., Cambridge, 1969.

Berque, Jacques, *Les Arabes d'hier à demain*, Paris, 1960.

———————— *L'Orient second*, Paris, 1970.

Berque, Jacques; Charnay, Jean-Paul, ed., *Normes et Valuers dans l'Islam contemporain*, Paris, 1966.

———————— *L'Ambivalence dans la culture arabe*, Paris, 1967.

Binder, Leonard, *The Ideological Revolution in the Middle East*, London-New York, 1964.

Brockelmann, C., *Geschichte der arabischen Litteratur — 3. Supplement band*, Leiden, 1942.

Carré, Olivier, *L'Idéologie palestinienne de résistance*, Paris, 1972.

Caspar, R., 'Le renouveau mo'tazilite', *MIDEO*, V (1957), pp.141-202.

Chejne, A.G., 'The Use of History by Modern Arab Writers', *Middle East Journal*, XV (1960), No.4, pp.382-396.

Corm, Georges G., *Contribution à l'étude des societés multiconfessionelles, Paris, 1971.*

'La culture arabe contemporaine', *Cahiers d'Histoire mondiale*, XIV (1972), No.4.

Daniel, Norman, *Islam and the West*, Edinburgh, 1960.

————————— Islam, Europe and Empire, Edinburgh, 1966.

Djaït, Hitchem, *La Personnalité et le Devenir arabo-islamiques*, Paris, 1974.

Ferid-Ghazi, Mohammad, 'La littérature tunisienne contemporaine', *Orient*, No.12, 1959, pp.131-197.

Germanus, A.K.J., 'Trends of Contemporary Arabic Literature', *Islamic Quarterly*, III (1956), pp.88-108; IV (1957), pp.29-42, 114-139.

Gibbs, H.A.R., *Modern Trends in Islam*, Chicago, 1947.

————————— 'Studies in Contemporary Arab Literature', *BSOAS*, IV (1926-1928), pp.745-760; V (1928-1930), pp. 311-322, 445-466; VII (1933-1935), pp.1-22.

Grünebaum, G.E. von, *Modern Islam: The Search for Cultural Identity*, Berkeley and Los Angeles, 1962.

Haïm, S.G., ed., *Arab Nationalism: An Anthology*, Berkeley and Los Angeles 1962.

Hanna, Sami A.; Gardner, George H., *Arab Socialism*, Leiden, 1969.

Hilan, Rizkallah, *Culture et Développement en Syrie et dans les pays retardés*, Paris, 1969.

Holt, P.M.; Lewis, B., *Historians of the Middle East*, London, 1962.

————————— Political and Social Change in Modern Egypt, London, 1968.

Hourani, Albert, *Arabic Thought in the Liberal Age 1789-1939*, London, 1962.

————————— A Vision of History, Beirut, 1961.

IPALMO, *La coscienza dell'altro: contraddizioni e complementarieta tra cultura europea e cultura araba*, Florence, 1974.

Issawi, Charles, ed., *The Economic History of the Middle East 1800-1914, A Book of Readings*, Chicago-London, 1966.

Karpat, Kemal H., ed., *Political and Social Thought in the Contemporary Middle East*, New York, 1968.

Kerr, Malcolm H., *Islamic Reform: The Political and Legal Theories of Muhammad Abduh and Rashid Rida*, Berkeley and Los Angeles, 1966.

Khemiri, T.; Kampffeyer, G., 'Leaders in Contemporary Arabic Literature: A Book of Reference', *Die Welt des Islams*, IV (1930), pp.1-40.

Laoust, Henri, 'Le réformisme musulman dans la litterature arabe contemporaine', *Orient*, X (1959), pp.81-107.

Laroui, Abdallah, *L'Idéologie arabe contemporaine*, Paris, 1967.

————————— La Crise des intellectuels arabes, Paris, 1973.

Lecerf, Jean, 'Le mouvement philosophique contemporain en Syrie et en Égypte', *Mel. Inst. Fr. de Damas*, I (1929), pp.29-64.

Lelong Michel, 'Aspects de la pensée tunisienne contemporaine', *IBLA*, XXIII, No.4 (1960), pp.453-62.

Lutfiyya, A.M., and Churchill, C.W., ed., *Readings in Arab Middle Eastern Societies and Cultures*, The Hague and Paris, 1968.
Miquel, André, *L'Islam et sa Civilisation*, Paris, 1968.
Montgomery Watt, W., *Islamic Political Thought*, Edinburgh, 1968.
Nuseibeh, Hazem Zaki, The Ideas of Arab Nationalism, Ithaca, 1956.
Qubain, Fahim, *Education and Science in the Arab World*, Baltimore, 1966.
Rodinson, Maxime, *Marxisme et Monde musulman*, Paris, 1974.
Said, Edward W., *Orientalism*, London: Routledge Kegan Paul, 1978.

MIDDLE EAST TITLES FROM ZED PRESS

POLITICAL ECONOMY

SAMIR AMIN
The Arab Economy Today
(with a comprehensive bibliography of Amin's works)
Hb

B. BERBEROGLU
Turkey in Crisis:
From State Capitalism to Neo-Colonialism
Hb and Pb

SAMIR AMIN
The Arab Nation:
Nationalism and Class Struggles
Hb and Pb

MAXIME RODINSON
Marxism and the Muslim World
Pb

GHALI SHOUKRI
Egypt: Portrait of a President
Sadat's Road to Jerusalem
Hb and Pb

CONTEMPORARY HISTORY/REVOLUTIONARY STRUGGLES

KAMAL JOUMBLATT
I Speak for Lebanon
Hb and Pb

GERARD CHALIAND (EDITOR), A.R. GHASSEMLOU, KENDAL,
M. NAZDAR, A. ROOSEVELT AND I.S. VANLY
People Without a Country: The Kurds and Kurdistan
Hb and Pb

ROSEMARY SAYIGH
Palestinians: From Peasants to Revolutionaries
Hb and Pb

BIZHAN JAZANI
Capitalism and Revolution in Iran
Hb and Pb

ABDALLAH FRANJI
The PLO and Palestine
Hb and Pb

RAYMONDA TAWIL
My Home, My Prison
Pb

INGELA BENDT AND JAMES DOWNING
We Shall Return:
Women of Palestine
Hb and Pb

MIRANDA DAVIES (EDITOR)
Third World — Second Sex:
Women's Struggles and National Liberation
Hb and Pb

NAWAL EL SAADAWI
The Hidden Face of Eve:
Women in the Arab World
Hb and Pb

NAWAL EL SAADAWI
Woman at Zero Point
Hb and Pb

JULIETTE MINCES
The House of Obedience:
Women in Arab Society
Hb and Pb

Zed press titles cover Africa, Asia, Latin America and the Middle East, as well as general issues affecting the Third World's relations with the rest of the world. Our Series embrace: Imperialism, Women, Political Economy, History, Labour, Voices of Struggle, Human Rights and other areas pertinent to the Third World.

You can order Zed titles direct from Zed Press, 57 Caledonian Road, London, N1 9DN, U.K.